D1022048

# Managing Component-Based Development in Global Teams

# Managing Component-Based Development in Global Teams

Julia Kotlarsky and Ilan Oshri

palgrave
macmillan

First published 2009 by
PALGRAVE MACMILLAN

Palgrave Macmillan in the UK is an imprint of Macmillan Publishers Limited, registered in England, company number 785998, of Houndmills, Basingstoke, Hampshire RG21 6XS.

Palgrave Macmillan in the US is a division of St Martin's Press LLC, 175 Fifth Avenue, New York, NY 10010.

Palgrave Macmillan is the global academic imprint of the above companies and has companies and representatives throughout the world.

Palgrave® and Macmillan® are registered trademarks in the United States, the United Kingdom, Europe and other countries

ISBN: 978-0-230-22244-1        hardback

This book is printed on paper suitable for recycling and made from fully managed and sustained forest sources. Logging, pulping and manufacturing processes are expected to conform to the environmental regulations of the country of origin.

A catalogue record for this book is available from the British Library.

A catalogue record for this book is available from the Library of Congress.

10   9   8   7   6   5   4   3   2   1
18   17   16   15   14   13   12   11   10   09

Printed and bound in Great Britain by
CPI Antony Rowe, Chippenham and Eastbourne

# Contents

| | | |
|---|---|---|
| *List of Figures and Tables* | | vi |
| *Preface* | | ix |
| 1 | Introduction | 1 |
| **Part I** | **The Essence of Globally Distributed Teams and Component-Based Development** | **13** |
| 2 | The Management of Globally Distributed Software Development | 15 |
| 3 | The Management of Component-Based Software Development | 35 |
| **Part II** | **How Leading Firms Managed Component-Based Development in Global Teams** | **65** |
| 4 | Observations of GD CBD at LeCroy Corporation | 69 |
| 5 | Observations of GD CBD at SAP | 99 |
| 6 | Observations of GD CBD at TCS | 125 |
| 7 | The Case of Baan: How Not to Manage Global Teams | 159 |
| **Part III** | **Component-Based Development in Global Teams: Learnt Lessons** | **199** |
| 8 | What Can Be Learnt From These Cases? | 201 |
| 9 | Towards a Framework of Successful Global Distributed CBD | 236 |
| *Appendices* | | 247 |
| *References* | | 257 |
| *Index* | | 268 |

# List of Figures and Tables

## Figures

| | | |
|---|---|---|
| 1.1 | Research focus | 7 |
| 1.2 | Related research streams | 8 |
| 2.1 | The Waterfall approach: traditional software development lifecycle | 19 |
| 2.2 | Scenario A – GDSD organised *by phase/process step* | 20 |
| 2.3 | Scenario B – GDSD organised *by product structure (product module)* | 21 |
| 2.4 | Scenario C – only well-defined tasks distributed across locations | 22 |
| 2.5 | Scenario D – GDSD based on *product customisation* | 22 |
| 2.6 | Potential factors that contribute to success in GDSD projects | 28 |
| 2.7 | Potential factors that contribute to success in GD teams | 34 |
| 3.1 | The main concepts behind components (adapted from Alexandersen et al. 2003) | 39 |
| 3.2 | V-cycle approach: CBD lifecycle (modified from Herzum and Sims, 2000) | 43 |
| 3.3 | A detailed V development process for CBD (adapted from Crnkovic et al. 2005) | 44 |
| 3.4 | Division of onsite/offshore work for development of the Skandia platform | 51 |
| 3.5 | Potential factors that may contribute to success in GD CBD | 63 |
| 3.6 | A question-led framework regarding success factors of CBD in global teams | 64 |
| 4.1 | Division of responsibilities between NY and Geneva offices | 70 |
| 4.2 | Major chronological phases of the Maui project | 71 |
| 4.3 | Maui product architecture (schematic) | 72 |
| 4.4 | Organisational structure of LeCroy software team (as of December 2001) | 74 |
| 4.5 | How LeCroy organises and manages GD CBD to be successful | 76 |

5.1   Organisational structure of KM Collaboration group          103
      (as of June 2002)
5.2   How SAP organises and manages GD CBD to be                  104
      successful
6.1   Quartz component-based architecture                         126
6.2   Technical overview of Quartz implementation                 127
6.3   Quartz product development and solution                     128
      implementation methodology
6.4   Skandia project: Apollo CB architecture                     129
6.5   Dresdner project: Investment and e-commerce bank            130
6.6   Typical organisational structure of the Quartz             132
      implementation project: Skandia and Dresdner
      projects
6.7   How TCS organises and manages GD CBD to                     133
      be successful
6.8   Skandia project: Onsite-offshore delivery model            136
7.1   Baan stock prices                                           160
7.2   Products included in the E-Enterprise suite                 163
7.3   Organisational structure of the E-Enterprise               165
      development group (as of March 2002)
7.4   Roles (people) involved in the management of each          169
      of the eight products comprising E-Enterprise
7.5   Compatibility between versions of different products       180
8.1   Inter-site coordination: Propositions                       212
8.2   Appropriate tools and technologies: Propositions            217
8.3   Social ties: Propositions                                   222
8.4   Knowledge sharing: Propositions                             228
8.5   Components management: Propositions                         233
9.1   Theoretical framework                                       237
9.2   How companies organise and manage GD CBD                   239
      to be successful

## Tables

2.1   Types of collaboration technology                           26
4.1   Contribution of managerial practices to success            77
      at LeCroy
5.1   Contribution of managerial practices to success at SAP     105
6.1   Contribution of managerial practices to success at TCS     134
7.1   The rise and fall of Baan Co.                               161
7.2   Capabilities of SD tools at Baan                            182

| 7.3 | Collaborative technologies used in Baan | 182 |
| 7.4 | Would adoption of CBD help to avoid the problems: Discussion | 193 |
| 8.1 | Similarities and differences between the studied cases | 202 |
| 8.2 | Managerial practices: Comparison of results across cases | 204 |
| 8.3 | Capabilities of SD tools: Comparison of results across cases | 213 |
| 8.4 | Requirement for ICT infrastructure: Comparison of results across cases | 214 |
| 8.5 | Collaborative technologies: Comparison of results across cases | 215 |
| 8.6 | Factors contributing to success (per success dimension) | 234 |
| 9.1 | Factors contributing to success | 238 |
| 9.2 | Checklist for managers | 243 |
| 9.3 | A guide to tools and technologies for managers of GD CBD | 244 |

# Preface

Globally Distributed Component-Based Development (GD CBD) is expected to become a promising area, as increasing numbers of companies are setting up software development in a globally distributed environment and at the same time are adopting Component-Based Development (CBD) methodologies. This process of globalisation and adoption of CBD methodology has introduced potential benefits as well as new challenges in the management of software projects.

On the one hand, it is expected that adoption of CBD will further facilitate globally distributed development of software products, as happened in industries such as aeronautics, automotive, electronics and computers hardware, where Component-Based (CB) architectures have been successfully used for setting up globally distributed design and production. Within the software industry, it is suggested that components could be developed in parallel independently by teams located in the same building or at remote locations. It has been argued that CBD enables each site to take ownership of particular components and work on them independently without much need for inter-site communication and coordination.

On the other hand, research on co-located CBD projects has reported difficulties associated with the management of CBD projects, such as lack of stable standards, lack of reusable components, and problems related to the granularity and generality of components. In the light of these problems, achieving the true potential of CBD, which is mainly about reusing components, is challenging even in co-located CBD projects. Globally distributed organisations may face the above-mentioned and additional challenges (caused by geographical, time-zone and cultural differences) when adopting the practice of CBD.

Being an emerging area, the management of GD CBD has evolved primarily on an *ad hoc* basis. We are happy to share with you the insights we have gained in the last eight years regarding the most effective practices companies should apply when organising and managing GD CBD.

# 1
# Introduction

Historically the demand for software services has outpaced supply. As we enter the era of e-business, companies are increasingly adopting complex software systems to support their internal and external processes. At the same time, we are also witnessing an exponential increase in the use of embedded software systems. For example, mobile phones, personal organisers and cars are equipped with sophisticated software which communicates over the web. Consequently, the demand for software and software developers is exploding in all parts of the world.

The imbalance between demand and supply is further exacerbated by the high levels of skill and training required for building software. Software engineering organisations have always had trouble meeting the growing demand for high quality software (Shachaf 2008). Although numerous improvements have been introduced to software engineering practices, Brook's (1987) claim that 'building software will always be hard' is now generally accepted. Brooks (1987) listed four unique properties of software that make software development more difficult than other systems engineering disciplines. Software systems are *complex, unvisualisable,* and are constantly subject to *change.* Finally, software systems are expected to *conform* to the continuously changing environment in which they operate. These 'inherent' difficulties of software make software engineering a complex discipline, and consequently, large software development projects are regularly delayed and show huge budget overruns (Willcocks et al. 2002; Wallace and Keil 2004). As a result, highly skilled software engineers and experienced software project managers are scarce and expensive in most regions of the world.

1

## Globalisation in the software industry

In order to build quality software faster and more cheaply, companies in industrialised countries are turning to globally distributed software development projects.

Emerging countries such as India and China are known to have large pools of highly trained software engineers at relatively low cost. Moving parts of the development process to these emerging countries can not only decrease development costs, but can also provide access to scarce development manpower and resources (Sarker and Sahay 2004; Kotlarsky and Oshri, 2008). Another advantage of global distribution could be reducing project lifecycle by using time-zone differences to organise 'follow-the–sun' (or 'round-the-clock') development (Carmel 1999; Evaristo and van Fenema 1999; Herbsleb and Moitra 2001).

Global distribution of software development has become widespread over the last decade. There are a number of economic and technical drivers that are likely to further accelerate the growth of distributed software development. For economic and financial considerations, many companies are switching to globally distributed development and/or offshore outsourcing of products and services. For instance, in the software and electronics industries offshore outsourcing of development (in the software industry) and manufacturing (in the electronics industry) is very common. Outsourcing of services such as call centres to English-speaking developing countries is becoming increasingly common. Many companies are opening R&D or manufacturing centres in countries where costs are low and yet skills and expertise are available (e.g. India, China). The recent trend towards mergers and acquisitions can also result in globally distributed organisations. Global distribution is also useful whenever a software product needs to be customised for a local market. Proximity to the customer may be necessary in such cases (Carmel 1999). On the technological side, ongoing innovations in Information and Communication Technologies (ICT) increase the possibilities to cooperate in a distributed mode.

However, the geographical distance, time-zone and cultural differences associated with global distribution has caused problems for globally distributed software teams, such as the breakdown of traditional coordination and control mechanisms, commonly used in co-located software teams, asymmetry in distribution of information between dispersed sites, misunderstandings and loss of communication richness (Carmel 1999).

Despite the problems and breakdowns that the people involved in Globally Distributed Software Development (GDSD) projects have experienced, more and more companies are becoming involved in GDSD. Gartner Group predicts: 'Globalization is inevitable, IT groups that plan their responses to the challenges raised by this complex issue have a better chance of succeeding in the increasingly competitive environment of software development' (Lyengar 2004).

## Adopting component-based development methodology

Typically, software systems have a long lifetime, of at least several years, during which such systems are upgraded and enhanced with more features, and released as different versions. Changes, improvements, and enhancements leading to new software design releases cause a software system to evolve (Peters and Pedrycz 2000). As a result, a software system needs to be updated and changed many times over the period of time that a system lives (Brooks 1987; Crnkovic and Larsson 2002). Therefore, the software industry has recently started to adopt a more modular or Component-Based (CB) architecture that facilitates development of software products with a long lifetime.

In terms of system structure, CB system architecture is considered to be a key to the success of systems with a long life cycle. As compared to a monolithic software system, a CB system is considered to be flexible, extensible, and reusable (Crnkovic and Larsson 2002). Furthermore, a CB system is easier and more effective to maintain, because it can be maintained in parts (by components), as opposed to a monolithic system that needs to be maintained as a whole (Verbraeck et al. 2002; Kotlarsky 2007).

Component-Based Development (CBD) has its roots in manufacturing. The trend to develop products that have *component-based* or *modular* architecture is well established in the automotive, electronics, aeronautic and other manufacturing industries. Since the mid-60s when the concept of modular production was introduced, modular (later referred to as component-based) product architectures have become dominant in several manufacturing industries.

In the software industry, CBD is a relatively new trend. It emerged in the mid-90s with the introduction of software component technologies such as Enterprise JavaBeans, Microsoft COM and CORBA, and is increasingly becoming a major trend in software development (Peters and Pedrycz 2000; Kim 2002; Kotlarsky, Oshri et al. 2008).

> **Component-Based (Software) Development** involves (i) development of software components and (ii) building software systems through the planned integration of pre-existing (developed in-house or procured from the component market) software components (Bass et al. 2000).

Initially, CBD methodology was presented as a revolutionary approach to software development, promising dramatic improvements in software development efficiency, such as better quality, shorter time-to-market, and lower development costs. The main advantage expected from adopting a CBD methodology was the possibility to reuse components (Bass et al. 2000; Crnkovic and Larsson 2002; Ravichandran and Rothenberger 2003; Vitharana 2003; Kotlarsky, Oshri, van Hillegersberg et al. 2007).

However, empirical research on CBD has challenged these benefits and shown that 'it often took longer to develop a reusable component then to develop a system for a one-off purpose' (Huang et al. 2003). It was argued that the benefits of reuse are difficult to achieve in the first place; and they cannot be achieved immediately, but only in the long run (Crnkovic and Larsson 2002). Reuse of components allows companies to improve the productivity and quality of products; however, it may take a long time to develop software components, before they can be reused in a number of products.

Moreover, it was expected that adoption of CBD would further facilitate globally distributed development of software products, as happened in industries such as aeronautics, automotive, electronics and computer hardware, where CB architectures have been successfully used for setting up globally distributed design and production. For example, in the computer industry, Dell products include components produced by different vendors in various locations. In the automotive industry, the design of a car and the manufacture of car components involve designers and component suppliers at various dispersed locations (Olin et al. 1999). Even a very large and complex product such as an aircraft could be developed from remote locations, as in the case of Boeing-Rocketdyne (Malhotra et al. 2001), Boeing 777 (Yenne 2002) and Airbus.

Within the software industry, it was suggested that components could be developed in parallel independently by teams located in the same building or at remote locations. It was argued that CBD enables each site to take ownership of particular components and work on them independently without much need for inter-site communication and coordination (Colbert et al. 2001; Repenning et al. 2001). Carmel (1999) argued that adoption of component technology and CBD would facilitate globalisation in the software industry because components could be developed remotely with minimum coordination across dispersed locations:

> The software technology itself will continue to have an impact on global dispersion. Software globalization and dispersion will continue because of continued changes in underlying software technology. The industry is moving slowly, though unevenly, to a paradigm of software components. Small software components will be built and sold like subassemblies to be put together and made into larger, more comprehensive packages. Each of these small components will easily connect to other components. **These characteristics will allow distant teams of software developers to develop software components with only minimal coordination with others.** One future scenario is that low-cost nations will build the components and sell them to software design centres in industrialized countries for assembly (Carmel 1999:22; authors emphasis).

## Why study globally distributed component-based development

Nowadays, Globally Distributed Component-Based Development (GD CBD) is expected to become a promising area, as increasing numbers of companies are setting up software development in a globally distributed environment and at the same time are adopting a CBD methodology. Thus, being an emerging area, the management practice of GD CBD is evolving primarily on an *ad hoc* basis. At this time there is a lack of coherent, theory-based approaches for managing GD CBD.

This process of globalisation and adoption of CBD methodology has introduced potential benefits as well as new challenges in the management of software projects. Numerous potential benefits can be associated with GD CBD. First, such a practice creates an expectation that companies involved in GD CBD will enjoy traditional benefits related to global distribution, such as lower development costs and shorter time-to-market. Second, globalisation of CBD promises to solve problems associated with CBD, such as lack of skilled professionals. In this respect GD CBD opens an opportunity to employ software engineers with required skills to work on a project from dispersed geographical locations. Lastly, there is an expectation that the adoption of CBD by globally distributed organisations may mitigate coordination problems associated with traditional (non CB) GDSD.

On the other hand, research on co-located CBD projects has reported difficulties associated with the management of CBD projects, such as lack of stable standards, lack of reusable components, and problems related to the granularity and generality of components (Vitharana 2003). In the light of these problems, achieving the true potential of CBD, which is mainly about reusing components, is rather challenging in the context of co-located CBD (Crnkovic and Larsson 2002). Globally distributed organisations may face the above-mentioned and additional challenges (caused by geographical, time-zone and cultural differences) when adopting the practice of CBD.

So far, researchers in the Information Systems (IS) field have studied only limited aspects of the phenomenon of GD CBD: some have focused on the impact of globalisation on the management of traditional (non CB) software development projects, while others have focused on the management of CBD in co-located projects. Research on management of GD CBD projects that combine these two streams is just emerging and is still in its early stages (e.g. GD CBD project by IBM described in Carmel (1999); Skandia's project described by Alexandersen et al. (2003), lessons learned from GD CBD at Cisco Systems described by Turnlund (2004) and several articles discussing GD CBD published by the authors of this book).[1]

## The main objective of this book

This book aims to develop a comprehensive understanding of the *management of Globally Distributed Component-Based Development projects*. We focus on understanding **how companies organise and manage Component-Based Development in a globally distributed environment to be successful?**

To answer this question, the following objectives are set and steps undertaken:

- First, to understand *what factors contribute to success in GD CBD projects*. A theoretical lens that indicates potential factors contributing

---

[1]Kotlarsky (2007), Kotlarsky, Oshri, van Hillegersberg et al. (2007) and Kotlarsky, Oshri et al. (2008)

to success in GD CBD is developed based on the existing literature; it serves as a starting point for the empirical investigation.

• Second, to collect *managerial practices that illustrate how companies organise and manage GD CBD projects*. Managerial practices are collected in four companies.

Based on the results of the empirical investigation, the theoretical lens is revised and a theoretical framework is proposed. Furthermore, managerial practices that describe how companies organise and manage CBD in globally distributed environment are presented.

## The focus of this book

The focus of this book is on the management aspects of GD CBD projects, as described in Figure 1.1

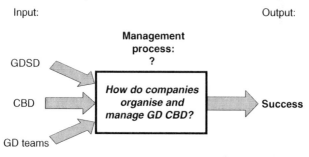

*Figure 1.1*   Research focus

A theoretical basis for studying the phenomenon of GD CBD draws upon the following related research streams (as illustrated in Figure 1.2): (i) research on traditional (non CB) GDSD which studies in depth the influence of global distribution on the management of software development projects; (ii) research on management of co-located and globally distributed CBD that discusses issues specific to CBD; and (iii) Organisational Behaviour (OB) research on collaboration in Globally Distributed (GD) teams that examines the importance of social aspects in global collaborations.

Different types of GD CBD can be distinguished: GD CBD for commercial purposes, component markets on the Internet, and Open Source Software development.

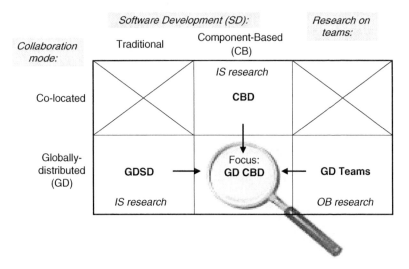

*Figure 1.2*   Related research streams

## Commercial GD CBD projects

Commercial GD CBD projects are projects that develop software for commercial purposes, i.e. for specific customers or a large market of potential customers. GD CBD for commercial purposes can involve several sites of a multinational company (for example, in-house GD CBD by SAP and Microsoft that involve sites in USA, Europe and India), or it can involve several geographically dispersed companies that work together as a joint venture or based on an outsourcing agreement. *This book focuses on commercial GD CBD projects that involve several sites of a multinational company.*

## Component Markets

Software component markets allow bidding, buying and selling of components from geographically dispersed locations over the Internet. They have been suggested to be the most effective way to gain the benefits of components reuse (Szyperski 1998; Traas and van Hillegersberg 2000), and the most appropriate marketplace to buy and sell components is the Internet: 'an international, freely accessible network which is perfectly suited for offering, promoting and distributing components' (Traas and van Hillegersberg 2000:114). Producers of components and intermediary organizations offering components for sale are globally distributed. The Internet allows users to link these globally distributed entities on one web-site.

Software component markets on the Internet represent a globally distributed trade (buying and selling) of individual components, and not of projects of development of CB systems. Thus, component markets on the Internet are considered as a possible source (supplier) of components for projects developing CB systems, but not as an instance of such projects.

### Open Source Software Development

Open Source Software (OSS) 'is a software whose source code is distributed without charge or limitations on possible modifications and distributions by third parties' (Crowston and Scozzi 2002:3). OSS has emerged from the hacker community (Wang and Wang 2001) facilitated by the Internet and the Web (Murugesan 1999). As stated on the Open Source community Web-site:[2]

> The basic idea behind open source is very simple: When programmers can read, redistribute, and modify the source code for a piece of software, the software evolves. People improve it, people adapt it, people fix bugs.

After the success of several OSS projects such as Linux and Apache, the interest of the academic and commercial worlds in OSS has grown (Murugesan 1999; Crowston and Scozzi 2002; de Vries et al. 2008). Development of OSS is entirely global and in most cases component-based: programmers from dispersed locations contribute to OSS via the Internet. Many OSS projects use component technologies, e.g. Java-Beans. However, as opposed to commercial GD CBD projects that are driven by business goals and involve paid staff, participation in development of OSS is voluntary (Murugesan 1999), and developers contribute to OSS 'for the sake of peer recognition and personal satisfaction' (Crowston and Scozzi 2002:3). Therefore, despite the fact that OSS is indeed an example of successful GD CBD, OSS and commercial GD CBD projects are different in their nature, and thus they need to be considered separately.

---

[2]www.opensource.org

## What academics and practitioners can learn from this book?

### Academic contribution

The research we have conducted over the last eight years which its results are presented in this book has three main contributions. First, it offers a theoretical framework that identifies factors contributing to success in GD CBD.

Second, managerial practices that describe how companies successfully organise and manage CBD in a GD environment are offered. The framework and the managerial practices suggest a more structured (theory-based) approach to studying the management of GD CBD projects than the current research tradition.

Third, this book provides an integrated view on the phenomenon of GD CBD which combines three areas of research: (i) research on *traditional* (non-CB) GDSD projects, (ii) research on the management of *co-located* CBD, and (iii) research on collaboration in GD teams.

### Practical contribution

The this book is also relevant to management practice for the following reasons.

First, managerial practices perceived as contributing to success in the studied GD CBD projects are of high relevance to managers. Other companies involved in GD CBD could learn from these practices how to organise and manage GD CBD in their organisations.

Second, a checklist for managers is proposed. It identifies specific activities that help to implement the above-mentioned managerial practices in the management of actual GD CBD projects.

Third, this book brings excellent examples from firms who have implemented CBD in their GD environments alongside an example of a failure case.

## The outline of this book

The book is divided to three parts. The first part reviews the main perspectives and aspects relating to component-based development in globally distributed teams. More specifically, Chapter 2 provides an overview of globally distributed teams and Chapter 3 explores component-based development in co-located teams, while considering the context of global teams. Part II in this book presents the results of a longitudinal study we have carried out in the last eight years. Chapter 4 brings insights regarding the management of component-based development in globally distributed teams at LeCroy, Chapter 5 at SAP, Chapter 6 at TCS and Chapter 7 at Baan. The third part of this book opens with Chapter 8 that provides an in depth analysis of the insights provided in the earlier chapters. The aim is to identify the most effective practices for GD CBD. Last but not least, Chapter 9 reflects on the learning generated in this book by revising the theoretical framework and by offering a checklist to managers.

# Part I

# The Essence of Globally Distributed Teams and Component-Based Development

# 2
# The Management of Globally Distributed Software Development

Research on Globally Distributed Software Development is just emerging and the discussion of aspects relating to Component-Based Development in distributed environments is even more limited. However, there are streams of research that have been looking into various aspects relating to globally distributed software development and to some extent into component-based development. First, there has been research on GDSD and the influence of global distribution on the management of software development projects. Second, there has been research on co-located CBD, and additional research on GD teams which addresses the importance of human and social issues for success in globally distributed teams and alliances. We bring these insights together in order to assess the most critical factors that play a role in the management of globally distributed teams.

*Globally distributed software development projects* are projects that consist of two or more teams working together to accomplish project goals from different geographical locations. In addition to geographical dispersion, globally distributed teams face timezone and cultural differences that may include but are not limited to different language, national traditions, values and norms of behaviour (Carmel 1999).

Research on the management of GDSD started to emerge in the second half of the 1990s as a subset of research on management of globally distributed projects and, by the late 90s (e.g. Carmel 1999; Karolak

15

1999), established itself as a separate research area. Historically, it has focused on traditional (non CB) software development.

Despite growing experience in the area of GDSD, research on this topic is still limited. Existing research is very fragmented and focuses on different aspects of distributed collaboration and at varying levels of analysis. For example, some studies focused on the various stages in GDSD, such as requirements analysis (Crowston and Kammerer 1998; Damian et al. 2007), while others considered issues related to offshore outsourcing of software development (Kumar and Willcocks 1996; Carmel 2003a, 2003b; Oshri, Kotlarsky and Willcocks 2007b; Oshri, van Fenema et al. 2008). Also, the unit of analysis used in IS development research varies among these studies: some studies considered the *organisation* as the unit of analysis (e.g. Grinter et al. 1999; Kobitzsch et al. 2001; Orlikowski 2002); others focused on globally distributed software development *projects*, as we do in this book.

The relevant literature reported problems and breakdowns encountered in GDSD projects, and practices that helped to overcome these difficulties (e.g. Carmel 1999; Karolak 1999; Smith and Blanck 2002). The main issues addressed in this literature include problems and breakdowns in GDSD projects, and different managerial practices offered to overcome the problems imposed by global distribution. These practices focused on activities to improve inter-site coordination, such as strategies for division of work, coordination and control mechanisms, communication patterns. Furthermore, technical support by means of (generic) collaborative tools and software engineering tools is suggested. Finally, some papers address issues related to inter-personal relationships and knowledge sharing and management. We will discuss these aspects in the following the sections.

## Problems and breakdowns in GDSD

Traditionally, past studies on management of GDSD tended to focus on issues pertaining to the geographical dispersal of work. Naturally, because of several constraints associated with globally distributed work, such as *distance, time-zone* and *cultural differences*, traditional coordination and control mechanisms tend to be less effective in global development projects (Rafii 1995; Carmel 1999; Karolak 1999; van Fenema and Kumar 2000; Espinosa and Carmel 2003; Herbsleb and Mockus 2003; Kotlarsky, van Fenema et al. 2008). *Distance* reduces the intensity of communications, in particular when people experience problems with media that cannot substitute for face-to-face communications. *Cultural differences* expressed in different languages, values, working and communication habits and implicit assumptions are believed to be embedded in the collective knowledge of a specific culture (Baumard 1999), and thus may cause misunderstanding and conflicts. *Time-zone differences* reduce opportunities for real time collaboration, as response time increases considerably when working hours at remote locations do not overlap. Therefore, receiving an answer to a simple question may take far longer than in co-located projects because of time-zone differences.

The literature also reports about problems and breakdowns in additional areas relating to GDSD projects, and in some cases elaborate on the practices that help overcome such challenges (e.g. (Carmel 1999; Karolak 1999; Smith and Blanck 2002; Oshri, Kotlarsky and Willcocks 2007a). The main problems and breakdowns reported in GDSD projects are:

- Breakdown of traditional coordination and control mechanisms (Carmel 1999; van Fenema 2002; Cheng et al. 2004; Lee, Delone et al. 2006).
- Loss of communication richness (Carmel 1999; van Fenema 2002; Cramton and Webber 2005; Iacovou and Nakatsu 2008).
- Limited opportunities for interaction (Espinosa et al. 2007).
- Leaner communication media (Espinosa et al. 2007).
- Lack of understanding of counterpart's context (Orlikowski 2002; Espinosa et al. 2007) and lack of communication norms in coordinating distributed teams (Ghosh et al. 2004; Lee, Delone et al. 2006).
- Language barriers (different competency in language) (Sarker and Sahay 2003; Kotlarsky and Oshri, 2005).
- Misunderstandings caused by cultural differences (different conversational styles, different subjective interpretations) (Battin et al. 2001; Olson and Olson 2004; Lee, Delone et al. 2006; Lee-Kelley and Sankey 2008) and language differences (Shachaf 2008).
- Dissonance or conflict: task and interpersonal conflict (Hinds and Mortensen 2005; Lee-Kelley and Sankey 2008).
- Loss of team cohesion and motivation to collaborate: decreased morale and lack of trust (Jarvenpaa and Leidner 1998; Carmel 1999; Karolak 1999; Shachaf, 2008).
- Asymmetry in distribution of information among sites (Carmel 1999; Kotlarsky, van Fenema et al. 2008).
- Difficulty in collaborating due to different skills and training, expertise in different tools and technologies, mismatch in IT infrastructure (van Fenema 2002; Sarker and Sahay 2004; Lee, Delone et al. 2006).

- Lack of informal, inter-personal communications (Herbsleb and Grinter 1999; Cramton and Webber 2005; Kotlarsky, Oshri and Willcocks 2007).
- Lack of effective work processes and poorer perceived performance (Cramton and Webber 2005).
- Difficulties to work in different time zones (Karolak 1999; Kobitzsch et al. 2001; Lee-Kelley and Sankey 2008).
- Risk factors in collaborative software development such as trust, culture and collaborative communication (Mohtashami et al. 2006). Iacovou and Nakatsu (2008) summarise the top risk factors of offshore-outsourced development project in three major categories: client-vendor communication (i.e. miscommunication of original set of requirements, language barriers and poor change controls), client's internal management issues (i.e. lack of top management commitment, inadequate user involvement, lack of offshore project management know-how, managing end-user expectations and failure of consider all costs), and vendor capabilities (i.e. lack of business and technical know-how by the offshore team).
- Delays in distributed collaborative work processes: unproductive waits for the other side to respond with clarification or feedback (caused by time zone differences and different interpretations) (Jarvenpaa and Leidner 1998; Herbsleb et al. 2000; Herbsleb and Mockus 2003).

The surveyed studies report on successful and unsuccessful experiences of companies engaged in GDSD projects and recommend a number of practices that would help these companies to reduce some of these problems imposed by global distribution. These practices will be discussed in the following section.

## How to organise and manage GDSD

### Software development methodology: background

Software development requires a multiplicity of tasks to be performed by multiple actors (Kraut and Streeler 1995). Typically, the structure of a software development process 'relies on a guiding set of principles or methodology that defines roles, tasks, and their inter-relationships over time' (Beath and Orlikowski 1994).

Historically, software systems have been developed following a Waterfall approach, which prescribes a number of phases to be followed in a sequential manner: requirements analysis and specifications, conceptual design, coding and testing, as illustrated in Figure 2.1.

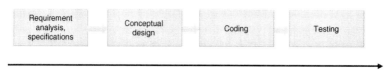

*Figure 2.1*    The Waterfall approach: traditional software development lifecycle

The increasing complexity of current IS, combined with the demand for shorter project development cycles, has led to alternative approaches, such as parallel (concurrent) development based on organising tasks in an overlapping (parallel) mode (Terwiesch and Loch 1996). For contract-driven software (developed for a specific customer, as opposed to off-the-shelf, sometimes customisable, software systems), methodologies aiming to increase user participation in the development process have been developed (Hirschheim and Klein 1994). Examples of these methodologies include Joint Application Development (JAD), Rapid Application Development (RAD) and prototyping (Carmel et al. 1993; Trevor 1994; Beynon-Davies et al. 1999; van Fenema 2002).

The choice of a development methodology (e.g. Waterfall and/or parallel) has implications for the way development work is divided and integrated (Kraut and Streeler 1995; van Fenema 2002). In particular, organising sequentially dependent tasks to be conducted in parallel changes the way tasks are coordinated and controlled. For example, overlap between tasks means that developers cannot check output from preceding tasks and compare them to standards, and therefore they need rely on inter-personal communications (van Fenema 2002). In a globally distributed environment, work is divided between teams and individuals at multiple geographically dispersed locations, and thus coordination and integration of work need to be done across these remote locations. This resulted in the delay of work completion time as distributed works appear to take longer time to complete compared to similar works that are collocated (Herbsleb and Mockus 2003). However, Holmström et al. (2006) find that agile practices seem to be useful for reducing delays associated with communication, coordination and control problems in global software development.

As discussed in the previous section, GDSD projects suffer from coordination breakdowns. The literature on GDSD has suggested a number of practices that would help to organise and manage GDSD projects to overcome (potential) problems and breakdowns (these practices are discussed in the following two sections). These practices mainly focus on *inter-site coordination*, aiming to improve coordination between remote sites, and *tools and technologies* that make it possible to collaborate in a distributed mode.

### Inter-site coordination in GDSD projects

Managerial practices for inter-site coordination in GDSD suggested in the literature involve (i) strategies regarding *division of work*, which aim to make easier coordination and integration of work conducted at remote locations, (ii) specific *coordination mechanisms* adapted for a distributed environment, and (iii) *communication patterns* aiming to make inter-site coordination more efficient, through planning systematic communication between remote counterparts and establishing rules of communications. These three groups of practices are now discussed below.

### *Division of work*

In GDSD, work-packages assigned to remote sites need to be managed and coordinated to ensure a successful outcome. Typically, strategies to divide work between locations suggested in the IS literature on management of GDSD projects aim to reduce needs for inter-site coordination and communications. In particular, strategies recommended for division of work are:

- Division of work by *phase/process step* when globally dispersed sites engage in different phases of a project in a sequential manner (i.e. work is handed over to a remote site after completing certain process steps) (Carmel 1999; Grinter et al. 1999; Taweel and Brereton 2006), as illustrated in Figure 2.2 (Scenario A).

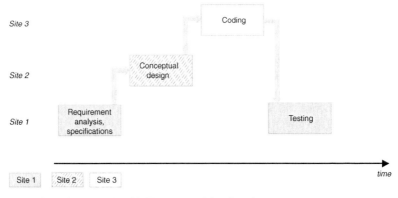

*Figure 2.2*   Scenario A – GDSD organised *by phase/process step*

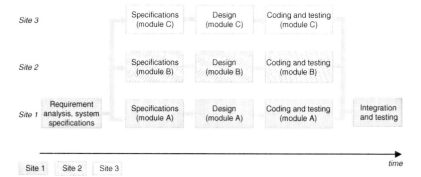

*Figure 2.3*   Scenario B – GDSD organised *by product structure (product module)*

- Division of work by *product structure (product module)* when each product module/feature is developed at a single site (Carmel 1999; Grinter et al. 1999). This approach allows for different sites to work on different modules in parallel. Figure 2.3 illustrates a possible scenario (Scenario B), when a system is divided into modules (typically different product functions) and each module is allocated to a different site.

Structured, well-defined tasks are more suitable to be allocated by *phase/process step*, while abstract (unstructured, loosely defined) tasks are more appropriate to be allocated *by product structure (product module)* (Carmel 1999; Karolak 1999; van Fenema 2002).

- Division of work that *minimises requirements for cross-site communication and synchronisation* in the context of particular types of product architecture and mechanisms for coordinating work (Ebert and De Neve 2001; Repenning et al. 2001; Herbsleb and Mockus 2003). To achieve this, it was recommended that 'tightly coupled work items that require frequent coordination and synchronisation should be performed within one site' (Mockus and Weiss 2001). Figure 2.4 illustrates a possible scenario (Scenario C) with tasks that require frequent coordination: requirements analysis and specification, conceptual design and integration and testing are conducted at one site, and only well-defined tasks (coding and testing of different modules) are conducted at two locations in parallel.
- Division of work based on *product customisation*, so that one site develops the product and other sites perform customisation, i.e. changes such as adding features and enhancements for specific customers (Grinter et al. 1999). In this case, often sites that customise

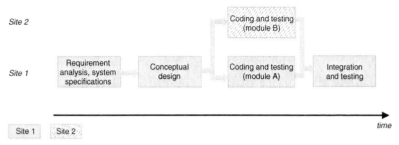

*Figure 2.4*   Scenario C – only well-defined tasks distributed across locations

the product are in the proximity of a customer. Figure 2.5 illustrates a possible scenario (Scenario D) when a system is developed in one location (site 1), and other globally dispersed sites customise the system for specific customers (site 2) or local markets, i.e. large number of potential (local) customers (site 3).

- Division of work across time zones; where a task is passed from one person at the end of a working day to another person 'across time zones' (Taweel and Brereton 2006) in order to reduce the project completion time and improve the resource utilisation through 24 hours development (Jalote and Jain 2006).

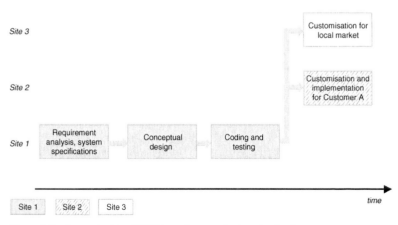

*Figure 2.5*   Scenario D – GDSD based on *product customisation*

## Coordination mechanisms

A number of coordination mechanisms are recommended to overcome problems and breakdowns in GDSD projects. These are, in particular:

- A more explicit, documented and formalised project process: standardising and documenting the development methodology, distributing it across sites and storing it in a shared repository; educating all team members in the chosen methodologies (Carmel 1999; Karolak 1999; Mockus and Herbsleb 2002; van Fenema 2002; Amrit and van Hillegersberg 2008).
- Promoting task-related interaction by encouraging interdependence and reliance on one another among the members of distributed teams (Hart and McLeod 2003).
- Providing approaches that can coordinate distributed software development tasks such as Integration Centric Development (Taxen 2006).
- Adopting a more structured project management approach. Ghosh and Varghese (2004) propose a project management framework that is based on Process Restructuring, where it can be used for managing and tracking distributed development of a large product efficiently. A development team according to both is organised as Centers of Excellence which can be geographically dispersed. Lee-Kelley and Sankey (2008) support that such approach will provide role clarity and increase predictability in expected behaviours and quality performance.
- Encouraging visits to remote sites and face-to-face meetings (Carmel 1999; Malhotra and Majchrzak 2005; Oshri, Kotlarsky et al. 2008; Lee-Kelley and Sankey 2008). However, some argued that face-face-meetings do not necessarily create the social relationships that can overcome structural impediments. Rather, the importance of the situational context while retaining the impact of demographic occupational and individual factors needs to be reintroduced. Despite obvious difference, it is possible for people to create a shared identity and culture (David et al. 2008).
- Establishing liaisons between remote locations (Battin et al. 2001; van Fenema 2002).
- Rotating team members (Carmel 1999; Carmel and Agarwal 2001; Smith and Blanck 2002).
- Creating transparency in project goals and company vision (Carmel 1999; Ebert and De Neve 2001).
- Building awareness of the work conducted at remote sites (e.g. making project plans accessible over the Web); of remote teams (e.g. creating a web-page for each team member with personal information); and

of local context (e.g. providing information about local working hours and holidays) (Kobylinski et al. 2002; Mockus and Herbsleb 2002; Smith and Blanck 2002; Espinosa et al. 2003).

- Identifying different modes of task assignment mechanisms: self-assignment, assigning to others and consult with others (Crowston et al. 2007).
- Raising cultural awareness and empathy through careful team selection (e.g. some members must have prior exposure and experience in distance working so that they can help other members who are new to virtual projects dealing with possible language, accent or attitudinal differences) and tailored personal development programmes and team building exercises (Oshri et al. 2005; Lee-Kelley and Sankey 2008).

### *Communication patterns*

Communication patterns recommended for GDSD teams include the following:

- Scheduling systematic phone/video meetings between remote counterparts (managers and team members) (Karolak 1999; Herbsleb and Mockus 2003; Oshri, Kotlarsky et al. 2008).
- Establishing communication protocols that cover ground rules and expectations concerning communications (e.g. for emails) (Carmel 1999; Olson and Olson 2004; Sarker and Sahay 2004; Oshri, Kotlarsky and Willcocks 2007a).
- Providing appropriate training and access to computing and communication technologies, so that efficacy and willingness to communicate are actively encouraged (Lee-Kelley and Sankey 2008).
- Communicating laterally (Carmel 1999; Smith and Blanck 2002; van Fenema 2002; Herbsleb and Mockus 2003).
- Being clear and patient in communications, as counterparts might not be able to comprehend and communicate in English (Espinosa et al. 2003; Paasivaara 2003; Oshri et al. 2005).
- Investing in language and cultural training (Battin et al. 2001; Smith and Blanck 2002; Kotlarsky, Oshri and Willcocks 2007).

### Tools and technologies to support GDSD

Tools and technologies suggested to overcome problems and breakdowns in GDSD and enable collaboration in a distributed environment comprise (i) a powerful *ICT infrastructure* that allows the transfer of data at high speed, (ii) *generic collaborative technologies* enabling remote colleagues to connect and communicate, and (iii) *software engineering tools* that support software development activities conducted in parallel at remote locations.

## ICT infrastructure

A reliable and high bandwidth ICT infrastructure is required to ensure connectivity between remote sites (Carmel 1999). ICT is a tool that facilitates the process of boundary crossing to overcome the challenges presented by remote and culturally diverse team members. ICT particularly mitigated the negative impact of intercultural miscommunication and supported the positive impact on decision making (Shachaf 2008). Whereas Paul (2006) suggested that ICT, particularly telemedicine can help organisations manage different facets of collaborative activities in the form of knowledge transfer, discovery, and creation: depending on the type of projects engaged in and the technology utilised.

## Collaborative technology

Collaborative technology can be used to improve collaboration in GDSD teams. The most commonly suggested collaborative technologies are:

| | References: |
|---|---|
| • **Teleconferencing combined with e-meeting** | (Shachaf 2008)<br>(Lee-Kelley and Sankey 2008) |
| • **Virtual whiteboards** | (Kotlarsky, van Fenema |
| • **Bulletin boards** | et al. 2008) |
| • **Email** | (Oshri, Kotlarsky and Willcocks |
| • **Chat (Instant Messaging)** | 2007a) |
| • **Phone / audio conference** | (Lee, Delone et al. 2006) |
| • **Videoconference** | (Paul 2006) |
| • **Internet/intranet** | (Taweel and Brereton 2006) |
| • **Group calendar** | (Kotlarsky and Oshri 2005) |
| • **Discussion list** | (Malhotra and Majchrzak 2005) |
| • **Electronic meeting system** | (Sarker and Sahay 2004) |
| | (Herbsleb and Mockus 2003) |
| | (Smith and Blanck 2002) |
| | (Herbsleb et al. 2002) |
| | (van Fenema 2002) |
| | (Carmel and Agarwal 2002) |
| | (Mockus and Herbsleb 2002) |
| | (Handel and Herbsleb 2002) |
| | (Ebert and De Neve 2001) |
| | (Battin et al. 2001) |
| | (Herbsleb et al. 2000) |
| | (Carmel 1999) |
| | (Karolak 1999) |

Typically, collaborative technologies recommended for GDSD teams are classified according to the time/space dimension: the two-by-two same/different place and same/different time matrix proposed in computer mediated communications literature (DeSanctis and Gallupe 1987) was widely supported in the research on GDSD projects to classify collaborative technologies (e.g. Carmel 1999; Smith and Blanck 2002). This matrix

*Table 2.1*   Types of collaboration technology (adapted from Huis et al. 2002)

| | Setting | | |
|---|---|---|---|
| | **Different place/ different time (off-line)**, i.e. *support between encounters* | **Different place/ same time (on-line)**, i.e. *support for electronic encounters* | **Same place/same time**, i.e. *support for face-to-face meetings* |
| **Communication Systems:** *aim to make communications between remote people easy, cheap and fast* | • fax<br>• email<br>• voice-mail<br>• video-mail | • telephone<br>• mobile phone<br>• desktop-video<br>• video/audio-conferencing systems (multi-point)<br>• chat system | |
| **Information sharing systems:** *aim to make the storage and retrieval of large amounts of information quick, easy, reliable and inexpensive* | • document sharing systems<br>• computer conferencing | • tele-consultation systems<br>• application for searching remote information sources | • presentation systems |
| **Collaboration systems:** *aim to improve teamwork by providing document sharing and co-authoring facilities* | • co-editing systems | • shared white-board, CAD, word-process or spread-sheet | • Group Decision Support Systems |
| **Coordination systems:** *aim to coordinate distributed teamwork by coordinating work processes* | Synchronisers:<br>• group calendar<br>• shared project planning<br>• shared workflow system | • awareness/ notification systems (e.g. 'active batch') | • command and control centre support systems |
| **Social encounter systems:** *aim to facilitate unintended interactions* | | • media spaces<br>• virtual spaces | |

contains four categories and corresponding technologies: *same place/same time* (collocated group decision support), *same place/different time* (workflow systems), *same time/different place* (telephone, chatting), *different place/different time* (bulletin board). However, this framework does not take recent technical progress into account, e.g. mobile technology and advanced collaborative tools such as Groove (http://www.groove.net).

A more advanced classification of collaborative technologies was suggested by Huis et al. (2002): the authors distinguish between several types of collaborative technology that support different needs of globally distributed teams in different time/place settings, as illustrated in Table 2.1.

### Tools to support software engineering

In addition to collaborative technologies that are generic to a great extent, a number of tools specific to software development are suggested to support GDSD teams. The most commonly suggested tools include the following:

|  | References: |
|---|---|
| • **Tool to detect socio-technical coordination problems i.e. Socio-Technical Patterns** | (Amrit and van Hillegersberg 2008) |
| • **Graphical design tool (Component Workbench (CWB)) for easy composition of applications** | (Kotlarsky, Oshri, van Hillegersberg et al. 2007) (Lee et al. 2006) (Arato et al. 2005) (Cheng et al. 2004) |
| • **Configuration and version management tool** | (Smith and Blanck 2002) (Carmel and Agarwal 2002) |
| • **Source-management system** | (Mockus and Herbsleb 2002) |
| • **Document management system** | (Handel and Herbsleb 2002) (Ebert and De Neve 2001) |
| • **Replicated databases/ repositories** | (Battin et al. 2001) (Herbsleb et al. 2000) |
| • **CASE tools that support modelling and visibility of design** | (Carmel 1999) (Karolak 1999) (Grinter 1999) |
| • **Integrated Development Environment (IDE) toolset, which combines tools such as editor, compiler, debugger** | (Grinter 1995) |

These tools ensure consistency in the product and development environment across dispersed locations.

Furthermore, adding collaborative capabilities such as email, Instant Messaging (IM), screen sharing, and a configuration management tool to the Integrated Development Environment (IDE) toolset was recommended by Cheng et al. (2004) to deal with breakdown in communication and coordination among developers. Cheng et al. (2004) argue that integrating collaborative capabilities into IDE holds great potential for easing programmers' development activities. However, this integration introduces a number of technical and design challenges, in particular: (i) building for extensibility, interoperability, and flexibility; (ii) choosing and designing the 'right' set of collaborative features; and (iii) supporting transitions between individual and group work.

### The management of GDSD projects: summary

Past research suggests that the proper application of technical and operational mechanisms, such as tools, technologies and coordination mechanisms, is the chief factor that may lead to successful GDSD projects. Figure 2.6 illustrates schematically the potential factors that contribute to success in GDSD projects.

Overwhelmingly, the solutions proposed to support globally distributed teams are technical in nature, involving little attention to the human and social aspects involved in globally distributed work (Karolak 1999; Battin et al. 2001; Ebert and De Neve 2001; Espinosa and Carmel 2003; Oshri, Kotlarsky and Willcocks 2007a). Furthermore, in the few studies that focused on the social aspects of globally distributed work, trust and social communications were indicated as barriers to achieving success between globally distributed teams. For example, Jarvenpaa and Leidner (1998) indicated that a lack of trust is likely to develop between

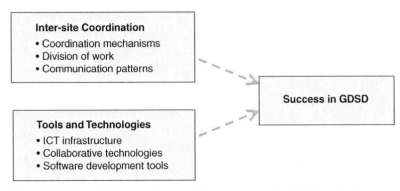

*Figure 2.6*   Potential factors that contribute to success in GDSD projects

globally distributed teams, while Carmel (1999) raised a concern about possible breakdowns in communications that may cause coordination problems because of language barriers, cultural differences, asymmetry in distribution of information among sites, and a lack of team spirit. In essence, past research is rather concerned with the barriers that social aspects present to globally distributed collaboration (Jarvenpaa et al. 1998; Jarvenpaa and Leidner 1998).

While, traditionally, the main focus of the IS literature on globally distributed projects has been on coordination and technical aspects related to the management of GDSD projects, OB research has acknowledged the importance of social-related aspects in global collaborations, such as trust and inter-personal relationships (Storck 2000; Child 2001). Avram (2007) for example concludes that human is the decisive factor for the success of projects in distributed teams environment. Furthermore, it is suggested that knowledge sharing is important for success in globally distributed teams (Faraj and Sproull 2000; Orlikowski 2002; Kotlarsky and Oshri 2005; Oshri, Kotlarsky and Willcocks 2007b; Oshri, van Fenema et al. 2008).

The following section will elaborate on the role of social aspects and knowledge sharing for success in GD teams.

## Social aspects in globally distributed teams

Among the many social-related factors contributing to collaboration, past studies have considered formal and informal communications (e.g. Dyer 2001; Kotlarsky, van Fenema et al. 2008), trust (e.g. Arino et al. 2001; Jarvenpaa and Leidner 1998; Brown et al. 2004), motivation (e.g. Child 2001) and social ties (e.g. Granovetter 1973; Storck 2000; Kotlarsky and Oshri 2005; Avram 2007). As argued above, past studies related to software development in the context of globally distributed teams have mainly raised concerns about managers' ability to overcome geographical, time-zone and cultural differences. For example, according to Smith and Blanck (2002:294), 'an effective team depends on open, effective communication, which in turn depends on trust among members. Thus, trust is the foundation, but it is also the very quality that is most difficult to build at a distance'.

---

*Trust* is defined by Child (2001:275) as 'the willingness of the one person or group to relate to another in the belief that the other's action will be beneficial rather than detrimental, even though this cannot be guaranteed'.

Trust is more likely to be built if personal contact, frequent interactions and socialising between teams and individuals are facilitated (Arino et al. 2001; Ba 2001; Child 2001). However, establishing trust in virtual team can be complicated as members may have no record of past collaboration to build and may never even meet face to face (Greenberg et al. 2007).

Rapport, another imperative factor contributing to collaboration between project teams and individuals, is more likely to be fostered in a co-located environment (Gremler and Gwinner 2000).

> ***Rapport*** is defined as 'the quality of the relation or connection between interactants, marked by harmony, conformity, accord, and affinity' (Bernieri et al. 1994).

It has also been argued that informal communications play a critical role in coordination activities leading to success in co-located software development (Kraut and Streeler 1995). As the size and complexity of IS development increase, the need for supporting informal communications also increases dramatically (Herbsleb and Moitra 2001). Consequently, in distributed development projects the amount of such communication is greatly reduced as a result of time, cultural differences and geographical distance (Kotlarsky et al. 2006): this, in turn, leads to the majority of problems reported in GDSD projects. For example, lack of interpersonal communications between remote team members and limited mutual knowledge are argued to be factors contributing to breakdowns in coordination and communication (Cramton 2001; Hansen 2002; Kotlarsky et al. 2006).

Furthermore, a related study on distributed social networks by Herbsleb and Mockus (2003) suggested that distributed social networks may be less effective than local social networks.[1] Their research reveals that (i) distributed social networks are much smaller than same-site social networks, (ii) there is far less frequent communication in distributed social networks compared to same-site social networks, (iii) people find it much more difficult to identify distant colleagues with necessary expertise and to

---

[1]Herbsleb and Mockus (2003) define *social network* as a network of people with whom one interacts with a frequency that varies from more than once a day to a few times a year. A *distributed social network* is a social network that involves people from dispersed locations, while a *same-site social network* is a social network that involves people from one location.

communicate effectively with them, and (iv) people at different sites are less likely to perceive themselves as part of the same team than people who are at the same site.

By and large, most studies tend to treat the social aspects involved in globally distributed IS development projects as constraints, while some have offered evidence suggesting that factors such as trust and rapport have a positive impact on global collaboration (Storck 2000; Child 2001; Kotlarsky and Oshri 2005; Oshri, Kotlarsky and Willcocks 2007b).

### Knowledge sharing in globally distributed teams

Past studies on knowledge sharing in IS development projects have focused mainly on co-located sites (e.g. Faraj and Sproull 2000; Massey et al. 2002), whereas the discussion of knowledge-sharing mechanisms and the contribution of knowledge-sharing activities to success in the context of distributed IS teams is still limited. Existing studies on GDSD have reported on the problems caused by lack of shared knowledge (e.g. Kobitzsch et al. 2001; Herbsleb and Mockus 2003; Kotlarsky, Oshri and van Fenema 2008).

However, organisational behaviour studies on GD teams have recognised the importance of knowledge sharing for the success of such teams (Majchrzak et al. 2000; Storck 2000; Cramton 2001; Hansen 2002; Orlikowski 2002; Cummings 2004). For example, Storck (2000) claims that sharing knowledge is important to building trust and improving the effectiveness of group work. Herbsleb and Moitra (2001) reiterate this observation, claiming that without an effective sharing of information, projects might suffer from coordination problems leading to unsuccessful project outcomes. Hill (2005) however, argues that knowledge sharing between team members is positively related to shared leadership, and this relationship will be partially mediated by trust. Lee, Delone et al. (2006:51) agree that 'capturing, storing, transferring, sharing and assimilating knowledge across location is vital for capitalizing the distributed knowledge across diverse development teams'. In addition, Espinosa et al. (2007) support that shared knowledge of the team and presence awareness could lessen the negative effects that geographic distance has on coordination. Meanwhile, Joshi and Sarker (2007) observe that knowledge transfer is critical to success of organizational initiatives, where multiple stakeholders with varying knowledge and backgrounds need to create a shared frame of reference. The creation of this reference depends on how the individuals involved share knowledge and learn from each other.

Other studies have described the complexity involved in sharing knowledge in co-located sites. For example, it has been acknowledged that the sharing of knowledge is a rather difficult task because of the idea that knowledge can be tacit (Polanyi 1967). The knowledge transformation model proposed by Nonaka and Takeuchi (1995), who conducted their research in co-located sites of electronic goods companies in Japan, is one example that demonstrates the complexity involved in transforming tacit to explicit knowledge and vice versa.

Paul (2006) however argues that collaborative activities in virtual settings can facilitate the leveraging of the knowledge assets by enabling the communication and application of tacit knowledge without failure to convert it into explicit knowledge.

Additional support to the above view is provided by Faraj and Sproull (2000), who claim that instead of sharing specialised knowledge individuals should focus on knowing where expertise is located and needed. Such an approach towards knowledge sharing is also known as *transactive memory* (Wegner 1987; Oshri, van Fenema et al. 2008).

---

*Transactive memory* is defined as the set of knowledge possessed by group members coupled with an awareness of who knows what (Wegner 1987).

---

Transactive memory was found to positively affect group performance and collaboration by quickly bringing the needed expertise to knowledge seekers (Faraj and Sproull 2000; Storck 2000; Kotlarsky and Oshri 2005; Oshri, van Fenema et al. 2008). The transactive memory of a globally distributed team implies that team members know the composition of a remote team (the people and their roles) and know the areas of expertise of their remote counterparts.

Joshi and Sarker (2007) propose that knowledge source attributes: capability, credibility and extent of communication could affect knowledge transfer within information system development teams. However their empirical study found that capability it not a significant role in knowledge transfer.

Further implications for knowledge sharing may arise when teams are faced with cultural, geographical and time-zone differences in globally distributed work. Herbsleb, Mockus et al. (2000:3) described in their study how one global IS development project was facing major challenges to identify who knows what:

There was a nearly total absence of informal, unplanned communications across sites. The difficulties of knowing who to contact about what, of initiating contact, and of communicating effectively across sites, led to a number of serious coordination problems.

Similarly, a need to know whom to contact about what was reported in a number of studies (e.g. Grant 1996; Orlikowski 2002; Kotlarsky and Oshri 2005; Oshri, van Fenema et al. 2008).

Indeed, research has suggested that such hurdles in managing distributed projects could be avoided through the build-up of *collective knowledge* (also referred as *common knowledge*), which comprises elements of knowledge that are common to all members of an organisation (Grant 1996). In the case of GD CBD projects, the 'organisation' involves all people participating in the globally distributed project from their remote locations.

---

*Collective knowledge* comprises the profound knowledge of an environment, of established rules, laws and regulations and 'knowledge of an unspoken, of the invisible structure of a situation, a certain wisdom' (Baumard 1999). It includes language, other forms of symbolic communication and shared meaning (Grant 1996).

---

Collective knowledge is based on the wisdom of social experience (Baumard 1999). In co-located organisations this would mean the development of a collective mind (Weick and Roberts 1993; Crowston and Kammerer 1998; Weick et al. 1999) through participation in tasks and social rituals (Orr 1990; Orlikowski 2002).

Cummings (2004) argues 'that the value of external knowledge sharing increases when work groups are more structurally diverse. A structurally diverse work group is one in which the members, by virtue of their different organisational affiliations, roles, or positions, can expose the group to unique sources of knowledge'.

### Social aspects in globally distributed teams: summary

The literature offers several factors, such as trust, rapport, transactive memory and collective knowledge, that may positively affect collaboration through social activities and personal interactions. Figure 2.7 illustrates schematically the potential factors that may contribute to success in GD teams. The following chapter will examine aspects relating to CBD.

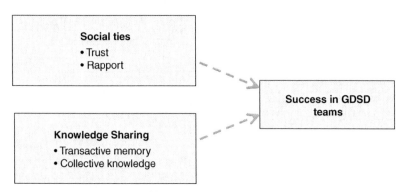

*Figure 2.7*    Potential factors that contribute to success in GD teams

# 3
# The Management of Component-Based Software Development

*The whole idea is that we can take the bunch of different components and create a different instrument within weeks is kind of optimistic, but within a few months rather than in a few years.*

(Director of Software Engineering, LeCroy)

CBD has its roots in manufacturing. The trend to develop products that have a *Component-Based* or *modular* architecture is well established in automotive, electronics, aircraft and other manufacturing types of industries.[1] Since the mid-1960s, when the concept of modular production (Starr 1965) was introduced, modular (later referred to as component-based) product architectures became dominant in manufacturing industries.

> In manufacturing, **components** (or *modules*)[2] are defined as parts of an assembly, chunks that 'implement one or a few functional elements in their entirety' (Ulrich and Eppinger 2000).

> A **Component-Based system** is a system that has two properties: (1) components, and (2) connections (interactions) between components that are well defined and are generally fundamental to the primary functions of the product (Ulrich and Eppinger 2000).

---

[1]In manufacturing, a product is assembled from parts, as opposed to process industries, where a production process is based on mixing raw materials and/or chemical processes (e.g. chemical, pharmaceutical, food industries).
[2]There is some confusion among practitioners as well as academics regarding the definition of a *component* and a *module*. Typically, *components* imply finer granularity than *modules* (a module could consist of a number of components). However, in practice and academic literature these two terms are often used interchangeably.

As opposed to a monolithic system, a CB system potentially has a number of advantages for production, and can increase the competitive advantage of a company in the market.

First, a CB system allows changes to be made to isolated functional elements of the product without affecting the design of other components (Ulrich and Eppinger 2000). Thus, changes in a product could be made fairly easily and quickly (as changes in different components could be done in parallel and without causing unwanted side-effects).

Second, from a marketing perspective, having a CB system enables easier customisation by facilitating different product configurations for different users and different markets (e.g. the same car model designed for different countries can be somewhat different), and increases product variety (the range of product models). In particular, a CB system architecture (structure) makes the integration of components easier, which is important for:

(i)    upgrades (the possibility to replace a component, typically by a more recent version), as technological capabilities or users' needs evolve;

(ii)   add-ons (adding components by a third party) according to a user's needs; and

(iii)  flexibility in use, as some products can be configured by users to provide different capabilities (e.g. many cameras can be used with a different lens and flash options).

In each of these cases, a CB architecture allows a minimisation of the physical changes required to achieve a functional change (Ulrich and Eppinger 2000). In a CB system components could be integrated relatively easily either by a *vendor* or by an *end user*:

- *Vendor integration:* Dell is an example of a vendor that assembles computers from pre-defined components, according to the specific choice of a customer.

- *End-user integration:* Many products are sold by a manufacturer as a basic unit, to which users can add components, often produced by third parties, according to their specific needs. For instance, the computer is a basic unit to which third-party storage devices (e.g. CD-RW, memory key, zip drive) could be added according to customer needs and personal preferences.

Third, standardisation of components allows the use of the same component in multiple products, thus reducing time-to-market, and production costs (Ulrich and Eppinger 2000; Lau and Wang 2007). Time-to-market is shorter because reusing components saves the time required for design and quality assurance of these components. Production costs are lower, because fixed costs for setting up production lines and equipment are divided over more components as batch size increases. Similarly, suppliers often give a quantity discount for larger quantities of components to be procured. Moreover, knowledge and experience invested in the design of a component that is later reused in a number of products implies reuse of this knowledge and experience.

Adopting CB design facilitated globalisation in manufacturing industries, because a CB system is relatively easy to develop from dispersed locations and/or it is possible to buy parts from suppliers located all over the world. For instance, in the computer industry, Dell products include components produced by different vendors in various locations. In the automotive industry, the design of a car and the building of car components involves designers and component suppliers at various dispersed locations (Olin et al. 1999). Even a very large and complex product such as an aircraft could be developed from remote locations, as in the case of the Boeing Rocketdyne (Malhotra et al. 2001), Boeing 777 (Yenne 2002) and Airbus.

In the light of CB systems, a number of similarities could be observed between the manufacturing and software worlds. Similar to manufacturing, in the software world a system can be integrated from components by a vendor or an end-user. For example, an end-user can buy separately Internet Explorer, Adobe Acrobat and Microsoft Office and plug (install) them together. In addition, vendors (e.g. SAP, PeopleSoft) of complex software systems, such as ERP (Enterprise Resource Planning), SCM (Supply Chain Management) and CRM (Customer Relationship Management) systems, typically integrate components required by a customer for that customer.

The next section will elaborate on CBD trends in the software industry.

## CBD in the software industry: background

In the software development industry CBD is a relatively new trend. CBD emerged in the mid-90s with the introduction of *software component technologies* such as Enterprise JavaBeans, Microsoft COM and CORBA, and is increasingly becoming a major trend in software development.

*Software component technology* includes the software that provides a runtime environment for software components (sometimes called a component *framework*), as well as other tools useful for designing, building, combining, or deploying components or applications built from components (Bass et al. 2000).

Information Technology (IT) providers are turning to software component technologies as the most promising way of meeting demands for increased productivity, reduced time-to-market and improved system quality (Peters and Pedrycz 2000; Kim 2002).

---

*Component-Based (Software) Development* involves (i) development of software components and (ii) building software systems through the planned integration of pre-existing (developed in-house or procured from the component market) software components (Bass et al. 2000). CBD also involves reusing application frameworks, which provide the architecture for assembling components into a software system (Vitharana 2003).

*CBD Methodology* comprises (i) software component technology and technical steps for (ii) designing and implementing software components, (iii) assembling systems from pre-built software components, and (iv) deploying assembled systems in their target environment (Bass et al. 2000).

---

As a result of applying CBD methodology, a *Component-Based system* is developed.

---

On a conceptual level, a ***component-based system*** could be described as consisting of components that are integrated by means of interfaces (similar to a CB system in manufacturing). On a more detailed level, there are numerous ways to design and integrate components.

---

The next section will elaborate on the definitions and main characteristics of software components, and explain how components can be integrated into a CB system.

## A component-based system

### What is a software component?

Similarly to manufacturing, in software development there is some confusion about what a *component* is:

> Industry doesn't speak consistently to the question of what a software component is. Some equate commercial-off-the-shelf (COTS)

software packages with components. Some consider the use of some underlying technology such as Microsoft's COM to be the defining criterion for component. Quite apart from these conceptual categories is the question of size. Some consider components to be the small-scale equivalent of objects in object-oriented programs, while others consider components to be the large-grained equivalent of subsystems or larger (Bass et al. 2000).

To clarify this confusion, we integrate several definitions of software components; these definitions emphasise different aspects of components, such as interfaces, the component market, replacement and reusability (discussed below).

### *The concept of components*

The main concepts behind components are shown in Figure 3.1.

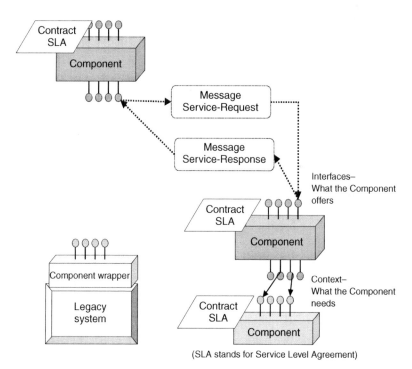

*Figure 3.1*   The main concepts behind components (adapted from Alexandersen et al. 2003)

- *Components* are units of independent production, acquisition, and deployment that interact to form a functioning system (Szyperski 1998).
- *Components* are executable units of code that provide a set of services through a specific interface (Vitharana 2003). They offer a precisely defined set of services to their environment. The combination of these services is referred to as the component interface.
- *Components* are self-contained units. Data and process are encapsulated in a component – each component stores its own data (as opposed to a database coupling in traditional structured software development).
- *Components* are replaceable parts of a system (Crnkovic and Larsson 2002).

Being self-contained and replaceable units that communicate and connect with other components via interfaces, components could be reused in a number of products, and be replaced by more recent and advanced versions of components in a 'plug-and-play' manner, as long as the interfaces are across the components comprising the products.

### Types of components

The concept of components within the IS world originated within the area of *technical system components*, but is also applicable to *business (software) components*:

- A *technical component* implements a general function/service, independent of a business domain. For example, a technical component could be a network socket component that offers the service of transmitting a file to another point in a network.
- A *business component* implements an autonomous business concept/ function or business process. For example, a business component could be a business function such as Human Resources, or an Accounting function in an ERP system that supports a variety of business processes for the corresponding organisational unit. Or it could be a mathematical function component that provides a specific mathematical function.

Components can be bought, installed and integrated locally, or they can be hosted by a third party. For example, a currency converter is a business component typically hosted by a third party and accessed over the Web.

### Granularity

Components can be *fine-grained* to *large-grained*. Typically, technical components are of finer granularity than business components (in system developed using component technology, business components contain fine-grained technical components) (Crnkovic and Larsson 2002; Alexandersen et al. 2003). The possibility to reuse components is considered to be one of the main advantages of CBD. Initially the focus was on reusing fine-grained components. However, the drawback was that search and integration costs easily outweighed the benefits of reuse. Recently the focus has shifted to reusing large-grained components (Alexandersen et al. 2003; Elfatatry 2007). In this book we discuss the development and reuse of components of different levels of granularity: fine-grained components (in the LeCroy and SAP cases) and large-grained components (in the TCS case).

### Communication via interfaces

Components communicate with each other by sending and receiving messages. A middleware technology is used to route and deliver messages between components. Currently much work is ongoing to standardise message syntax and semantics (Alexandersen et al. 2003). Although some technical standards have emerged, for most business domains semantic standards are still at an early stage (Bass et al. 2000; Kim 2002). As a result, component integration usually needs to be done manually. As more domain standards emerge, component integration will become smoother and plug-and-play components may become more of a reality (Alexandersen et al. 2003).

Usually software components need to interact with legacy systems that generally do not have interfaces and clear service specifications. In these cases, a component wrapper has to be built, which exposes the functionality of the legacy system so that it can be viewed as a component (Kim 2002; van den Heuvel et al. 2002).

### Deployment

A software component can be deployed independently and is subject to further assembly by third parties (Pfister 1997). Therefore, for proper integration and functioning, extensive information about components is needed. Component documentation should clearly specify interfaces (the services they provide), (encapsulated) functionality, and the states of components and in which state and which function they could be used. Furthermore, non-functional properties, such as the reliability, performance, security (and pricing, if intended for sale) should also be specified in the component documentation. Although components should be designed to be as independent as possible, they often require the services of other components to function. Thus, context requirements should be explicitly stated in the component documentation. Sometimes, examples of use and reference models (e.g. if used for calculations) that the application is based on, should be documented as well.

### Characteristics of a component-based system

Typically, software systems have a long lifetime of at least several years, during which upgraded software systems with more features are released under different release versions. Changes, improvements, and enhancements leading to new software design releases cause a software system to evolve (Peters and Pedrycz 2000). As a result, a software system is updated and changed many times over the period of time that a system lives (Crnkovic and Larsson 2002). Therefore, the main aim in a software design process is to provide a clear and relatively simple structure of a system, which is *flexible* (facilitating changes to accommodate new needs), *extensible* (essentially open and easily revised to satisfy increasing demands or additional services), *portable* (can be made to execute on different platforms with reasonable effort), *reusable* (the architecture can be extracted from one application and inserted into a new application with reasonable effort) (Peters and Pedrycz 2000), *adaptable* (ability to respond to changing requirements in different applications or in an application during its lifecycle, *substitutable* (related to contractual interfaces and dependencies) and *expandable* (ability to add new interfaces to existing components, or ability to add new components) (Törngren et al. 2005).

In terms of system structure, CB system architecture is considered to be key to the success of systems with a long lifecycle. As compared to a monolithic software system, a CB system is considered to be more flexible, extensible, and reusable (Crnkovic and Larsson 2002). Furthermore, a CB system is easier and more effective to maintain, because it can be maintained in parts (by components), as opposed to a monolithic system which needs to be maintained as a whole (Verbraeck et al. 2002).

### The CBD approach: process overview

The Waterfall model is too rigid and linear, therefore it does not support iterations, parallel development, incremental delivery or flexibility in software development supported by component technology (Graham et al. 1997). Mahmood et al. (2007) suggest that CBD approach is quite different from the traditional waterfall approach, and it should not only focus on system specification and development, but requires additional consideration for overall system context, individual components properties and component acquisition and integration process. An approach that is common for CBD is referred to as *V-cycle*: it defines the main steps in CBD, which are requirements, analysis, design and implementation, and four different levels of testing – for each of the four previous steps (Herzum and Sims 2000). Figure 3.2 illustrates the main steps of CBD as a V-cycle approach. The V-cycle is a simplified and linearised representation of a complex development process reality; however it has proved a convenient way to introduce many concepts and deliverables of the CBD process (Herzum and Sims 2000).

As Figure 3.2 illustrates, the first two and last two stages, i.e. system requirements, analysis and two corresponding types of testing, focus on a *system*. These stages are concerned with the design, assembly, and testing of a system using business components. It can also include selection of pre-existing components that can be reused in the system. By contrast, the intermediary four stages, i.e. design, implementation and two

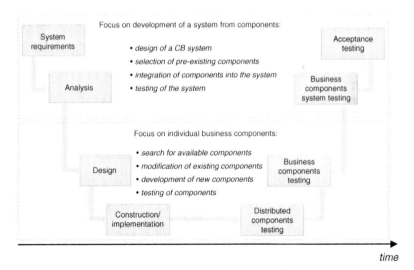

*Figure 3.2*   V-cycle approach: CBD lifecycle (modified from Herzum and Sims, 2000)

corresponding types of testing, focus on *business components*.[3] These stages are concerned with the designing, building and testing of individual business components (Herzum and Sims 2000). Design and implementation can also include the search for available components, internally or from component markets, and the customisation of components to suit the needs of a system being developed.

Crnkovic et al. (2005:323) criticised the V-cycle model described above for being a 'simplified and idealized process'. They argue that it is based on the assumption that there are components available to select from which fit the design. However in practice available components might only partially fit the overall design. Therefore processes of finding and adaptation of components need to be introduced. Then, modified components need to be tested before they can be integrated into the system.

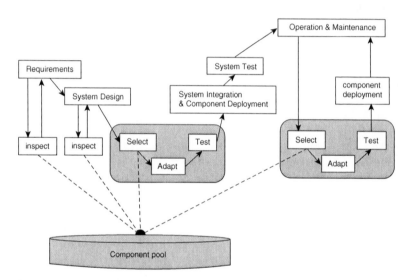

*Figure 3.3* A detailed V development process for CBD (adapted from Crnkovic et al. 2005)

---

[3]Herzum and Sims (2000:556) define *business component* as 'the software implementation of an autonomous business concept or business process. It consists of all software artefacts necessary to represent, implement, and deploy a given business concept as autonomous, reusable element of a larger distributed information system'. Business components are large-grained. They contain fine-grained components (referred to by Herzum and Sims (2000) as '*distributed components*', defined as 'a software artefact that can be called at run-time with clear interface, and clear separation between interface and implementation').

Figure 3.3 illustrates a detailed V development process for CBD suggested by Crnkovic et al. (2005) which takes into account these processes. Crnkovic et al. (2005) argue that independent of the system development process organisations should pursue a process of component development which should aim to develop reusable components. The next section will discuss the benefits and challenges associated with CBD.

## Reuse in CBD: benefits and challenges

Initially, the CBD methodology has been presented as a revolutionary approach to software development, promising dramatic improvements in software development efficiency. The main advantage expected from adopting CBD methodology is the possibility to reuse components (Bass et al. 2000; Kunda and Brooks 2000; Crnkovic and Larsson 2002; Ravichandran and Rothenberger 2003; van Hillegersberg 2003; Vitharana 2003; Crnkovic et al. 2005; Kotlarsky 2007; Lau and Wang 2007; Kotlarsky, Oshri, Kumar et al. 2008). Nevertheless, it is argued that component reuse strategy contributes toward fewer opportunities to learn about new technologies in R&D environment (Oshri and Newell 2005; Oshri et al. 2007).

A company developing a CB system can apply different modes of component reuse in terms of *source* of components:

- Internal reuse – reuse of components developed in-house (e.g. Crnkovic and Larsson 2002; Bertoa et al. 2006).
- Reuse from component markets – reuse of components procured from component markets to develop the CB system (Traas and van Hillegersberg 2000).
- Hybrid reuse – combination of internal reuse and reuse from component markets (e.g. Homann et al. 2004).

Furthermore, the reuse concept can be used on different levels in terms of *granularity* (Herzum and Sims 2000; Crnkovic and Larsson 2002):

- Reuse of small-size components (high granularity, mostly technical components).
- Reuse of business components (encapsulating business functions).
- Reuse of complete products that are integrated in complex systems.

Crnkovic and Larsson (2002) argue that, on each level of reuse, the demands on the reusable components, on the component management and on the integration process are different.

The possibility to reuse components influences directly the efficiency of the development process, in particular:

- Better quality – reliability of products increases when components are reused in a number of products (van Hillegersberg 2003; Vitharana 2003; Mahmood et al. 2005; Crnkovic et al. 2005; Selby 2005; Bertoa et. al. 2006).
- Improved productivity – shorter time-to-market, because, first, a new product could be developed faster when (some) components are reused in a number of products. Second, the variety of products increases because it is easier to customise, upgrade, and add new features to existing products (Bass et al. 2000; Kunda and Brooks 2000; Crnkovic and Larsson 2002; Kim 2002; Huang et al. 2003; Ravichandran and Rothenberger 2003; Vitharana 2003; Mahmood et al. 2005; Selby 2005; Lau and Wang 2007). Lee, Banerjee et al. (2006) state that modular architecture allows fast and flexible integration of multiple system components, thus contributes to the agility of project management. Furthermore, development time could be reduced because components could be developed in parallel independently by teams located in the same building or at remote locations (Repenning et al. 2001).
- Lower costs – development costs are lower when components are reused in a number of products (Kunda and Brooks 2000; Ravichandran and Rothenberger 2003; van Hillegersberg 2003; Mahmood et al. 2005; Bertoa et al. 2006; Lau and Wang 2007; Kotlarsky, Oshri, van Hillegersberg et al. 2007). Moreover, component markets provide an alternative to in-house development: the components are procured from component markets for a lower price than they would cost to develop in-house.

However, empirical research on CBD has challenged these benefits and shown that 'it often took longer to develop a reusable component then to develop a system for a one-off purpose' (Huang et al. 2003). Oshri, Newell and Pan (2007) also find that component reuse triggers redesign feedback loops in other modules which resulted in additional time and more man-power dedicated to making modifications in other modules. It was argued that the benefits are difficult to achieve in the first place, and that they cannot be achieved immediately, but in the long run (Crnkovic and Larsson 2002). Empirical research on co-located CBD reported a number of challenges that companies faced, trying to achieve the benefits of reuse:

- Before the components can be reused, a sufficiently large pool of reusable components needs to be developed (Bass et al. 2000).

- Often, there is a gap between requirements and available components. If some components can be found neither in-house nor on the component market, then cost-benefit analysis, and possibly negotiation with a customer, is needed to decide whether to adjust the requirements to the available components or to develop customised components (Vitharana 2003; Crnkovic et al. 2002).
- There are a multitude of component repositories (Traas and van Hillegersberg 2000). Therefore, effective classification and coding schemes are needed in order to develop advanced searching mechanisms and enable component seekers to locate components (Vitharana 2003).
- Often, requirements of the components are not well understood, which brings an additional level of complexity. Crnkovic and Larsson (2002) explain that long-life products are most often affected by evolution of different kinds: evolution of system requirements; evolution of technology used in software products and other related domains; business changes and organisational changes (Grinter 1998). 'As a result of new requirements for the products, new requirements for the components will be defined. The more reusable a component is, the more demands are placed on it' (Crnkovic and Larsson 2002).
- Stable standards for component technology and certified components are lacking (Bass et al. 2000; Kim 2002) and components from different producers are often incompatible.
- Software or component adaptation is widely known to be one of the crucial problems in Component-based Software Engineering (CBSE). Incompatibilities between the behavioural interfaces of software components may lead to the problem related to interface and behavioral mismatch (Bracciali et al. 2005; Brogi et al. 2006).
- A need to decide on the level of granularity of components (large- or fine-grained), to achieve (i) a higher reuse rate (for internal reuse in-house), and (ii) a higher demand (for commercial components) (Alexandersen et al. 2003; Vitharana 2003).
- A need to decide how generic (or how specific) a component should be (Vitharana 2003; Törngren et al. 2005). On the one hand, to be reused, a component has to be generic enough to be appropriate for different products. On the other hand, if a component is too generic, it might not be reused at all if it is not associated with any particular business or functional domain. Elfatatry (2007:39) claims that 'a major limitation of building flexible software using components has been the way components are specified. Proprietary standards and implementation-dependent specification of components have

hindered component-based development from achieving its primary goal facilitating reuse'.

- A need to verify how a component will behave correctly in a new environment; which will include testing and formal verification (Törngren et al. 2005).
- A need to decide on required documentation: what should be included in the documentation?
  - Interfaces – how should interfaces be described? Should UML be used for interface documentation (van Hillegersberg 2003)? There are no widely accepted standards and guidelines about this (Bass et al. 2000; Vitharana 2003).
  - How detailed should documentation be? Documenting in-house developed components for internal reuse takes time and is often considered as an administrative overhead. However, documentation is needed to ensure that a component and the logic behind it can be understood in case modifications or bug fixes are needed.
  - Should documentation include the source-code (i.e. 'white-box' documentation) (van Hillegersberg 2003)? On the one hand, the source-code could be used for understanding how a component functions and could increase the sales of the component because customers can see what they are buying. On the other hand, revealing the source-code is a potential threat to the intellectual property of an organisation.
- A need to decide on building vs. buying: to buy a component from the component market or build a needed component in-house (Vitharana 2003)? A cost-benefit analysis is required to evaluate and compare the alternatives. Developing components in-house might take longer and cost more. However, searching for required components to buy could also take time and cost money; components available from the market might require some modification, and their price might be per use (i.e. per product, so each internal reuse costs money).

As described above, the empirical research on CBD reports on the difficulties in achieving reuse that challenge the potential benefits. This literature is mostly based on case studies in co-located CBD projects.

In the light of globally distributed software development, it has been argued that CBD enables each site to take ownership of particular components and work on them independently without much need for inter-site communication and coordination (Carmel 1999; Colbert et al. 2001; Repenning et al. 2001). Thus, the adoption of CBD by organisations involved in globally distributed projects might ease coordination problems faced in traditional (non CB) GDSD projects caused by geographical dispersion, time-zone and cultural differences. On the other hand, the difficulties of achieving reuse reported in co-located CBD projects might be relevant in GD CBD projects as well.

## How to organise and manage CBD in a globally distributed environment

Despite the fact that increasing numbers of companies are setting up software development in a globally distributed environment and at the same time are adopting a CBD methodology, research on the management of GD CBD is just emerging. Majority of research on the management of CBD is conducted on co-located settings, and at present little is known about the management of GD CBD.

This section will give an overview of issues addressed in the literature on the management of CBD, co-located and globally distributed; and will discuss potential factors contributing to success in GD CBD. These factors cover (I) *Inter-site coordination in GD CBD*; (II) *Tools and methods to support CBD*; (III) *Human, social and organisational issues in CBD*; and (IV) *Knowledge sharing in CBD*. To distinguish between the findings from co-located and from globally distributed CBD, each factor/issue is discussed first as addressed in the co-located CBD, followed by the findings from GD CBD research.

### Inter-site coordination in GD CBD

*Co-located*

As discussed earlier, research on co-located CBD suggests that components can be developed remotely with minimum coordination across dispersed locations (Carmel 1999; Colbert et al. 2001; Repenning et al. 2001).

*Globally distributed*

Despite the expectation that components could be developed without much need for inter-site communication and coordination, existing studies of GD CBD point out that in GD CBD still much coordination between sites is required (Carmel 1999; Turnlund 2004; Kotlarsky 2007; Kotlarsky, Oshri, van Hillegersberg et al. 2007; Kotlarsky, Oshri, Kumar et al. 2008). For example, Carmel (1999) describes the difficulties faced by IBM in a globally distributed project developing software based on Java-Beans component technology. Initially, IBM tried to organise 'follow-the-sun' development, so that during the USA daytime the USA head-quarters site set up specifications for each JavaBean and assigned it to one of the remote locations (in China, Belarus, Latvia or India). Then, the remote locations worked on the code during their daytime and by the end of the day (by the morning in the USA) sent it back to the USA site for successive rounds of reviews and feedback. After testing in the USA, instructions were sent to the remote location for the next iteration. However, this arrangement did not work because the USA site was handling too many tasks sending components back and forth. As a result, instead of a 'follow-the-sun' approach, the ownership of components was delegated to the remote sites, and the USA head-quarter's role was reduced to managing the complicated coordination process. Carmel (1999:32) suggested that 'the essence of making this complicated coordination process work was a good collaborative technology infrastructure'.

Furthermore, it is reported that in a globally distributed environment, granularity and interdependencies between components become an issue. For example, Turnlund (2004:30) pointed out that:

> At the surface level it is attractive to push every part of the system down into its own granular, self-contained entity. With a single physical location for development, a group can execute within this model. From a combinatorial aspect (geography, number of inter-connects, variability of execution) this 'trust everyone to understand the overall system' method becomes a disaster.

When too many relatively complex interrelationships need to be managed, effective parallel development is not possible any more: in this case the 'integration exercise becomes a complex, rework-ridden, lengthy, indeterminate majority of the development exercise' (Turnlund 2004:29). To reduce the complexity involved in dealing with too many fine-grained components across remote sites, Turnlund (2004) suggests 'logical geographic groupings of component control', so that each site can take care of its own components. This attempt to divide work between sites is similar to the approach to division of work in traditional GDSD, aiming to reduce interdependencies between work packages assigned to different sites.

However, dispersed teams can do only limited types of work independently: the majority of tasks still require a great deal of communications and coordination between the teams. For example, Figure 3.4 illustrates the division of work between *onsite* (customer site of Skandia

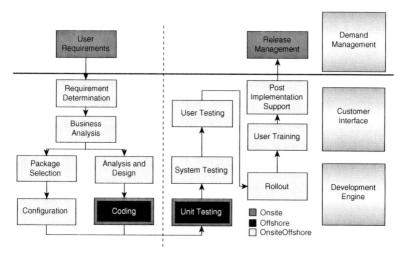

*Figure 3.4* Division of onsite/offshore work for development of the Skandia platform (adapted from Alexandersen et al. 2003)

Financial Concepts (SFC) in Zurich, Switzerland) and *offshore* (development centre of TATA Consultancy Services (TCS) in Gurgaon, India) for the development of Skandia's financial services platform, described by Alexandersen et al. (2003).

Alexandersen et al. (2003:17) explained the criteria that the division of work between onsite, onsite-offshore, and offshore work were based upon:

> First there was the need for direct customer contact and at the location of the customers. Thus user requirements and release management were primarily *onsite* activities. Second, those activities that were self contained, and could be conducted with minimal customer contact, such as coding and unit testing, were sent *offshore* to take advantage of the cost structures, quality, and availability of offshore personnel. Finally, activities that required co-work by client, SFC, and technical TCS personnel were conducted in a *mixed onsite-offshore* mode with frequent mediating contacts through communication technologies and site-visits.

As can be seen from Figure 3.4, the majority of activities required extensive communications, and onsite and offshore teams conducted them jointly. Only coding and unit testing was done independently at the offshore location.

## Tools and methods to support CBD

The majority of the literature on co-located CBD talks about the importance of automated tool support for successful CBD. Tools required for CBD include (i) tools for the development and management of components, (ii) configuration and version management tools, (iii) tools for tracing and tracking bugs, and (iv) tools for testing. In order to support CBD these tools need to provide the following capabilities:

### Development environment

*Co-located*
Research on the co-located CBD reports that development environment support is essential to enable editing, compiling, building, debugging and testing of components. Although recently more tools for CBD have emerged, the early adopters of CBD had to develop their own tools and integrated development environments to manage large scale CBD. For example, the company described by Crnkovic and Larsson (2002) developed their own software development environment: 'an internally built program package which encapsulates different tools, and provides support for parallel development'. Visual Basic for instance has proved to be a very successful development tool (Crnkovic 2003).

*Globally distributed*
It is more difficult to provide development environment support for GD CBD than for co-located CBD because the development environment would need to connect to remote sites (Kotlarsky 2007; Kotlarsky, Oshri, van Hillegersberg et al. 2007; Kotlarsky, Oshri, Kumar et al. 2008). This leads to the question: *how can development environment support be provided in GD CBD?*

In GD CBD, dispersed sites can be connected either under a single development environment, or by synchronising files across locations in a Web-based environment in a peer-to-peer distributed system. As opposed to the Open Source community which uses Web-based IDEs such as SourceForge to work in a distributed environment, commercially available IDEs (e.g. Java IDE) and modelling tools (e.g. Rational Rose) are usually client-server based systems designed primarily for a single user (i.e. only one person can work on a chunk of code or software design at a time). They offer only limited support for distributed development (Herrera 2002). Therefore, companies and researchers are working on how to design collaborative capability into IDSs (e.g. Cheng et al. (2004), and the research of John Grundy on JViews multiple user system, a component-based software architecture for multiple view).[4]

However, Morch et al. (2004) argue that IDEs are built for professional developers, resulting in shortcomings from the end user development (EUD) perspective. Therefore, they introduce a components approach to EUD that addresses ways to ease transition between using an application and tailoring it at different levels of complexity.

### Automated management of interdependencies between components

#### Co-located

In CBD there is a need to manage interdependencies between components: 'when it is about complex products, it is impossible to manually track dependencies between the components' (Crnkovic and Larsson 2002), and an automated tool for checking consistency is needed.

Coronato et al. (2005) propose two automatic tools (i.e Component Constraint Modeler (CoCoMod) and the Component Constraint Generator (CoCoGen)) to translate constraint models into source code that can provide a solution to the increase of developing time and costs, and the increase of software faults.

#### Globally distributed

In a globally distributed environment the need for automated tools to manage inter-dependencies between components becomes even more critical for success, because, in addition to managing interdependencies, components need to be synchronised across sites (Kotlarsky 2007; Kotlarsky, Oshri, van Hillegersberg et al. 2007; Kotlarsky, Oshri, Kumar et al. 2008). This leads to the following question: *how can components and their interdependencies be managed in a globally distributed environment?*

### Version and configuration management (tracing and tracking of components)

#### Co-located

It is suggested that the development of reusable components requires support for the development and maintenance of different versions of components for different product versions (Crnkovic and Larsson

---

[4]From the home-page of Prof. John Grundy http://www.cs.auckland.ac.nz/people/profile.php?id=jgru001

2002).[5] Therefore, version and configuration management process support is needed on two levels. First, on the component level, component versioning needs to facilitate the tracing of each component from inception to delivery, and (versions of) components used in multiple applications need to be coordinated. Second, on the product-integration (application) level, different versions of a product would have a different set of components, and different versions of components which need to be managed consistently (Crnkovic and Larsson 2002; Vitharana 2003). Furthermore, third party components (e.g. from the component market) used in a product have their own versioning that needs to be managed as well.

This requires an advanced version and configuration management process to be defined, and powerful Software Configuration Management (SCM) tools[6] to support this process (Crnkovic and Larsson 2002; Vitharana 2003).

Braga et al. (2006) propose an approach for accessing software components called Odyssey-Search Engine which provides flexibility, transparency and more accuracy in software component retrieval.

Meanwhile, Zhou et al. (2007) suggest a new rule-based semiautomated component parameterisation approach that performs code analysis to identify and adapt parameters and changes components into reconfigurable ones.

### Globally distributed

Existing SCM tools are designed for distributed development. The literature on co-located CBD suggests that SCM tools are needed to support people working in parallel from different work stations located at the same (or different) buildings (Crnkovic and Larsson 2002). However, in a globally distributed environment a more powerful network and server(s) are needed, and differences in tools or different versions of the same tools used at remote sites might cause difficulties such as lack of compatibility between files/versions developed at different sites (Kotlarsky, Oshri, van Hillegersberg et al. 2007; Kotlarsky, Oshri, Kumar et al. 2008). This lead to the question: how can version and configuration management be supported in GD CBD?

---

[5]It is important to note that version and configuration management is different from the automated management of interdependencies between components, discussed earlier. The former is concerned with tracing and tracking of versions of components, while the latter is concerned with technical interdependencies between components such as interfaces and messages (service request and service response).

[6]Version Control System (VCS) is part of SCM tools.

## Bug tracing and tracking

### Co-located

It is suggested that in co-located CBD there is a need to trace bugs on three different levels: first, on the *system* level, where customers report problems with their specific product; second, on the *product* level, where errors are detected in a specific product version; and finally, on the *component* level, where the fault is located (Crnkovic and Larsson 2002). The need to trace bugs is closely related to version and configuration management, because 'a modification of the component can lead to an explosion of new versions of different products which already exist in several versions. The relations between components, products and systems must be carefully registered to make possible the tracing of errors on all levels' (Crnkovic and Larsson 2002). This introduces additional requirements for an advanced SCM tool. The need to manage and maintain complex products is not unique to CBD: however, 'what is specific to the component-based approach is the mapping between products and components and the management of error reports on product and component level, the most difficult part of the management' (Crnkovic and Larsson 2002).

### Globally distributed

There are several tools that have Web-based interfaces, such as Rational ClearQuest that support bugs tracing and tracking in GD CBD. This, for example, allows customers to report problems using Web-based forms, independent from their geographical location, and to track the status of the problem (i.e. progress in resolving the bug reported).

In addition to a Web-based system to report bugs, companies involved in GD CBD need to be able to trace back bugs on product and component levels (as explained above) across globally dispersed locations (Kotlarsky 2007; Kotlarsky, Oshri, van Hillegersberg et al. 2007; Kotlarsky, Oshri, Kumar et al. 2008). This leads to the question: *how can bug tracking and tracing be supported in GD CBD?*

## Testing and quality assurance

### Co-located

Research on co-located CBD suggests that comprehensive tools and techniques are required for different types of testing:

- Component (unit) testing: 'almost like an individual application, though on a smaller scale, each component must undergo verification and validation testing throughout its development process' (Vitharana 2003).

- Application (integration) testing: Brenner et al. (2007) propose a more component-oriented approach to reduce verification process in component-based system, i.e. by using built-in testing (BIT) – test that are packaged and distributed with prefabricated, off-the-shelf components. The approach 'consists of a method that defines how components should be written to support and make use of running-time test, and a resource-aware infrastructure that arranges for tests to be executed when they have a minimal impact on the delivery of system services (Brenner et al. (2007: 151)).
- System testing.

Furthermore, in order to assure the quality of a final product, quality certification is needed for third party components used in the product (Vitharana 2003; Mahmood et al. 2005; Bertoa et al. 2006). ISO/IEC 91 26 Quality Model defines the quality of a software product in terms of six major characteristics (Functionality, Reliability, Usability, Efficiency, Maintainability and Portability), which are further refined into 27 sub-characteristics (Bertoa et al. 2006).

*Globally distributed*
This issue is not mentioned in the literature on the management of GD CBD. Typically, tools for testing would be part of the development environment. Testing in a globally distri-buted environment might be more difficult to organise than in a co-located one, because components developed at remote sites need to be tested together (in particular for application and system testing). This leads to the question: *how can testing be supported in GD CBD?*

In addition to the tool capabilities discussed above, the literature on co-located CBD mentions the need for a commonly accepted standard method for CBD.

### Methods for CBD

*Co-located*
The literature on co-located CBD suggests that 'what is needed by the CBD project team is a commercial-level CBD methodology that covers a whole lifecycle process and provides practical guidelines' (Kim 2002). In addition, a methodology is needed to aid in composition of reusable components so that the correctness of the composed software system can be assured (Sinha and Hanumantharya 2005).

There are several CBD methodologies, such as Catalysis (D'Souza and Wills 1999) and Componentware Methodolog.[7] Furthermore, Firesmith and Henderson-Sellers (2001) have proposed OPEN Process Framework – a meta-process that can be tailored to a CBD approach. Existing methodologies are based on different technical standards and different component technologies, while a commonly accepted standard reference model for an engineering method to consistently guide CBD is lacking (Bass et al. 2000; Kim 2002).

At present companies are trying to find their own way to succeed in CBD. For example, in order to support CBD and facilitate component reuse in Korea, a nationwide Component Industry Promotion (CIP) project was launched by the Korean Ministry of Information and Communication (Kim 2002). Kim (2002) reported that the CIP project developed a standard reference model for 'a whole lifecycle CBD methodology' that comprised four main stages of CBD: (1) planning the project and comprehending requirements, (2) developing components, (3) developing an application using existing components, and (4) deploying a CB application. Each stage was broken into phases and further into activities. The reference model combined the main features of existing methods, such as Catalysis and Componentware, and added new techniques based on CBD projects in Korea which participated in the nationwide CIP project.

Taking into account the difficulties related to component reuse, Crnkovic and Larsson (2002) suggest:

> The reuse orientation requires a systematic approach in design planning, extensive development, support of a more complex maintenance process, and in general more consideration being given to components. It is not certain that an otherwise successful development organisation can succeed in the development of reusable components or products based on reusable components.

A standard CBD method/methodology would provide a structured and systematic approach for CBD and would facilitate reuse. Rodriguez et al. (2004) present a methodology to estimate the impact of modifying software system design. In order to perform this task, the designer

---

[7]Available on Carnegie Mellon Software Engineering Institute web site: http://www.sei.cmu.edu

defines the system in terms of its components, their dependencies, the properties they fulfil and the properties each component requires to other components. The methodology enables the evaluation of software system reusability as well as coupling of its components.

Lee and Shirani (2004) claim that existing software design methodologies often lack the Web focus and explicit support for componentisation. Therefore, they propose a methodology for requirements analysis and high-level design, specifically for component-based Web applications. The proposed methodology introduces page and component classification, and a set of tags to implement link semantic. Based on these constructs, it then specifies procedures for requirement analysis and design.

Arato et al. (2005) introduce an extended component-based methodology that includes both hardware and software components, where both of them are handled in a uniform way by using a generic component notion focusing on functionality, and by using software-like interface adapters for hardware. This methodology is called component based hardware-software co-design (CBHSCD).

Apart from that, Bracciali et al. (2005) present a formal methodology for adapting components with mismatching interaction behaviour. Three main ingredients of the methodology are (i) the inclusion of behaviour specifications in component interfaces, (ii) a simple, high-level notation for expressing adaptor specifications, and (iii) a fully automated procedure to derive concrete adaptors from given high-level specifications.

Vergara et al. (2007) on the other hand, discuss the problems involved in dealing with component adaptation within the context of Model-Driven Web Engineering and show how design patterns can help addressing it. They identify the major interoperability problems that can happen when integrating third-party application or legacy systems into Web systems, and then propose the mechanisms that need to be put in place at the design level to generate the appropriate specification of adapters that compensate for the possible mismatches and incompatibilities.

*Globally distributed*
Methods for GD CBD are not addressed in the literature. This leads to the question: *What methods can support the lifecycle of GD CBD, in particular aspects that are unique to GD CBD, such as methods to support division of work between site, integration procedures?* For example, to support working in a globally distributed environment, these methods should be web-enabled.

## Human, social and organisational issues in CBD

### Co-located

It is suggested that designing components requires unique skills that involve in-depth knowledge of CB technologies, design principles and decisions different from those used in traditional software development (Vitharana 2003). Furthermore, CBD allows separation of skills which in turn results in new roles, for example infrastructure builder, component developer or application assembler (Bass et al. 2000). Therefore, in companies/teams who switch from traditional software development to CBD, top management needs to invest significant resources in retraining current personnel and/or hiring new personnel (Vitharana 2003).

Kunda and Brooks (2000) have studied the adoption of CBD from a socio-technical perspective, aiming to identify (i) problems experienced by organisations implementing CBD on individual, group and organisation levels, and (ii) factors influencing CBD success. Based on case studies in three companies adopting CBD, Kunda and Brooks (2000) report problems related to cognitive skills, disincentives, organisational politics and organisational culture. They identified factors that affect CBD success as follows:

- *Human factors*, which include motivation, enthusiasm, incentives, cognitive skills, and customer ownership.
- *Social factors* are: different perceptions, different goals, and interactions and communication between group members.
- *Organisational factors* are: political issues, organisational and business strategy; organisational resources and support; organisational setting and management style, and organisational culture. These results are supported by Huang et al. (2003), who studied the importance of organisational cultures and sub-cultures in the success of CBD adoption.

Despite the findings of Kunda and Brooks (2000) regarding the importance of human, social and organisational issues in the success of CBD, the majority of the literature on the management of CBD emphasises the importance of tools and technologies for successful CBD, while the social and human issues involved in CBD are typically neglected (Kunda and Brooks 2000; Huang et al. 2003).

### Globally distributed

Research on the management of GD CBD does not address issues related to human, social and organisational factors. It is possible that the same problems related to cognitive skills, disincentives, organisational politics and organisational culture identified in co-located CBD projects will be faced by globally distributed teams. Moreover, the implications of global distribution, such as geographical distance and cultural differences, may make these problems more severe. This leads to the following questions: *what is the impact of human, social and organisational factors on success in GD CBD, and how should these factors be managed in GD CBD?*

### Knowledge sharing in CBD

*Co-located*

Huang et al. (2003) report that intensive knowledge sharing and collaboration throughout a whole development lifecycle are required for the successful adoption of CBD. The authors suggest that sharing knowledge and creating 'knowledge redundancy' is 'a critical step in reducing conflict resulting from misunderstandings between and within stakeholder groups' (Huang et al. 2003: 96) involved in the development process. Oshri, Newell and Pan (2007) argue that knowledge man-agement and expertise development processes that coexisted in harmony and maintained coherence within the product development process create a high cost to learning and often lead to technological development redundancy.

*Globally distributed*

Existing research on the importance of knowledge management in GD CBD is limited (e.g. Kotlarsky, Oshri, van Hillegersberg et al. 2007; Kotlarsky, Oshri, Kumar et al. 2008). Taking into account that misunderstandings and conflicts often happen in globally distributed teams, it is likely that knowledge sharing is more difficult to achieve in GD CBD. This leads to the questions: *what is the impact of knowledge sharing on success in GD CBD, and how can knowledge sharing be facilitated in GD CBD?*

This section has given an overview of what is known about the management of CBD, co-located and globally distributed, based on the existing literature. Taking into account that only a limited number of studies on GD CBD have been published, the findings from research conducted in co-located CBD were applied to globally distributed projects, suggesting possible scenarios and posting questions that need to be addressed in the context of GD CBD.

The next section will describe different measures used to evaluate the success of IS projects.

## Success in information system projects

Success in IS development projects has been studied from various angles. Some studies put the emphasis on the project outcome to assess success: for example, product delivery being on time and within the budget (Nelson and Cooprider 1996; Hoegl and Gemuenden 2001; Nellore and Balachandra 2001), and product and process quality. Others focus on the quality of interactions between project members to assess collaboration success, such as communications and team performance (Nelson and Cooprider 1996; Hoegl and Gemuenden 2001).

In this sense, success is represented in this research as a combination of product outcome, people-related outcome and collaboration process quality.

---

Product success can be represented by various indicators, such as growth in sales, product delivery on time and within the budget (Nellore and Balachandra 2001; Andres 2002), short time-to-market (Datar et al. 1997) and increase in reuse of components (Crnkovic and Larsson 2002). In line with these indicators, *product success* is thus defined as the achievement of project objectives (Gallivan 2001).

---

This criterion for product success can either be objective, i.e. based on market or company data, or subjective, i.e. based on project participants' perceptions of product success.

While the IS literature on globally distributed teams has traditionally focused on technical tools, such as ICT, and their contribution to success (Carmel 1999; Karolak 1999; Herbsleb et al. 2002), some hints about other factors affecting product or project success have been provided by past studies that mainly focused on co-located teams. Among these factors, research has suggested knowledge sharing (Nelson and Cooprider 1996), informal communications and personal relationships (Hoegl and Gemuenden 2001), interactions between parties involved in the development, for example, customers or marketing and engineering specialists (Nelson and Cooprider 1996), and team cohesion (Rafii 1995; Hoegl and Gemuenden 2001).

A desired result of a distributed team can also be a people-related outcome (Hoegl and Gemuenden 2001) which entails meeting the psychological needs of the members (Gallivan 2001). Hoegl and Gemuenden (2001) and Gallivan (2001), for example, suggest that, in addition to performance objectives, teams must also work in a way that increases members' motivation to engage in future teamwork. There should be some level of personal satisfaction that motivates individuals and teams to continue their engagement in collaborative work despite geographical, time and cultural differences.

> In this research *personal satisfaction* is perceived as the outcome of a positive social experience. Such positive social experience can, for example, be in the form of stress-free communication rituals between remote counterparts and collegial relationships between remote teams.

Some factors that may foster people-related outcomes and thus may improve personal satisfaction are open and multiple informal communication channels (Hoegl and Gemuenden 2001), the encouragement of interactions between parties involved in the development process (Nelson and Cooprider 1996), and the cohesion of a team (Gallivan 2001; Hoegl and Gemuenden 2001).

The success of a distributed team can also be assessed in terms of the quality (efficiency) of a process through which dispersed team members collaborate.

The word 'collaboration' comes from the Latin words *com* (prefix *together*) and *laborare* (verb *to work*). It means that two or more individuals work jointly on an intellectual endeavour (Webster 1992).

> *Successful collaboration* is a complex, multi-dimensional process characterised by constructs such as coordination (Faraj and Sproull 2000), communication (Weick and Roberts 1993), and structure (Scott 1992; Adler and Borys 1996), which achieves a predefined goal (a product or desired performance) through group effort.

Furthermore, OB studies stress the importance of social aspects such as relationships (Gabarro 1990), trust (Meyerson et al. 1996) and shared meaning (Donnellon et al. 1986; Bechky 2003) for successful collaboration.

Naturally, geographical, cultural and time-zone differences pose additional challenges to globally distributed teams to achieve success, whether seen as a people-related outcome, a product outcome or a collaboration process quality. Managerial practices that involve inter-site coordination mechanisms and technologies help to reduce geographical, cultural and time-zone differences, and problems and breakdowns associated with these gaps. Therefore, in addition to product, process and people-related measures of success commonly used in IS research, in this book the success of GD CBSD is assessed based on the degree of success in bridging gaps between globally distributed teams.

> **Bridging of gaps** between globally distributed teams is assessed based on the perceptions of team members of gaps (geographical, time-zone and cultural) as being a problem.

## Conclusion: potential success factors of GD CBD

Past research in the IS field stresses the importance of tools, technologies and coordination mechanisms for successful GDSD projects (Carmel 1999; Karolak 1999; Herbsleb et al. 2002). Despite the fact that research on the management of GD CBD is very limited, existing studies on GD CBD recognise the importance of coordination mechanisms and technologies for success in GD CBD. Furthermore, the OB literature offers several factors, such as social ties and knowledge sharing, that may positively affect success through social activities and personal interactions.

Figure 3.5 illustrates schematically the potential factors that may contribute to success in GD CBD. These factors combine potential success factors identified in the research on traditional GDSD, research on GD teams and research on co-located and globally distributed CBD.

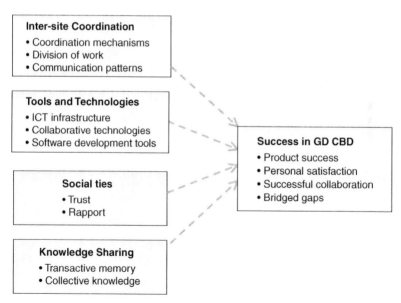

**Inter-site Coordination**
- Coordination mechanisms
- Division of work
- Communication patterns

**Tools and Technologies**
- ICT infrastructure
- Collaborative technologies
- Software development tools

**Social ties**
- Trust
- Rapport

**Knowledge Sharing**
- Transactive memory
- Collective knowledge

**Success in GD CBD**
- Product success
- Personal satisfaction
- Successful collaboration
- Bridged gaps

*Figure 3.5*   Potential factors that may contribute to success in GD CBD

Another way to represent the factors that could affect GD CBD is illustrated in Figure 3.6. In this figure, we focus on key questions regarding the four conceptual areas that could lead to successful CBD in global teams. We have used this framework during data collection and therefore will re-examine this framework each time we report on our findings per each firm.

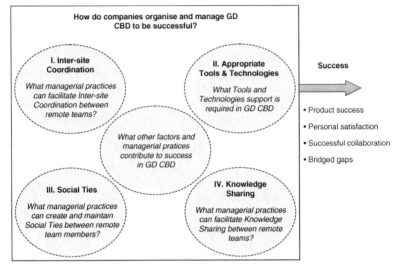

*Figure 3.6*   A question-led framework regarding success factors of CBD in global teams

# Part II

# How Leading Firms Managed Component-Based Development in Global Teams

## How this research was conducted

We have been studying global teams since 2000. This on-going research project involved the study of best practices relating to the management of global teams in four world leading software vendors; SAP, TATA Consultancy Service, Baan and LeCroy. We interviewed over 200 people, most of them top executives, software architects, middle managers and software developers from the above firms but also with experts from the industry. We collected data in India, the USA, Israel, Netherlands, Switzerland, Brazil, Luxemburg, Italy, the UK, Germany and other countries. Clearly, the scope of issues that emerged from these data collection activities was wide and often brought up topics that were not centered around component-based development in global teams. However, we have learned that many of the topics discussed in these interviews contributed to our understanding of the challenges that global teams face in the context of CBD and therefore should be reported in this book. Here we would like share with you how we selected the firms with whom we have conducted a longitudinal study on the topic of global teams. Additional information about the research methods applied in this book can be found in Appendix 1.

## The selection of the firms

The selection of the firms and projects to be studied was driven by the following criteria:

- The firm has introduced a CBD project globally distributed between at least two locations.
- The firm has successfully implemented a CBD project.

In our sample, three of the four cases investigated satisfy both criteria. One is a failure story that we considered as no less important to investigate and therefore report about in this book.

Naturally, the choice of projects which could be studied was limited, for a number of reasons. First, not many companies were involved in GD CBD when we started this line of research. Second, not many companies were ready to give access to such projects. Therefore, initially the case study selection was limited only by the above-mentioned criteria. However, as we got more familiar with the characteristics of GD CBD projects, we were able to locate additional projects that were suitable for this research projects and that allowed us to apply a comparable analysis method between the various cases. For this we needed to apply secondary requirements for selecting the other firms which were driven by the characteristics of the first case project (i.e. LeCroy):

(a) The type of project – new product development (i.e. innovative projects); interested in long-term collaboration between the distributed teams (as opposed to one-time outsourcing projects that do not plan to have long-term collaboration in the future between the same teams and individuals).
(b) The size of project team is 25–35 people.

Consequently, the following companies and projects were selected:

- **LeCroy** – development of a CB platform for a new generation of digital oscilloscopes; teams distributed between three locations – Geneva (Switzerland), New York (USA) and Maine (USA).
- **SAP** – development of collaborative tools; teams distributed between three locations – Walldorf (Germany), Palo Alto (USA) and Bangalore (India).
- **TATA Consultancy Services (TCS)** – development and implementation of a Web-based financial platform for Internet banking and the development of financial application for a large European bank. Three related projects were studied: the first project distributed between three locations – Gurgaon (India), Bombay (India) and Zurich (Switzerland); the second project distributed between Gurgaon (India) and San Francisco (USA); the third project between Amsterdam, Mumbai, Luxemburg and Sao Palo. The first two projects are related, therefore were analysed together as one 'embedded' case study.
- **Baan** – development of an e-Services platform; teams distributed between two locations – Hyderabad (India) and Barneveld (The

Netherlands). In January 2002, when data collection in Baan started, the studied project was described by Baan's contact person as a CBD project, and two teams in Hyderabad and Barneveld were working on the project. However, during data collection, which started from a visit to the Hyderabad office, interviewees reported that the e-Services platform was not a pure CB. Furthermore, in June 2002, when interviews with people in the Barneveld office were about to start, Baan started re-organising its development centres and activities. As a result, in July 2002 development of the e-Services platform in Barneveld was stopped, and later, the whole project was shut down and the Baan facility in Barneveld was closed.

Despite these aspects in the Baan case study, we think that including the story about Baan in this book gives an opportunity to compare managerial practices from the successful projects of LeCroy, SAP and TCS with practices that were, or, more importantly, *were not* in place in the unsuccessful project of Baan. However, taking into account that the Baan case study is not a classical CB and covers only one of two distributed sites, definite conclusions cannot be drawn from comparing the three successful projects with the unsuccessful project of Baan. With this in mind, we now present our observations regarding the management of GD CBD at LeCroy, SAP, TCS and Baan.

# 4
# Observations of GD CBD at LeCroy Corporation

> *The biggest problem is a people problem: if people from different sites don't have the respect and trust for each other, they don't work well together.*
>
> (Chief Software Architect, LeCroy)

## Background of LeCroy global organisation

Founded in 1964 by Walter LeCroy, a physicist, LeCroy Research Systems (in 1980 the name was changed to LeCroy Corporation) was quickly recognised as an innovator in instrumentation. In 1972 the company established an instrument design and production facility in Geneva, Switzerland. In 1976 the corporate headquarters moved to its present location in Chestnut Ridge, New York (NY).

Initially, LeCroy developed technology to capture, measure, and analyse sophisticated electronic signals in a stringent scientific environment. In 1985, the company began transferring this technology to a popular line of general-purpose instruments. Growth in the commercial test and measurement market really took off when the company introduced its first digital storage oscilloscope products. Since that time the core business of LeCroy has been the design and production of oscilloscopes and oscilloscope-like instruments – signal analysers, signals generators and others (see Appendix 2 for general information about oscilloscopes and products of LeCroy Corporation).

During the last 20 years, LeCroy has opened a number of sales offices in Europe (in France, Italy, Germany, Switzerland and the UK). These offices are responsible for sales in all Europeans countries. There are also offices in Japan, South Korea, China and Singapore (see LeCroy's organisational structure in Appendix 3). LeCroy now employs more about 400 people worldwide. In 2008 the company reported annual revenues of more than $160 million.[1]

Three teams – software, hardware and manufacturing – are involved in the production of oscilloscopes. Initially, all three teams were located in New York and Geneva and worked together from these two locations. In 1999 manufacturing and hardware were consolidated in NY. Software development stayed as it initially was, distributed between NY and Geneva. The case study focuses on the software development team, which is globally distributed between New York and Geneva. Figure 4.1 illustrates the division of responsibilities between the NY and Geneva offices since 1999, after hardware and manufacturing were consolidated in one location.

## Background of the project and product under study

The software for oscilloscopes developed by LeCroy during the period from the 80s until the 90s has grown into a monolithic system. In the first half of 1997 it was divided into three modules (operating system, Core software[2] and acquisition system[3]) that were linked together. Then, while producing scopes based on this modular system, between

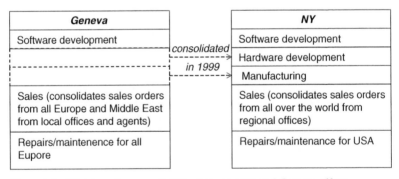

*Figure 4.1*   Division of responsibilities between NY and Geneva offices

---

[1]From LeCroy Annual Report 2008: this is the latest financial information available.

[2]*Core* contained the functions common to all oscilloscopes (analysis and display capabilities), regardless of the operating systems.

[3]*Acquisition system* is the heart of an oscilloscope; it captures signals. Each scope has a different acquisition system. The acquisition system is the part that changes every time a new scope is produced.

July 1997 and January 2002 LeCroy developed a Component-Based platform for a new generation of scopes, which is the focus of this research.

The project investigated in this case study concerns the Maui project ('Maui' stands for Massively Advanced User Interface). Maui is a software platform for new generations of oscilloscopes and oscilloscope-like instruments based on Windows. This case study covers the development of the Maui platform, and the development of the first products based on the platform. In particular, the focus is on the Aladdin product, the first in the new generation of digital oscilloscopes based on Windows. The launch of Aladdin (officially called WaveMaster) took place on January 10, 2002. Schematically, the major phases of Maui are presented in Figure 4.2.

### What is Maui?

Maui has been called several things. It is an *operating system for scopes*. But basically, it is an application, consisting of a collection of hundreds of components, each of which could have a place in the oscilloscope, or in oscilloscope-like instruments. In other words, Maui is also a *component tool box*: it is a repository of components (there were 508 on December 17th 2001); a scope is built by selecting from and integrating these components. 'That is Maui. However with those components you don't have a scope' (Larry Salant, Director of Software Engineering).

### How to create a scope in Maui

A specific oscilloscope product such as Aladdin or X15 can be constructed by integrating the components from Maui with an acquisition system and designing the user interface for a specific application. For example, the Aladdin scope would be built by combining the Aladdin Acquisition system and Aladdin Application with the components

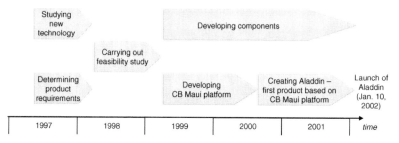

*Figure 4.2*   Major chronological phases of the Maui project

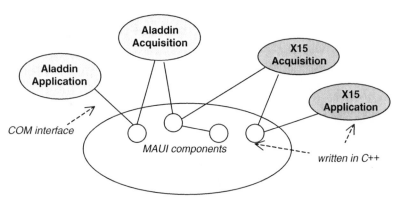

*Figure 4.3* Maui product architecture (schematic)

selected from the 'Maui toolbox'. The same would apply for another product called X15: it requires X15 Acquisition and X15 Application together with components from Maui.

The architecture of a product based on Maui consists of large numbers of Maui components (most of them common for all scopes), an Acquisition system and an Application. Figure 4.3 illustrates schematically Maui product architecture.

Basically, there are four types of components in products based on the Maui architecture. One category is called *processors*, with hundreds of mathematical functions, one component per functionality. A second category is *Graphical User Interface (GUI)*, components that are combined to provide the user interface. The third category of components is the *core components* that allow the systems to work together, and provide the basic instrument capabilities. And finally there are the components that comprise the *acquisition board driver*. These are responsible for controlling the acquisition hardware.

The components are written in C++ and the interfaces between them are in COM. Maui describes these interfaces, they are part of Maui architecture:

> I guess, really the root of Maui are these interfaces. There are maybe 30, 40, 50 interfaces which describe how these components talk to each other. That is really the heart of Maui. If you want to make a component for Maui – whether it will be something to display waveforms, to control the front panel, an acquisition system, any of these things – in order to integrate them into the system and to attach to the rest of the system, they have to implement or use one

of the Maui interfaces. It is a bunch of standards, and it is a tool kit (Anthony Cake).

As of December 17 2001, Maui architecture contained 508 components. This number had grown to 726 by January 15, 2003 (the number of components on the dates of the first and second round of interviews correspondingly).

## Background of the software team

### Working experience in a globally distributed environment

Since the mid 80s, the software for the oscilloscopes has been partly developed in Geneva, and partly in New York. Initially there were about 5–6 people in Geneva and 5–6 people in New York. These two teams interacted frequently. Originally, interactions involved shipping tapes and floppy disks between the two sites. Later, the software team used a 2400-baud modem to interchange files. The interactions progressed as the teams acquired email. Later on, they replaced modems with a Wide Area Network (WAN) connection between the two sites.

In 1999, LeCroy re-examined manufacturing in two very expensive locations. It was not as important to have the software team physically located close to manufacturing. Also, since the software team had developed very good ways of working together over distance (as opposed to the hardware team, which had problems working together over distance), it was decided to leave the software team in Geneva.

### Organisational structure of the software team

Software development is organised by feature/product function: some features are common in most products and product families (e.g. Core software), other features are developed for one specific product family (e.g. PXI Acquisition). A schematic illustration of an organisational structure of LeCroy software team is presented in Figure 4.4.

From a geographical perspective, the software team is distributed between three locations (numbers are correct as of December 2001):

1) New York (USA): head office with 13 software engineers
2) Geneva (Switzerland): 14 software engineers
3) Maine (USA): main software architect (one person)

There are two senior managers who are in charge of the NY team and the team in Geneva.

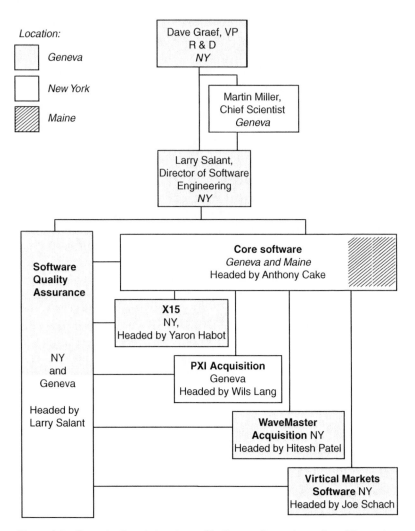

*Figure 4.4* Organisational structure of LeCroy software team (as of December 2001)

Also, there is a software architect of LeCroy, who telecommutes from Maine. One senior manager explained how this dispersed team is organised: 'he (the software architect) is sort of independent. He kind of works on everything. He is one of our architects so he basically reports to me'. This individual had worked in New York for many years and spent a year working in Geneva. He was living in Geneva at the time when the Maui project started. In 1999 his family decided to move back to Maine, where they were originally from. From Maine he carried on the work that he did in Geneva telecommuting. It worked out very well:

> He is online most of the day with either someone from New York or someone in Geneva talking. Because he is one of the architects of the system, he gets all the guys in Geneva when he wakes up in the morning. They have questions for him and they get on the line with him, and then in the afternoon he has guys in New York who get online (senior manager).

## How LeCroy organises and manages GD CBD: key observations

In this section the analysis and results of the LeCroy case study are presented and discussed. First, managerial practices perceived as important in GD CBD are presented followed by the contribution of these practices to success in GD CBD.

### LeCroy concept map

In total, 19 managerial practices were important for success in LeCroy's GD CBD project. These practices were classified around the following aspects: (I) *Inter-site coordination*, which focuses on the coordination activities and division of work; (II) *Appropriate tools and technologies*, which describes tools and technologies required in a GD CBD team; (III) *Social ties*, which focuses on people management and social aspects involved in GD CBD; and (IV) *Knowledge sharing*, which focuses on the needs to share knowledge between distributed teams. Furthermore, one more factor emerged from the data, which is (V) *Components management*.

The managerial practices are classified into the five above-mentioned areas and presented in the form of the concept map in Figure 4.5.

In addition to the managerial practices, the LeCroy concept map contains aspects representing success. We assess success in such projects based on the following criteria: *product success, personal satisfaction, successful collaboration* and *bridged gaps*. By examining this LeCroy project, two sub-themes of personal satisfaction were identified: *less communication effort* and *healthy environment*. Furthermore, two sub-themes of successful collaboration were identified from the data: *effective coordination* and *effective communications*.

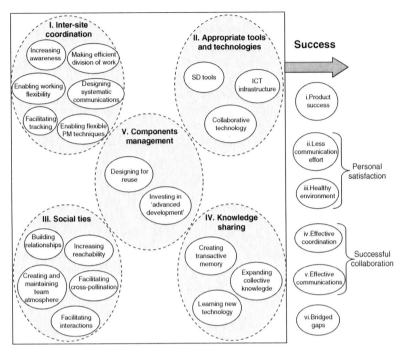

*Figure 4.5* How LeCroy organises and manages GD CBD to be successful

In the following sections, the influence of each area to success in GB CBD and its managerial practices will be discussed.

### Factors and managerial practices that contribute to success

Managerial practices linked by interviewees with success are presented in Table 4.1 (marked X in the table). We indicate in the table only the practice that was most frequently mentioned in connection to a particular factor.

From Table 4.1 it follows that the managerial practices that were most often explicitly connected to success by interviewees are *designing systematic communication* and *building relationships,* and knowledge sharing practices, such as *creating transactive memory* and *expanding collective knowledge*: they contributed to the majority of categories of success. Furthermore, *facilitating interactions* contributes in particular to reducing communication effort.

*Table 4.1* Contribution of managerial practices to success at LeCroy

| Managerial practices | Product success | Less communication effort | Healthy environment | Effective coordinat. | Effective communic. | Bridged gaps |
|---|---|---|---|---|---|---|
| | | Personal satisfaction | | Success. collabor | | |
| **I) Inter-site coordination** | | | | | | |
| 1 Increasing awareness | | | X | | | |
| 2 Making efficient division of work | | | | X | | |
| 3 Enabling working flexibility | | | | X | | |
| 4 Facilitating tracking of bugs and development tasks | | | | | | |
| 5 Enabling flexible PM techniques | | | | X | | |
| 6 Designing systematic communications | | X | X | | X | X |
| **II) Appropriate tools and technologies** | | | | | | |
| 7 Software development tools | | | | X | | |
| 8 ICT infrastructure | X | | | | | |
| 9 Collaborative technology | X | | | | X | X |
| **III) Social ties** | | | | | | |
| 10 Building relationships | X | X | X | X | | X |
| 11 Increasing reachability | | | | | | |
| 12 Creating and maintaining team atmosphere | | | | X | | |
| 13 Facilitating interactions | | X | | | X | |
| 14 Facilitating cross-pollination | | | X | X | | |
| **IV) Knowledge sharing** | | | | | | |
| 15 Creating transactive memory among team members | X | X | X | | X | |
| 16 Expanding collective knowledge of dispersed team | | X | X | X | | X |
| 17 Learning new technology | | | | | | |
| **V) Components management** | | | | | | |
| 18 Designing for reuse | X | | | | | |
| 19 Investing in 'advanced development' | | | | | | |

## Managerial practices: Description and evidence

In this section, managerial practices perceived by interviewees as important for success in GD CBD are described and illustrated using some statements made by interviewees.

### Inter-site coordination in GD CBD: managerial practices

Following are managerial practices dealing with inter-site coordination in GD CBD:

#### *Increasing awareness*

The interviewees indicated that increasing awareness of (i) what is going on in the company and the project, (ii) what everybody is working on in the local team; and (iii) progress made by remote teams, is important for success. For example, one senior manager explained about the philosophy software managers follow: 'we generally want that everyone knows what everyone else is working on. And if someone is held up because of a particular problem – somebody else may have a solution'.

Furthermore, increasing awareness by providing updated information to 'other departments (like Marketing and Production) on what we are working on' is considered important as well.

#### *Making efficient division of work*

An efficient division of work is important: it involves the principles that software managers follow (i) to divide work between teams in Geneva and NY, as well as (ii) to divide specific assignments (tasks) and responsibilities between individual team members. For example:

- To develop experience of new areas (new technology and new products), people who had most experience were chosen. One engineer explained: 'there were guys who wrote 15 years ago the original code. So they were also the natural guys to work on the next generation, or defining the next generation'. These people developed the basics of the new CB Maui platform.

- Software engineers specialise in different technical domains: 'each of us know really well one part of the system, so we have kind of specificities, we know better one domain than another one' (Senior manager, Geneva).

### Enabling working flexibility

Enabling working flexibility implies providing flexible working conditions in order to accommodate personal circumstances of team members, to make their working environment more convenient and comfortable. The interviewees suggested that working flexibility contributes to success. The example of Jon Libby, who has been telecommuting from his home in Maine (USA) since early 1999, illustrates working flexibility:

> When Jon and his wife decided that they want to move to Maine, we asked him if he wanted to telecommute. I have realised that this month [in December 2001] it is 3 years that he has been telecommuting. He has got a cable modem and he is probably online most of the day with either someone from NY or someone in Geneva talking (senior manager, NY).

### Facilitating tracking of bugs and development tasks

Tracking includes (i) having a constantly updated status about the stages in fixing a bug, or progress in a task, and (ii) knowing who is responsible for fixing the bug, or completing the task.

Tracking of bugs is important for developers as well as for people in sales offices.

At LeCroy, the in-house developed tool, BugBase is used for tracking bugs and development tasks. One top executive described:

> Everyone has access to BugBase, also all our sales offices, in Japan, for instance, they have a copy of it. They can enter the bugs and they can look at the status. And what happens is, as a bug gets fixed, the one who entered the bug gets notified that it was fixed. And every time one of the engineers changes the bug, as a manager I get notified that they updated it, and so I can see how they diagnosed it. So for management of bugs, BugBase is invaluable.

Furthermore, BugBase is used for tracking development tasks: 'sometimes we put into BugBase tasks for people, just because it is convenient later to track them'.

### Enabling flexible Project Management (PM) techniques

Flexible PM techniques are necessary to accommodate everyday dynamics. One engineer explained: 'the problem we find in huge projects is that there are so many dynamics – things are dynamically changing on any given day. If you try to fully maintain the project at micro level, it would be a full-time job for someone'. Therefore, a flexible PM technique includes:

- On a macro level: planning of major project activities (milestones).
- On a micro level: flexible and not too detailed planning.

### Designing systematic communications

Systematic communications are considered by interviewees as important for success. This practice includes organising frequent communications and designing rules aiming to make communications more effective, in particular:

- Scheduling systematic and frequent communications, such as regular teleconferences between software managers in NY and Geneva; a transatlantic videoconference with all team members every couple of months.
- Communicating directly to reach an appropriate person (i.e. no hierarchy in communications).
- Improving style and content of communications to achieve better understanding (and prevent conflict and misunderstanding) between remote counterparts.

For example:

> I have a lot of experience working with a lot of foreign cultures. In some cultures if you are on the phone explaining something to somebody and they don't understand it – they still say 'I understand'. So the way I try to ensure that the information was received correctly is through a very detailed process of describing the issue. For example I say, 'open this Web link. What do you see?' So it is very specific, very detailed (senior developer, NY).

### Appropriate tools and technologies in GD CBD: managerial practices

Managerial practices related to tools and technologies important in GD CBD are as follows:

### Software Development tools

Software Development (SD) tools include tools for the development and management of components, configuration and version management tools, and tools for testing and tracking bugs. In order to support

CBD in a globally distributed environment, SD tools need to provide the following capabilities.

| | |
|---|---|
| **Automated management of interdependencies between components and related files** | Managing interdependencies between components is not a problem as long as the number of components is small. In this case the dependencies could be modelled and understood visually. However, when the number of components becomes hundreds, visual understanding is no longer an option. As one software architect explained:<br><br>Imagine building one DLL in one project under Visual Studio. It is very easy to do. Building two or three project DLLs that depend on each other is also fairly easy to do. Building 300 or 500 of these things is impossible.<br><br>To this end, the LeCroy software team developed an in-house tool called COMProjMgr. COMProjMgr knows the dependencies between all the files in Maui (of which there were 5,000–6,000 in end of December 2001), and between the various components, and manages the entire project. |
| **Rapid update of changes** | There are many dynamics in the development environment: every day new components are developed, and existing components are modified. Components and files are inter-related, thus every new component and modification requires changes in the whole environment. In order to accommodate rapid changes in the development environment and ensure that everybody is working with the latest versions of files and components, |

the LeCroy software team compiled a build of components four times a day. The building does not apply to everything, as this would take too long. 'Right now [end of December 2001] building everything takes about six hours, even on a high-powered machine' (senior manager, NY). Therefore COMProjMgr builds only those files that have been modified or added, and those that depend on them. One engineer explained:

> What COMProjMgr will do is if one of these files changes, it knows the dependencies about everything from everything else. And it will go through the old build just looking for things that need to be built.

---

**Automated testing of components**

An in-house developed tool called SoftwareTestHarness is used for testing components. It runs automatic tests every day. One Quality Assurance manager:

> What it does is it shows you all the LeCroy developed components in your system, and you could say 'run a test for all of them' or 'run the test for any one of them'.

Each component LeCroy develops has interfaces that are standard for the component: one for a basic self-test, and one for an advanced self-test. There are special test components used for testing of other (functional) components. They typically contain 'a whole bunch of test cases' needed to make sure that the functionality of the tested component is correct. The Director of Software development commented 'We can test each component by itself in SoftwareTestHarness and that runs every single day automatically'.

| | |
|---|---|
| **Standardisation of tools and methods across locations** | Everyone working with Maui uses the same  tools and methods. One project manager described: |

All are identical, absolutely identical. We have one Version Control System [VCS], at least for Maui, which is located in Geneva: it is on the network, so everyone can get to it. The Lotus Notes system we use is on servers in NY and in Geneva. And they are replicated, so they are identical essentially. Everything is the same. Everyone working with Maui uses the same tools.

| | |
|---|---|
| **Centralisation of tools** | Centralisation of tools in one location ensures one single environment for all remote locations. For the LeCroy software team, there are no 'local' tools as such – all tools are located at one central place. For example: |

VCS – Perforce – exists in Geneva and guys access it here [in NY] the same way over WAN, so the only difference there is: from here it takes a little longer to access it, speed is slower. It doesn't matter where you are in the world, you still can access the same single VCS (senior manager, NY).

| | |
|---|---|
| **Creating a Guide that explains how to use tools and methods** | Maui Software Developer's Guide lists the tools used (Lotus Notes, Visual Studio, Perforce, ComProjMgr, Rational Rose, BugBase, SoftwareTestHarness) |

and explains how to create and debug components in Maui using these tools. This Guide is invaluable for new employees, and staff moved from previous products and starting work with Maui (during a transition period).

---

**Developing tools in-house**

The strategy regarding SD tools that LeCroy software managers follow is building tools in-house, if the required tools are not available on the market:

> Whenever we need a tool, we do try to buy it, but most of the time we don't find a proper solution. Then we made our own, and this goes for most of the tools that we have (senior manager, NY).

> Of the main four SD tools, Perforce is a commercial tool, and the other three – COMProjMgr, SoftwareTestHarness and BugBase (discussed above) – are all tools developed in-house by the LeCroy software team.

---

### ICT infrastructure

Interviewees stressed the importance of ICT infrastructure for success: 'no firm trying to execute GD CBD successfully can do so without the right infrastructure' (VP of IS, NY).

An ICT infrastructure enables connection between all remote sites. It includes Internet, WAN, server and applications pool, how resource shares are set up (i.e. sharing of databases, server, project repository), conferencing tools, and network speed and bandwidth. Furthermore, it includes capabilities aiming to support security requirements, such as firewalls and access rights.

In order to succeed in a globally distributed environment, the ICT infrastructure needs to support the following:

| | |
|---|---|
| **Quick access to the network** | Quick access to the network is required from all remote locations (in the office, and for those working from home). |
| **Shared databases** | Having one central database accessibleover WAN from remote locations ensures that everyone is working with the latest versions of files and components. One IS manager explained:<br><br>I don't have to build every component locally. If someone changes the hardcopy component and they put it back – it will be rebuilt on the server and then in the morning I can import that component and just use it. |
| **Web access and constant replication of databases** | Web access and constant replication of databases (over the Web) are required to provide updated information/data and allow tracking. LeCroy engineers have project databases based on Lotus Notes. As one senior manager explained:<br><br>Because we are working at separatelocations and Lotus Notes replicates databases, it is very good for us. The big databases are local to Geneva and here [NY] and they get replicated constantly over the Web. |

### Collaborative technology

The following are collaborative technologies used by LeCroy team to collaborate successfully over distance:

| | |
|---|---|
| **Online chat** | Every member of the software development group appears on the list of MSN Messenger. This tool enables real-time remote contact. One project manager described: |
| | During the day if you have a question or you need somebody's help, largely you use online chat. It is immediate, it does not matter where they are in the world – whether they are in the next cubical or whether they are in the next country, they use that system. |
| **Phone and teleconferencing** | If real-time collaborative tasks require more than a couple of lines of response, team members tend to communicate by phone: 'generally if it is more than a couple of lines of response, then we'll pick up a phone, and talk to each another' (Anthony Cake). |
| **Application Sharing** | The LeCroy software team uses the Net Meeting Application Sharing Tool (AST) for real-time collaboration, both co-located and remote collaboration. It allows developers to see what is on the screen of a remote computer, and to share and take over control. Software developers make extensive use of the tool for code reviews. One project manager observed: |
| | I have even seen it within this building, two guys in almost the next cubical to each other doing a |

code review: sitting next to each other, but they are sitting at their desks and looking at their own screen, working through the code. So, it is actually an interesting tool, and people are used to doing code reviews across the ocean or up to Maine.

System architects also use the AST frequently when designing a new feature or user interface: 'we have been working in Visual Studio when laying out a dialog for a product via AST when Anthony will be in Geneva and I'll be here [in NY],' (senior manager, NY).

AST is used for taking control of a computer mainly when somebody needs help with debugging. One software developer explained:

> If someone has a problem in Geneva and would like to work with me on finding the bug in the code, we use AST to go through the code together [NY and Geneva] while discussing the bug over the phone.

Typically, in such situations developers use AST to see what is happening on the computers, and at the same time they use the phone or voice chat capability of AST to discuss the problem.

| | |
|---|---|
| **Videoconference** | Since about one year before the launch of the Aladdin system (from early 2001), software managers have been Video Conferencing (VC) at least once a week to discuss progress and other issues. Furthermore, VC is used (i) for meetings with a remote team; and |

| | (ii) for meetings with all developers from both locations. |
|---|---|
| **Email** | Email supports low priority tasks and issues, and tasks that cannot be completed in real-time because of time-zone differences. |
| **Intranet** | The LeCroy team has access to its own Intranet environment where internal documents and other relevant information are posted. |

### Social ties in GD CBD: managerial practices

According to the opinions of the interviewees, rapport and trust contribute to success, as illustrated by the following quotations:

*Contribution of Trust*

One project manager explained the importance of trust:

> It makes a big difference, when the guys know each other. And more importantly – when the guys trust each other and they know what the others' capabilities are. I think that makes a huge difference. It is because there are very clever guys in the group. And when you get fairly clever guys talking to each other, there needs to be certain degree of trust, I guess respect is a better word for each other. And where that is lacking, there is really a communication problem. But when there is a lot of trust and respect, people get on very well, they are very productive.

*Contribution of Rapport*

One software architect explained the importance of rapport:

> We found over the years that whenever people had worked face-to-face, or even if it was only for a few days, the fact that you could put someone's face to it, made it that much easier for someone to pick up the phone and ask the question, than if it was just a name that you heard.

Following are the managerial practices that focus on social aspects and facilitate rapport and trust between remote counterparts.

### *Building relationships*

Building relationships involves building rapport and trust between remote team members: it is considered by interviewees very important for success. The following quotes illustrate the importance LeCroy top managers give to building relationships:

- 'We all got together in the mountains of France and it was a real fun week. It had two purposes: one was to teach us all this new technology [Microsoft COM]. The other, which was equally important, if not more important, was to try to build relationships between people' (senior manager, NY).
- 'The biggest problem is a people problem, or people from different sites, it happened, do not respect and trust each other, they don't work well together. But in most of cases that is not really an issue any more' (senior manager, NY).

### Increasing reachability

Increasing reachability implies making it easier to reach the right people at a remote location, in particular:

- to know whom to contact, i.e. who is the person who has knowledge (of a certain domain or issue);
- to know who is available, i.e. if the person is in the office on the given day or time.

For example, as everyone appears on the MSN Messenger list, this gives an indication to others, specifically in the remote locations, about who is at work (logged in MSN Messenger), and if the person is at his/her desk or away (status changed to 'away').

### Creating and maintaining team atmosphere

Creating and maintaining a team atmosphere implies making sure that all are 'plugged' into the project/company. It is important, in particular for the remote team in Geneva. One software engineer described:

What happened in Geneva is that among the guys there is a natural feeling that they are kind of unplugged from the rest of the company. Because it is an outpost! In order to handle that we organise regular meetings to let people know what is going on in the company, what everyone else is working on. It is a big help. Every several months we have a transatlantic videoconference with the software guys in NY and Geneva. It helps everyone, I think, to feel we are working as a team and that they are part of the LeCroy team.

### Facilitating interactions

Facilitating interactions between people at remote locations is important. It includes (i) facilitating personal face-to-face interactions and (ii) organising regular and frequent interactions over distance.

LeCroy software managers try to facilitate interactions and create relationships between remote counterparts.

For example, meetings in person are considered important. One project manager explained:

> Meeting and getting to know each other has got a lot to do with trust and respect. In fact, I would say that most valuable time spent in this respect is probably in the local bar than in the meeting room. Because getting to know someone happens over a few beers. And that develops into the professional [area]. I think that's sort of an important thing, a very important thing. That was the idea behind the conference in the Alps, to get people in an environment where there was plenty time for that. It was pretty important.

### Facilitating cross-pollination

Cross-pollination implies that people from the one group spend significant amounts of time in the other group (other location) and vice versa.

One of the interviewees emphasised the importance of cross-pollination by giving an example of unsuccessful collaboration of the LeCroy hardware team. Initially the hardware team was distributed between NY and Geneva, the same as the software team. This person said:

> I think, part of the problem was – there was no kind of cross-pollination. There was nobody from the NY group who spent a significant amount of time in the Geneva group or vice versa. So there were already two separate groups. How to explain, they just didn't get on. Really didn't have any respect for each other.

In the software team, one of the advantages was that a couple of members of the Geneva software group originally worked in New York. Anthony Cake started in NY in 1986, and only later moved to Geneva. Another senior person – Martin Miller, the chief scientist currently based in Geneva – worked in New York for many years (he has been at the company since the late 1970s). Anthony Cake expressed his viewpoint: 'to take people with experience, I think, working in the group, and then move them into another group, is a good way to seed the other group, to make sure that everything works together'.

## Knowledge sharing in GD CBD: managerial practices

Interviewees consider knowledge sharing as contributing to success, in particular, building up collective knowledge through shared experiences, and creating transactive memory among team members at dispersed locations.

In LeCroy, team members had a history of working together, and some of the dispersed team members had an opportunity to meet in person: therefore at LeCroy global software team transactive memory and collective knowledge were developed to some extent before the case project started and were facilitated throughout the project.

Following are managerial practices seen as important for knowledge sharing between remote team members, supported by quotations from interviews.

### *Creating transactive memory among dispersed team members*

Creating transactive memory among team members located in NY and Geneva and Maine is considered important for success.

In LeCroy, a number of activities that facilitate interactions among dispersed team members were organised through which team members could get to know each other and further facilitate creation of transactive memory. These activities included an introductory course for Microsoft COM combined with a team-building exercise, where all team members met in one location, and also frequent visits of managers to remote locations.

The following statement illustrates the existence of transactive memory at the studied team:

> When a problem occurs it is important for the team, instead of finding the bug, to find quickly who knows best about the failing component.

### *Expanding collective knowledge of the dispersed team*

Expanding collective knowledge of the dispersed team is important for success. This practice includes learning about the national culture of remote counterparts, sharing knowledge of the overall product (beyond a specific area an individual team member is working on) and developing common technical knowledge.

Development of the Maui platform started in Geneva where the basics of the platform were developed; only later did the team in NY start working on Maui. Gilles Ritter, who was involved in the Maui project from the very beginning, explained how knowledge sharing about the

Maui platform was organised to ensure collective technical knowledge and common understanding of the evolving product:

> Initially, only a few people started in NY and they had always a lot of questions regarding the new platform. So they were always in contact from NY to Geneva. And when more and more people in NY started to work on the new platform, it was decided for me to come over here [to NY] for one year to facilitate the contact for everyone new in the new platform. [...] I know all the basics, the background of the platform. So, that's why I am here for one year to kind of teach all the other co-workers how to develop using the same tools.

To expand collective knowledge of the dispersed team members LeCroy managers facilitate sharing of experiences between the teams, as illustrated by the following quote:

> I am back and forth all the time, and Anthony as well. But occasionally, we do have people coming from Geneva here or from here going to Geneva for a week or two and we even have a few cases where we put someone over, we have one guy right now who is spending a year here from Geneva. And that is really useful sharing experiences and stuff (senior manager).

### *Learning new technology*

For the LeCroy software engineers, the new Microsoft COM technology and CBD methodology were very different from the approaches they used to develop software for earlier oscilloscopes. Therefore, one of dilemmas LeCroy faced while developing the CB Maui platform was how to move people onto the Maui project so that they could develop in Maui and, hopefully, be as productive as they were with the old system.[4] Thus,

---

[4]Anthony Cake explained:

> It's an interesting or it's a difficult step for a developer to make, when you were the master of your environment for such a long time, and you understood the entire system (and it is – we are talking about half a million lines of code). These guys knew this stuff [the old system], this was their world for 10–15 years, and all of a sudden someone says 'OK, forget all that, we are going to go to this new place which is completely different'. And it is using some standards by Microsoft, that we didn't create and that's not perfect but we have to live with them. And, everything that they were used to-day-to-day – changed. Some guys accepted that very, very quickly and some guys were up-and-running, maybe climbing the learning curve within a few weeks. Other guys, they took longer. Somebody from the original senior guys are still not really up to speed in this new environment – they never will be as productive as they were on the old stuff. So the younger guys find it a little easier, they came up to speed literally in weeks.

learning new technology was organised in several steps. First, the introduction of the Microsoft COM technology was organised, when all software engineers had an overview and some background about its principles and development methodology. The second step involved learning how to work with applications based on Microsoft COM technology. Finally, after the Maui platform was developed by a small group of experts, all software engineers were taught about what the Maui and how to develop a product (oscilloscope) in Maui. Furthermore, after the Maui platform was developed, a Guide that describes the environment and tools used to develop products in Maui was created. The Guide served as a reference framework for everybody and facilitated learning of the new platform.

## Components management in GD CBD: managerial practices

In addition to the four factors suggested in the theoretical lens, the *components management* emerged from the data as a factor contributing to success. Following are managerial practices seen as important for ensuring the successful components management in GD CBD.

### Designing for reuse

For LeCroy this practice aims to increase reuse of software components across a number of products in the long term. This involves analysis and long term planning for future products and product families, and making strategic decisions about the granularity level of components. The need to facilitate reuse through design derives from the major goal of LeCroy software managers.

### Investing in 'advanced development'

The development of the Maui platform was treated at LeCroy not as a typical product development project where product requirements are defined in the very beginning, but as a research project.

*Advanced development* included learning about available technologies, and conducting a feasibility study aiming to test whether or not a 'proof of concept' for the product can be achieved by applying available technology(ies). One software engineer explained:

> When Maui project started, we didn't really have a product in mind, not in the sense of the product that you can ship. But we knew that we wanted to use this [Maui platform] on several products that would be defined in the future.

## Success in GD CBD: evidence

This section presents evidence collected in interviews about the success achieved in the studied case. The evidence (quotations from interviews) is presented according to the categories of success illustrated in the LeCroy Concept Map (Figure 2.5).

### i) Product success

The Maui project was highly successful:

- LeCroy's WaveMaster 8600 was announced as Product of the Year 2002 by END magazine (among ten best products for test and measurement purposes).[5]
- The Maui CB architecture (platform) served as a basis for future products. One top manager commented:

> We began shipping both the WaveMaster 8300 and 8500 to customers in March, 2002. At the same time we also began shipping a Disk Drive Analyzer (DDA), which is based on the WaveMaster 8500.

- In January of 2003, LeCroy launched the WavePro 7000 series of scopes (7000, 7100, and 7300), which is also based on Maui.
- Due to the Maui architecture, LeCroy successfully partnered with three different commercial software companies during 2002 to further extend the analysis capabilities of LeCroy products.

### Personal satisfaction

*Healthy environment*

One project manager described his view regarding personal satisfaction:

> The job here is very demanding and challenging. I think that those who stay onboard are the engineers who share the same goal: to work on complex problems in cutting edge technologies. I think that that the fact we share this goal helps us to communicate well.

---

[1]http://www.e-insite.net/ednmag/index.asp?layout=article&articleid=CA263115&pubdate=12/12/2002

*Less communication effort*

A couple of project managers commented on communication efforts:

- 'We use MSN messenger from Microsoft – every member of the software development group, they appear on the list. So for having a chat with someone, wherever they may be in the world in the given time, you just need to double click on their name and start typing a line'.
- 'In Geneva, all senior guys speak English very well. Some of the junior guys speak English purely. So what we have done at their request, we paid English lessons for them. But locally they speak French. When I communicate with them in English, it is very rare that I cannot communicate my ideas or issues or so on'.

## Successful collaboration

*Effective coordination*

One manager commented on coordination activities in the project:

> Basically when we started the platform in Geneva we were only a few who developed the basement of the new platform [...]. And the other guys, the other workers who joined us after and had to learn how the platform works, now know who of the first guys knows well which parts, then go to ask questions. And sometimes, if it is not the right person, I'll just tell him to ask another guy who knows better than me, and this is how it works.

Having standards and centralised tools helps to make coordination more effective and efficient. For example, there is no need to build every component locally: all components are built on the central server. Furthermore, programming building of components four times a day allows the use of time-zone differences to work around-the-clock.

*Effective communications*

One senior manager from Geneva explained about his experience of working with remote counterparts:

> For example, when I control his machine, it doesn't respond as fast as on my computer. So it is a technical delay in terms of seconds, but the understanding is absolutely identical remotely or just on site.

## Bridged geographical, time-zone and cultural gaps

*Geographical distance* is not perceived as a problem:
For the LeCroy software team, geographical distance causes limited inconvenience, i.e. in extreme situations when physical presence is required: 'for an important meeting, people get on the plane and fly over for a meeting, but that is an extreme' (senior manager, NY). But on a regular basis, team members communicate remotely using different types of communication media.

*Time-zone differences* are not perceived as a problem:
Time differences are not perceived as a problem, rather as an advantage: 'we use the fact that we are not working together to allow us to work around-the-clock' (senior manager, Geneva). One manager explained:

> Generally it doesn't really matter, it is not a big advantage, not a big disadvantage. I would not say that time differences are a disadvantage, and close to a release or big milestone they can be a big advantage. Because problems, bugs fixes, can be passed on from time-zone to time-zone.

There is a six hours time difference between the USA East coast[6] (UTC –5) and Switzerland (UTC +1). Despite this six hours difference, 'generally we have quite an overlap. Because, the first guy that starts working in Geneva is in the office at about 6 am. And in times when we are close to getting a product out, or big milestone, they are there [in the office in Geneva] until midnight, so we get only a few hours when we are not overlapping somewhere' (senior manager, NY). Another manager had the same opinion:

> Of course we know that with Geneva, we have to work in the morning. And they have to work with us [with NY] in the day-after-noon. But after that constraint, I don't see any.

*Cultural differences* are bridged:
The software team is multinational: 'a lot of the people in the Geneva team are actually not Swiss. There are guys with Spanish origin, guys from other places. But, I would say, on a daily basis it doesn't change

---

[6]NY and Maine are in the same time-zone.

the way that things are done. And I think these differences are not obstacles any more' (senior manager, NY).

## Conclusions

In this chapter, the analysis and results of the LeCroy case study were presented and discussed. Managerial practices and quotations from interviews illustrating these managerial practices and their contribution to success, as perceived by the interviewees, were presented.

The results of the case study illustrate that interviewees considered four factors suggested in the theoretical lens, and the fifth factor (components management) that emerged from the data, as contributing to success in GD CBD.

In terms of managerial practices, *inter-site coordination* between NY and Geneva was effective and efficient: first, work was divided according to where expertise was located. Skill-based division of work was possible because team members had experience of working together from dispersed locations and had built relationships. This reduced the chances of misunderstandings and conflicts. Second, in order to increase awareness and keep remote teams updated all the time, systematic communications were organised on different levels (between managers and developers). Third, flexible project management techniques were adopted to accommodate everyday dynamics.

In relation to appropriate *tools and technologies*, first, interviewees stressed the importance of the ICT infrastructure. Second, standardisation and centralisation of software development tools enabled remote teams to work in one single development environment, and use similar tools and methods at all remote locations. Third, software development tools supported rapid update of changes by automatically (four times a day) building components that had changed; this enabled the utilisation of time-zone differences to speed the development process. Fourth, using various collaborative technologies, team members in LeCroy did not feel the differences between working with colleagues at the same office, and colleagues at a remote location.

Regarding *social ties*, in LeCroy, trust and rapport between remote counterparts were developed, first, because the software team had a long history of collaborating over distance; and second, because in the beginning of the project all team members had an opportunity to meet in person in an informal environment.

Concerning *knowledge sharing*, in the LeCroy team, transactive memory and collective knowledge were developed through the shared experience of working together over distance. LeCroy managers emphasised the importance of systematic communications and interactions (e.g. short visits and meetings in person) in order to further facilitate knowledge sharing between remote team members.

It was particularly remarkable how *components management* was organised in LeCroy: in order to maximise reuse across products, they invested time and resources in analysis to identify the most common functionalities for the product family they intended to develop. This design-for-reuse strategy enabled the LeCroy team to achieve the benefits of reuse and be more efficient in developing new products based on the Maui platform.

The LeCroy case clearly illustrates that the possibility of components reuse changes the concept of *product* in the software industry. What is a *product*? Is a component procured from a component market a *product*? Or, is a CB system that comprises commercial and in-house developed components a *product*? As Larry Salant said about products based on the CB Maui architecture:

> What is the product? That, I guess, is really the key. So the products are – we have X15 as a product, WaveMaster or Aladdin is a product. But most of the components are the same in both. These are literally hundreds of these components.

# 5
# Observations of GD CBD at SAP

> *To span a project crossing Palo Alto, India and Germany is a night-mare for the people who have to work on this. 13 hours time differences. There is no overlap. It is a pain. So, you have to have really good reasons to do something like this.*
>
> (Director of KM Collaboration Group, SAP Portal)

## Background of SAP global organisation

Founded in 1972, SAP is a recognised leader in providing ERP and other collaborative business solutions, industry-specific and cross-industry solutions, for small and medium-sized businesses, and providing technological platforms that allow for integrating heterogeneous systems. Its largest competitors are Oracle Corporation and Microsoft. SAP employs more than 32,000 people in more than 50 countries.[1] With operations in Bulgaria, France, India, Israel, Japan, and North America, SAP Labs integrate ideas and leading-edge technologies that address the needs of specific industries and geographic regions, and maintain SAP and its customers at the forefront of e-business success.[2] In 2008, revenues from software sales were 3.6 billion Euros (that is 31% of the total revenue: the other 69% of the total revenue came from software maintenance, consultancy and training).[3]

This case study focuses on the SAP Collaboration tools project developed by the Knowledge Management (KM) Collaboration group, which is part of the Enterprise Portal Division.

---

[1] From SAP web-site http://www.sap.com/company/; numbers are correct for April 2005.
[2] From SAP web-site http://www.sap.com/company/saplabs/
[3] From SAP Annual Report 2008, this is the latest financial information available.

## Background of the project and product

The goal of the SAP Collaboration tools project was to develop a comprehensive collaborative platform that would enable both individuals and teams in different locations to communicate in real time and asynchronously, and to support the teamwork of any distributed project teams. The SAP Collaboration tools were developed to be part of the next generation application and integration platform (that is, SAP NetWeaver), and to allow integration with various tools of different providers.

The architecture of the SAP Collaboration tools aimed to be component-based, to allow independent upgrade of different features and, as a result, more flexibility in customizing solutions for specific customers and reduced time-to-market for new versions.

The development of SAP Collaboration tools started in September 2001. By June 2002, the first version of SAP Collaboration tools was released and the group was working on the second release.

### SAP Collaboration tools

SAP Collaboration tools provide groupware capabilities and support synchronous (real time) and asynchronous communications. Groupware capabilities include virtual work spaces (collaboration room), team folders and discussions lists, a team calendar, task assignment and tracking. They offer real-time collaboration capabilities such as desktop and application sharing that enable online meetings, remote support and co-browsing; chat; email; and video and audio conferencing capabilities, e.g. voice-over IP. Furthermore, SAP Collaboration tools offer a unified calendar function that enables task coordination (e.g. to schedule meetings) and synchronisation with user's personal calendars in MS Exchange or Lotus Notes.

SAP Collaboration tools provide individuals and groups with a single point of access for documents and information sharing: 'collaboration capabilities retain project information in context and within one location, which currently is most likely distributed among file servers, email accounts'.[4] Information located in different places is delivered to a user on one single screen via SAP Portal.[5]

---

[4] From SAP web-site.
[5] SAP Portal 'provides people-centric integration of all types of enterprise information, including SAP applications, third-party applications, databases, data warehouses, desktop documents, and Web content and services. It provides employees, supply chain partners, customers, and other communities with immediate, secure, and role-based access to key information and applications across the extended enterprise' (from SAP web site). A user sees all this information on one screen.

## Software components in SAP Collaboration tools

SAP Collaboration tools have a CB architecture that is open and extensible. The components can be integrated with third-party collaboration tools like WebEx from WebEx Communications Inc., so portal users can collaborate with non-portal users. This allows users to work with familiar tools, protecting their existing technology investments.

The development architect explained about the components included in the SAP Collaboration tools:

> These are rather small components compared to something like a component in an ERP [solution] like a finance or HR as a component. We have smaller components: for example, email details are in one component, a portal component. This is a stand-alone component in the sense that it can run stand alone, and within the Portal as well. And it can be replaced by a functionally equal component, the system will still run as it did before. There are thousands of components in the product.

Information from different sources that is consolidated on the screen of the user is generated by portal components, which sit on top of the portal platform. The portal components are called iViews.[6] Each element of the screen is a component. For example, Christoph Thommes explained that three views included in the Outlook mailbox – a folder list (on the left side of a screen), a list of emails (on the right side), and a detailed view of an email (on the bottom of the screen) – are components. Components are packaged together within one communication package (officially called iView Studio). The communication package consists of the different iViews and 'connectors' that put together different components of the package. There are two types of connectors: connectors to third party components (e.g. Microsoft Exchange or Lotus, which provide group-ware functionality), and connectors to the technical (Portal) platform that provides the user interface (i.e. images that the user actually sees on the screen).

## Background of the software team

### Working experience in a globally distributed environment

In September 2001, when the Collaborative tools project started, key players (managers and architects) and team members from remote

---

[6]In the SAP Glossary, iView is defined as a 'self-contained, XML-based presentation element. A well-defined set of interfaces displays content and the personalisation of the content elements presented as part of a portal page'.

locations did not know each other. They did not have a history of working together. Some of the team members had previous experience of working in a globally distributed environment, but not necessarily with Indian/German/American cultures: for the majority of key players and team members this cross-cultural setting was new.

The geographical distribution of the Collaborative tools project between Germany, India and USA was the result of a merger. As the director of the KM Collaboration group explained: 'To span a project crossing Palo Alto, India and Germany is a nightmare for the people who have to work on this. Thirteen hours time differences. There is no overlap. It is a pain. So, you have to have really good reasons to do something like this'. For the KM Collaboration group the key reason was a merger between SAP and Top Tier. As one project manager explained:

> I didn't have an alternative: we inherited already working teams from totally different set-ups, and, based on this merger, we consolidated them at that time. [...] If I had really started out a project from scratch, I would have done it differently. But that was no question – if you are merging, you are not starting from scratch, but you have teams or locations and try to set up something that way and form a unit that is at the end of the day able to execute, somehow.

By the time the interviews in Germany were completed, in June 2002, the key players had been working together for nine months.

### Organisational structure of the software team

The KM Collaboration group, where the case study was conducted, is part of SAP Portal. SAP Portal is a product organisation. Different groups are responsible for different parts of a product (solution). The KM Collaboration group is responsible for SAP Collaboration tools, which are part of mySAP Enterprise Portal solution: 'we are responsible for different collaborative tools within every release. We have product cycles. Within these product cycles, we have currently several tools we have to deliver' (senior manager).

A schematic illustration of the organisational structure of the KM Collaboration group is presented in Figure 5.1.

Development managers of each team report directly to the director. Two development architects, Christoph Thommes and Martin Moser, work on the conceptual design of the architecture. Their responsibility is to drive the architectural design and ensure that everything fits together.

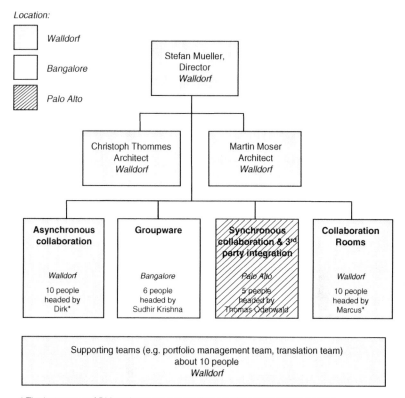

* The last names of Dirk and marcus are not disclosed for confidentiality reasons

*Figure 5.1* Organisational structure of KM Collaboration group (as of June 2002)

From a geographical perspective, the software team is distributed between three locations (numbers are correct as of June 2002), and each team is working on a different part of the Collaboration project:

1) Walldorf (Germany): head office with two teams that work on asynchronous collaboration and SAP Collaboration Rooms: ten people each
2) Bangalore (India): develops Groupware: six people
3) Palo Alto (USA): develops synchronous collaboration and third party integration: five people

Furthermore there are various supporting teams, like the portfolio management team and the translation team, which include in total about ten people. These teams provide partial support for direct development. They are most of the time assigned to one specific product, but they are separate branches of the organisational chart and so report to different managers.

## How SAP organises and manages GD CBD: analysis and results

In this section we present the key managerial practices that were central to SAP implementation of CBD in its GD teams.

### SAP concept map

There were 16 managerial practices that SAP applied in order to successfully implement GD CBD.

The managerial practices are classified into five areas and presented in the form of the concept map in Figure 5.2. In addition, evidence of success is presented in the concept map.

In the following sections, we discuss each area contributing to success in GD CBD and its key managerial practices.

### Managerial practices that contribute to success

Managerial practices linked by interviewees with success are presented in Table 5.1. We indicate in the table only the practice that was

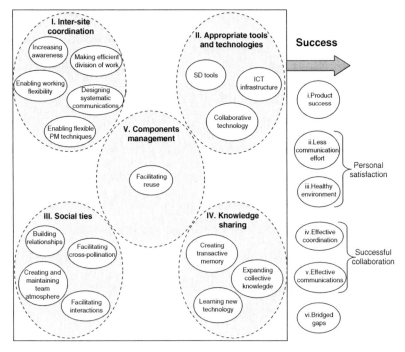

*Figure 5.2*   How SAP organises and manages GD CBD to be successful

most frequently mentioned in connection to a particular factor (marked by X in the table).

From Table 5.1 it follows that managerial practices that were most often explicitly connected to success by interviewees are *building relationships,*

Table 5.1    Contribution of managerial practices to success at SAP

| Managerial practices | Product success | Less communication effort | Healthy environment | Effective coordinat. | Effective communic. | Bridged gaps |
|---|---|---|---|---|---|---|
| | | Personal satisfaction | | Success. collabor | | |
| **I) Inter-site coordination** | | | | | | |
| 1 Increasing awareness | | | X | | | |
| 2 Making efficient division of work | X | | | | | |
| 3 Enabling working flexibility | | | | | | |
| 4 Enabling flexible PM techniques | | | X | | | |
| 5 Designing systematic communications | | X | X | | X | X |
| **II) Appropriate tools and technologies** | | | | | | |
| 6 Software Development tools | | | | | | |
| 7 ICT infrastructure | | | | | | |
| 8 Collaborative technology | | X | X | | X | X |
| **III) Social ties** | | | | | | |
| 9 Building relationships | | X | X | | X | X |
| 10 Creating and maintaining team atmosphere | | | X | | | |
| 11 Facilitating interactions | | X | X | X | X | X |
| 12 Facilitating cross-pollination | | | | | | X |
| **IV) Knowledge sharing** | | | | | | |
| 13 Creating transactive memory among team members | | X | X | | X | X |
| 14 Expanding collective knowledge of dispersed team | | X | X | | X | |
| 15 Managing 'by intuition' | | X | | | | |
| **V) Components management** | | | | | | |
| 16 Facilitating reuse | | | | X | | |

*facilitating interactions, systematic communications*; and knowledge sharing practices, such as *creating transactive memory* and *expanding collective knowledge*: these contributed to the majority of categories of success.

## Managerial practices: description and evidence

In this section, managerial practices perceived by interviewees as important for success in GD CBD are described and illustrated using quotations made by the interviewees.

### Inter-site coordination in GD CBD: managerial practices

Following are managerial practices dealing with inter-site coordination in GD CBD.

#### Increasing awareness

The interviewees indicated that increasing awareness of (i) what is going on in the company and the project and (ii) about remote team members and the environment, are important for success.

(i) Increasing awareness of the management team and key players about the 'entire vision' is specifically important when setting up a new organisation (as in this case, when three teams were merged into one group).

(ii) Increasing awareness concerning remote team members and the local environment is important, in particular because the teams in India, USA and Germany had not worked together before, and many of the team members were not familiar with the culture of their counterparts. One manager gave a perspective of the team in Bangalore about the importance of building awareness:

> For us it's more of building awareness of the whole team through Stefan, because he heads all the teams [the entire group] so he [Stefan] needs to have a good picture of how the team composition is, what each individual is like or what different people are like.

In the early stages of the project, this manager organised a visit to Bangalore for key players from Germany and Palo Alto, who participated in the team-building exercise together with the local team. The manager had the following expectations for this visit:

> For them it is also getting to know the infrastructure itself and the environment in which we work, because in a situation when there is a problem, then it's easy to visualise what is happening. Then, even

if videoconferencing stops working all of a sudden, then you can still imagine where the people are sitting, what it looks like, you know what is going on.

### Making efficient division of work

An efficient division of work and responsibilities is considered important for success. Principles that software managers follow involve (i) giving full ownership of a product feature for each remote team and (ii) division of technical and 'social' responsibilities, which include establishing reporting channels across the globe:

(i) Work is divided feature-wise, providing full ownership and responsibility for distributed teams. One manager commented: 'you are responsible for what you have taken up and nobody is going to hold back anything'. Each of the four teams has full responsibility for an entire block of functionality: groupware, asynchronous collaboration, synchronous collaboration, and third-party integration. It is important, in particular for offshore teams, to have full ownerships of work. It gives them a feeling of being valuable and the motivation to collaborate.

(ii) A clear division of technical and 'social' supervision (i.e. management of local teams) between the technical architect located in Walldorf and the local development manager aims to ensure the quality of the product and effective team management. For example, two development architects located in Walldorf serve as technical contact persons for the remote teams: one is a contact person for the Bangalore team, and one is a contact person for the Palo Alto team. The architects provide technical supervision for the assigned remote team, and are responsible for technical issues and the quality of software developed by this team. One of them explained that because a technical architect drives the overall product architecture, he is the most appropriate person to provide technical supervision and to control the quality of the product:

> I'm in a position where I have to supervise sometimes what they [Bangalore team] are doing from a technical point of view, I need to point out certain weaknesses in whatever they're doing, from a code perspective for example.

The local development manager of each team is responsible for team management: he divides specific assignments (tasks) between team members and resolves social issues. The development manager and team members are of the same culture. This makes it easier for the development manager to understand and deal with the team members. As one engineer explained:

> I'm not responsible for people, people management is completely up to Sudhir. He deals with the team: assign tasks to the team members, reviews tasks, gives a performance feedback. If there is a technical conflict, there is an agreement that because of my role as a development architect, I'm the one to take the last final decision call on technical issues.

### Enable working flexibility

The interviewees suggested that working flexibility, in terms of (i) providing flexible working conditions such as working from home and (ii) flexible working hours, are important for success. For example, one product architect explained how he uses flexible working hours to increase overlap in working hours with India:

> I start quite early in the morning: they [in Bangalore] come to the office maybe at 9 something and I start at 7 something so it's $1^{1}/_{2}$ hours where they cannot reach me and they stay quite long.

### Enabling flexible Project Management (PM) techniques

Flexible PM techniques help to accommodate everyday dynamics. They include:

- On a macro level: Planning of major project activities (milestones). One project lead explained: 'We have project phases – three to six to, maybe, 12 months, depending on the part of the project'. On a macro level planning includes setting up clear objectives for teams (what features each team should deliver) by the project manager and development architects. Then, within each team planning of work is done by the local development manager:

> I set up clear objectives, but then I give them [local development managers] an entire area for which they are responsible: this means that I am also not buying excuses if they don't deliver. I give them an entire block of functionality, and I give them full responsibility to plan properly, to execute, to tell them what they are actually getting developed. So I put the requirements, what we need, feature-wise, and then judge them from what they really deliver. What they do with the team, how they do it – I

don't care. I tell them to send me updates, and we can adjust the plan if they want. If they don't tell me anything – I take this for granted – this is our culture, this is how we decide what we will deliver.

- On a micro level: Flexible and not too detailed planning.

As one senior manager explained:

We do not plan exactly on a daily basis: maybe it's giving an estimate of how long the task might take and assign someone, who is responsible for the specific task. So it is not in days, but it is more or less weekly milestones.

### Designing systematic communications

Systematic communications considered by interviewees as contributing to success. The design of systematic communications involves the following:

- Scheduling systematic and frequent communications, such as regular teleconferences between software managers in Walldorf, Bangalore and Palo Alto, transatlantic videoconferences with all team members every couple of months.
- Communicating directly to reach an appropriate person. For example, on the question of what is most important in a globally distributed environment, one project manager replied:

Quick and direct communications as far as possible, is the most important thing. 'Direct' means: do not communicate through other people but with the people directly. If you have one contact person who distributes all the information, you lose some amount of information, just because you do not reach the right people.

- Setting up rules of communications

Setting up rules of communications helps people to adjust to communication styles and reduces misunderstandings and confusions that typically happen as a result of a different cultural backgrounds. For example:

  ○ Agreement was reached that the Indian team members would not take it personally when Germans are too direct, because, compared to Indians, Germans usually are very direct and 'brutally precise' in communicating what they have in mind and, typically, this is one of the biggest challenges in German-Indian teams.

○ One manager based in Germany explained about his experience with another manager based in India regarding communication styles; how helpful it was to ensure successful communications over distance:

What I did with him in the very beginning, I told him: 'I am explicit, I am forgiving – if you tell me in the beginning that something is going wrong. Because it is not just me having to deal with an Indian team, changing my style totally. I will try to adapt but because of time-constraints I am not going to adapt exactly to what you are expecting. Otherwise you tell me if you have a problem'. That was easy. That is what we did on the face-to-face meeting when he was here in Germany. He said that this is clear, and now we can see that it worked.

Furthermore, communicating over distance, it is important to make communication 'precise'. Another manager commented on this:

Being precise means being very explicit: making clear statements, especially when you are not meeting face-to-face. If you look at me when I have a telephone call, you would say 'you are brutally precise': I say [by phone] 'yes', 'no', 'no', 'no', 'yes' and there is no answer such as 'maybe': 'maybe' just doesn't work.

**Appropriate tools and technologies in GD CBD: managerial practices**

Managerial practices related to tools and technologies identified in SAP as important in GD CBD are as follows:

*Software Development (SD) tools*

In order to support CBD in a globally distributed environment, SD tools need to provide the following capabilities:

| | |
|---|---|
| **Standardisation of tools and methods across locations** | Everyone in the KM Collaboration group uses the same tools and methods. |

| **Centralisation of tools and web access** | Centralisation of tools under a single environment accessible from all remote locations over the Web is important to make sure that everybody is working with the same, most updated versions. For example, one manager from India explained that SAP Intranet (called SAPNet) serves as a central place that has links to all updated information: all the documents are accessible from SAPNet while in practice they are located at Perforce – a VCS that is linked to SAPNet via a Web server. He said: |
| | We use SAPNet for storing the information: we store mostly all the documents in Perforce, and we have a Web server that accesses the Perforce; this Web server is linked to SAPNet. So SAPNet is a central medium – when a user clicks on a link at SAPNet, it takes him to the appropriate machine and shows him the document. |

## *ICT infrastructure*

ICT infrastructure implies high bandwidth reliable connections between all remote sites to support the following:

| **Quick access to the network** | Quick access to the network is required from all remote locations. Powerful servers are used to allow quick access for multiple users from remote locations. |
| **Quick and easy connectivity across locations** | Quick and easy connectivity between locations is important. For example, setting up internal phone lines across |

the globe (five digits number between Bangalore and Walldorf) makes it easy to contact remote counterparts.

| | |
|---|---|
| **Shared server and project repository and Web access** | There is one server that can be accessed from remote locations, therefore sometimes team members pass bug fixes from one team to another to take advantage of time-zone differences. One manager from India explained how it was done:<br><br>Typically that's what we do: if I get an email sometime in the afternoon or evening 'there is a problem, can you look into it?', I say 'OK, by tomorrow morning your time it will be done'. Because Walldorf is sleeping and at that time we log in and finish the issue, so that there is an advantage.<br><br>There is also a central project repository on SAPNet accessible over the Web and the project plan is also accessible; it ensures that everyone has updated information. |

### Collaborative technology

The following are collaborative technologies used by SAP team to collaborate successfully over distance:

| | |
|---|---|
| **Phone and teleconferencing** | The phone is used for urgent matters, regular updates between managers and to resolve misunderstandings. |
| **Application Sharing** | Typically an AST is used remotely (i) for discussions that involve showing slides (usually, in such situations |

remote counterparts use AST to show presentation slides, and at the same time they use the phone to explain the slides and to discuss issues and questions); and (ii) for discussing technical issues (e.g. code reviews, debugging): in this case the AST is used for taking control of a computer remotely.

**Videoconference**

VC sessions that involve managers and developers in all three locations are used to discuss progress and other issues; they are organised twice a month. One manager explained:

> Whenever a new colleague joins in our team or any of the teams in the other locations, in the next VC which we have, we have an introduction round like 'these are new colleagues that have joined'. So though you have not met them physically, you get to know that this is the person, he exists there, things like that.

He continued describing the use of VC for design reviews:

> If no major changes required, then it is not necessary to have a VC. But if the issues are critical, than we certainly need to have a VC. To discuss 'why do you propose such and such a design?', it's better to talk face-to-face [over VC] and explain face-to-face, than to keep sending emails.

**Email**

Email supports low priority tasks and issues, and tasks that cannot be completed in real-time because of time-zone differences. Email is used as documentation (record) as well.

| | |
|---|---|
| **Intranet** | The team has access to SAP internal Intranet environment (SAPNet), where internal documents and other relevant information are posted. |

### Social ties in GD CBD: managerial practices

According to the opinions of interviewees, rapport and trust contribute to success, as illustrated by the following quotations:

*Contribution of Trust*

> Right now I know people pretty well. With India I had a problem in the beginning, until Sudhir and I got to the level of confidence that he is able to interpret my reaction and I am able to deal with him (project manager, Germany).

*Contribution of Rapport*

> I need to have good relationships with the people I am working with [...] the better you know the people the easier it gets. I know Sudhir and Thomas I think by now quite well (product architect, Germany).

The following are managerial practices that focus on social aspects and facilitate rapport and trust between remote counterparts.

#### Building relationships

Interviewees consider building relationships between remote team members very important for success. For example, it was important to build relationships between the team in Bangalore and the team in Germany. The development manager of the team in Bangalore explained that it was very important that the development manager from Germany met and got to know personally the whole team in Bangalore, and team members got to know him, because:

> He is the person to whom all of us email, regarding any technical issue. We don't say 'you all have to mail me then I will mail to him', we all email to him directly.

### Creating and maintaining team atmosphere

Creating and maintaining a team atmosphere is important, in particular for offshore teams in Bangalore and Palo Alto. One manager from Palo Alto explained that it is important to show team members that:

> There is no fear, that I am not playing tricks with them, that I am trying to be an ambassador, that we have visibility, that our product is wanted, that we get the respect of the other teams, that we are properly embedded within the overall management group, that there is enough room to grow – this is what they [team members] expect [from the head of the group]. It was pretty hard to establish among them [all teams] a 'no-fear environment' because they see me at videoconferences and that's like a lecture, this is the only way to do a videoconference with about 30 people at three locations: not much discussions, or the communication just fails.

Visits to remote locations help to create and maintain the team atmosphere. For example, during a team-building exercise, letting team members of the Bangalore team meet and spend some time together with key people, specifically with the head of the group gave the team members a feeling of belonging, of being part of the KM Collaboration group, and equally important, as the other teams in Palo Alto and Walldorf. This was one of the goals Stefan Mueller had during his visit to India – to give confidence to the team members in Bangalore that they are important and they are part of the KM Collaboration group and part of SAP Portal: 'the team-building for me was for them to show 'yes, you as a remote location are valuable', to give the overall organisational confidence'.

### Facilitating interactions

Facilitating interactions between people at remote locations is important. It includes (i) facilitating personal face-to-face interactions and (ii) organising regular and frequent interactions over distance. For example, personal face-to-face interactions are particularly important in the beginning of a new collaboration, as in this case when several teams were merged into one group. One manager from Germany explained:

> With Sudhir, we are now about nine months working with each other. With Thomas in the USA, in Palo Alto, it's the same. With Marcus, in here [in Walldorf], it is much easier to get accustomed to

working habits, because he is just sitting in the next office right now. And then it is much easier for him to understand how the director [Stefan Mueller] reacts, and why he reacts, why he is so pushy or not pushy, or doesn't react. That what I learned with Sudhir. But just because Sudhir came over here. So, this 'develop confidence' is something you have to set up once in the face-to-face meeting, or even a longer stay.

### Facilitating cross-pollution

Interviewees considered cross-pollination (i.e. that people from the one group spend significant amounts of time in the remote group and visa versa) to be important for success. In particular, it was helpful to deal with cultural differences between German and Indian cultures, because, usually, it takes a long time to get to know and get used to these differences. Sudhir Krishna worked several years in Germany and knew about German culture and the German way of working and communicating before he got involved in the development of SAP Collaboration tools. One manager from Germany explained:

> Sudhir had an advantage – he was here [in Germany] for two years, so he already knew Germans, and this is a big advantage. The most he has to deal is with is – German habits, dictatorship German habits. And that is what I knew. And that is what he also told me.

### Knowledge sharing in GD CBD: managerial practices

We learned that knowledge sharing was considered as contributing to success; in particular, building up collective knowledge through shared experiences, and creating transactive memory among team members at dispersed locations.

The globally distributed teams in Walldorf, Bangalore and Palo Alto did not have a history of working together before they were merged into KM Collaboration group. The transactive memory and collective knowledge in this group had been developing since the project started (i.e. since the merger).

The following are managerial practices seen as important for knowledge sharing between members of remote teams.

### Creating transactive memory among dispersed team members

Creating transactive memory among team members in Walldorf, Palo Alto and Bangalore was considered important for success.

Transactive memory is important because it influences the amount of information that needs to be shared, and has an impact on the efficiency of communications, as illustrated by the following statements:

> A simple one-line question can result in a ten-page answer. It can be a very lengthy answer, or he [the person who answers] can simply cut it up by giving a one-line reply. And as to what detail you get in an answer depends on how well you know that person. Because if the person knows me very well and he knows in what areas I am working, then he can decide how much information I will need. Is one-line good enough for him or should I explain to him over three pages so that he knows what is happening? (project manager).

Furthermore, in a globally distributed team transactive memory enables staff to coordinate efficiently across locations. For example, a project manager from Germany explained:

> What I did in the past was – this was in the very early phase of the project, I sent requests only to Sudhir and he would distribute the issues between people. But by now, after six months, I know quite well what everybody is doing. So after a time, you just know who's doing what.

### Expanding collective knowledge of the dispersed team

Expanding collective knowledge of the dispersed team is important for success; in particular it was important to create collective knowledge about differences in the national cultures of people involved in the project: Indian, German and American cultures. For example, during team meetings people are encouraged to reflect on their perception of cultural differences they experienced when visiting a remote location and/or communicating with remote counterparts, as one developer experienced during his visit to Walldorf.

Furthermore, in the beginning of the project, there was a knowledge and experience gap between people involved in the project. One manager from India explained:

> People have different profiles: here [in Bangalore], the maximum experience is five years. But if you take these three colleagues travel-ling to the team-building exercise, the two of them have about 12–15 years of experience, and the minimum experience here [in

Bangalore] is about 2¹/₂ years, so that's a huge experience gap that they have to bridge.

One of the goals of the team-building exercise organised in the beginning of the project was to bridge this gap and create collective knowledge in the globally distributed team. As the counterpart manager from Germany reflected:

> It [team-building] was a pretty good experience for myself: learning the culture and also how the team internally works. So my understanding of what you can expect from the team, and what you cannot expect, is very important for the project.

### Managing 'by intuition'

Management 'by intuition' is based on catching signals and sensing (feeling) that something is working or not working properly. The ability to manage 'by intuition' is important for success. It is illustrated by the following extract from the interview with one manager from Germany, who had nine years of experience in the management of software development at the time the interview was conducted:

---

*Manager*: Quality, time-line, this is what you see. This way you feel if something is not working properly.

*Researcher*: Could you also feel if something is not working properly in the very beginning?

*Manager*: No. If I had led this unit five years ago, I would be in deep shit. This is what you have to learn. With experience you know the signals: they are not written, they are not formal and nobody tells you: 'it is something missing today, it is too quiet, it cannot be that quiet because there have to be some problems'. And it is experience, it is guidance, connecting with other people, supporting, helping them to overcome these problems. But for the other areas that are working – don't touch them.

*Researcher*: To sense this, you probably need to know very well your development managers and architects?

*Manager*: Sure, you also need to know what they tell you, what they don't tell you, how they react. You read between the lines.

---

To enable management 'by intuition' in globally distributed environment, a manager needs to know his/her subordinates personally and to have a rapport with them. Then he/she might be able to catch and interpret signals when a subordinate sends too many or too few progress reports, or perhaps too many or too few clarification requests.

### Components management in GD CBD: managerial practices

In addition to the four factors suggested in the theoretical lens, *components management* emerged from the SAP data as factor contributing to success. The following is a managerial practice seen as important to enable reuse of components.

#### *Facilitating reuse*

It was indicated that facilitating the reuse of *knowledge* and reuse of *components* across locations are important for success in GD CBD. For example, as one developer from India explained:

> The team in Walldorf should be aware of what is being developed in Bangalore or Palo Alto, so that we don't reinvent the wheel again and again. So we basically communicate about what are the things that are being done, and is there something reusable which we are developing, or have they developed something which somebody else can use. Maybe some of the packages which we have developed might be useful for the team in Palo Alto. Maybe they are developing some application which needs a package smaller, maybe a half a package can fit into that. Then you are not rewriting the whole product again and again. Maybe they can just use our package that is available, make some changes according to what they need, and use it. For things like that we need to interact with each other.

## Success in GD CBD: evidence

This section presents evidence collected in interviews about success achieved in the studied case. The evidence is presented according to the categories of success illustrated in the SAP Concept Map.

### Product success

> We just went through a merger, so setting up a global project was not an easy task. Despite all the difficulties we managed to have a successful second software release in eight months (product manager, Germany).

Furthermore, there is external evidence of project success:

• According to JupiterResearch, a leading research and consulting company in emerging technologies, SAP Enterprise Portal is the third largest software solution, with 17% of the USA market. The studied project developed SAP Collaboration tools as one of the main features of the SAP Enterprise Portal.

**Personal satisfaction**

*Healthy environment*

The team-building exercise was a way to show that we care about remote locations. The end result of that exercise was that the entire team [globally distributed] feels more comfortable to work together. Now they know each other and trust each other better (product manager, Germany).

*Less communication effort*

One senior developer from Bangalore team expressed his team's perspective on the team-building exercise:

The team-building exercise improved relationships among the KM Collaboration group [between the team located in Bangalore and their remote colleagues], because earlier communications were only in a formal way, and after the team-building activity we really knew people much better, it became easier to communicate and communications became more informal.

As one manager from Germany explained:

It's a lot easier to pick up the phone, from my experience, to pick up the phone and call someone if you at least met him once. Or if this is not possible due to cost reasons, at least see him via the Video-conference. If you see someone, at least for me it's completely different to communicate later via the phone.

**Successful collaboration**

*Effective coordination*

I am not controlling in details. On the other hand, I am pretty much in line with their daily activities, and take action if I see problems popping up (project manager, Germany).

*Effective communications*

After the key players visited the Bangalore site and got to know remote team members personally, centralised communications were replaced by direct communications. One manager from Germany explained:

> From a code perspective for example, what I did before I met all of them [team in Bangalore] in person was to send all things to Sudhir and he was the one to distribute it within the team, and this has changed now. I address most of the things directly to the team members.

## Bridged geographical, time-zone and cultural gaps

*Geographical distance* creates limitations for face-to-face meetings. The costs of travel limit opportunities for team members to meet in person. To overcome geographical distance the following practices are adopted:

- For managers: 'we generally keep travelling at least once in every three months. But if there is a need or there is an urgency, then we travel any time' (manager, India).
- For developers: 'the idea is that every developer travels across [to Walldorf] and meets everybody once for the reason to get to know each other in person rather than just by name' (Manager, India).

*Time differences* cause problems, but sometimes can be used as an advantage:

Time differences between Germany and India are not seen as a problem, and are sometimes even used as an advantage:

> Sometimes we find it advantageous, especially if there are demo systems in Walldorf, if you are to send data for demos, its really easy for us. Because by that time Walldorf is sleeping, we have $4^{1}/_{2}$ hours where we can finish our stuff and log off. And then people in Germany fight for that (Manager, India).

Also problems (bug fixes) sometimes are passed across time-zones. However, people in Waldorf and Bangalore find it very difficult to work with Palo Alto:

- 'for us it is definitely a problem: we sleep and they wake up' (Manager, India)

- 'because you cannot communicate the information in time' (Manager, Germany).

For the team in Palo Alto, which mostly has to communicate via email, answers are always delayed (at least for one day): they do not have a possibility to call when a question arises, but need to plan calls in advance:

> The biggest disadvantage is that both Walldorf and India are sleeping when they are awake, so the information flow for them is even more difficult – they have to specifically request for a telephone call and they have to plan it in advance (Manager, India).

One of the ways adopted to reduce time-zone differences was to fly some people from India to Walldorf during the last stages of the project (before product release) so that they could finish the project working from only two locations: Walldorf and Palo Alto. This reduces time differences from 13 hours to nine (that is the time difference between Walldorf and Palo Alto). As one manager from Germany explained:

> Jyothi is here at the moment, he will stay another four weeks, and Sudhir and Akhilesh will arrive in two weeks [to Walldorf]. They are going to finish a project here and work closely together, which is a lot easier. Since the time difference of 11 or 13 hours, depending on when you start coming to the office, it's easier to finish the project here [in Walldorf].

*Cultural differences* are bridged to a great extent:
Team members in Bangalore are Indian: team members in Walldorf are mostly German. The team in Palo Alto is multinational: 'there are Chinese guys, Ukrainian guys, somebody from India, a German manager of the team plus also other units' (Manager, Germany). As indicated by the interviewees, differences between German and Indian cultures are mostly in the way of working, way of communicating, and values. A team-building exercise helped to bridge cultural differences, as one manager from India explained:

> From my perspective, it was a new thing for Stefan and Christoph to get to know how Indians work, their values – a cultural thing. Thomas has worked for more than two years with Indians, so he was aware of our working style.

## Conclusions

In this chapter, the analysis and results of the SAP case study were presented and discussed. Managerial practices and quotations from interviews illustrating these managerial practices and their contribution to success were presented.

The results of the case study illustrate that interviewees considered the four factors suggested in the theoretical lens, and the fifth factor that emerged from the data as contributing to success in GD CBD.

In terms of *inter-site coordination*, the work was divided between the teams in Bangalore, Walldorf and Palo Alto based on product features, providing full ownership and responsibility for each team. There are two reasons why SAP gave full ownership to each of the remote teams, instead of dividing the work based on the expertise of individual team members. First, because when the project started remote teams did not have knowledge about the product: collaborative tools were developed from scratch. Second, because teams had just merged into one group, they did not have a history of working together. Thus, giving full ownership to each of the remote teams reduced dependencies and, therefore, the need for coordination between the teams.

Moreover, systematic communications between key people (architects located in the headquarters and development managers of the remote teams) were important to ensure quality of the product: that components developed by the dispersed teams fit together.

In relation to *appropriate tools and technologies*, remote teams used similar tools and methods across locations. Various collaborative technologies were available for dispersed team members, for example internal phone lines (a five digit number) between Bangalore and Walldorf made it easy to contact remote counterparts.

Regarding *social ties*, in SAP, three teams were merged into one group in the beginning of the studied project, and members of these teams had to build trust and rapport from scratch. Team-building exercise and short visits were organised to give developers and key players an opportunity to meet in person in an informal environment and get to know each other. This helped to create transactive memory and build relationships among the team members.

Concerning *knowledge sharing*, in the beginning of the project the SAP team did not have a transactive memory and collective knowledge. Therefore, interactions were particularly important to create transactive memory and collective knowledge about the cultures of the remote counterparts and of the evolving product. Interviewees from

SAP suggested that knowing who knows what at a remote location enables the organisation to reduce development lifecycle because response is quicker when team members know whom to contact for a specific problem. Moreover, the importance of intuition for managing GD CBD projects was emphasised. To be able to manage 'by intuition', extensive experience in the management of software development in general and globally distributed projects in particular is required.

In regard to *components management*, globally dispersed teams organised formal meetings, usually using VC tools, to discuss what each team has developed and to identify an opportunity to reuse knowledge and/or software components (applications).

# 6
# Observations of GD CBD at TCS

*We all speak Quartz language. It is a loss for us if somebody leaves Quartz because for somebody new it will take time to learn Quartz.*
(Offshore Project Leader, TCS)

## Background of TCS global organisation

Tata Consultancy Services (TCS) was established in 1968 as a division of Tata Sons Ltd (Tata Group). TCS is one of the biggest Indian software companies: it specialises in IT consultancy, services, and business process outsourcing, and is recognised among the 25 top IT consultancy companies in the world. TCS employs over 120,000 people in 42 countries, and it has 26 development centres all over the world: in India (11 centres), USA (eight centres), Canada, UK, Uruguay, Hungary, Australia, China and Japan. Sixteen of these centres have been assessed as operating at Level 5 maturity on the Software Engineering Institute's Capability Maturity Model (SEI CMM) scale. The main TCS industry practices include banking, financial services and insurance, telecom, manufacturing, transportation, and retail and consumer goods. The main service practices of TCS include e-business, architecture and technology consultancy, process consultancy, and application development and maintenance. TCS reported total revenues of $5.7 billion in 2008.

## Background of the project and product under study

This case study concerns the development and implementation of Quartz, an integrated financial platform aimed at providing solutions for financial institutions such as traditional and internet banks, brokerage/securities houses and asset managers.

125

**What is Quartz?**

Quartz is an integrated package and banking platform for the international financial industry. It was developed jointly by TCS and TKS (Teknosoft, a Swiss-based company that specialises in financial services), through a partnership in which the technical knowledge and experience of TCS in providing computing services was combined with the business knowledge of TKS of the financial industry and banking.

Quartz consists of a collection of architectural and business components that can be integrated with third party components to provide a solution according to the requirements of a specific customer. The Quartz architecture consists of (1) core banking components that are integrated into a Core Banking Engine, and (2) business components, which are added as an additional layer on the top of the Core Engine, as illustrated in Figure 6.1. *Core banking components* provide core banking functionalities, such as business relations, financial instruments, market information and parameterisation information: they can be (easily) adapted to a specific bank environment and integrated into the legal framework within which the bank operates. Additional functions offered as *business components* may be installed, omitted or replaced with third-party components. Together these two types of components ensure that

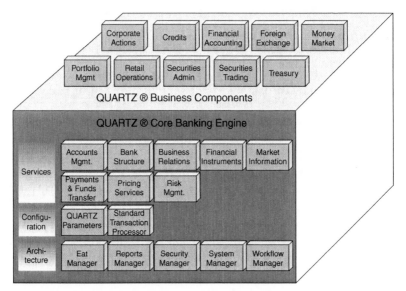

*Figure 6.1*   Quartz component-based architecture

the Quartz architecture provides a flexible package of the entire banking application.

The first implementation of Quartz took place in 1998. In March 2002, when we visited the Gurgaon office of TCS, TCS was implementing Quartz in several organisations. Two implementations, at Skandia Bank Switzerland (SBS) in Zurich, Switzerland, and Dresdner Bank in San Francisco, USA, were approaching completion: both projects were at the stage of end-user testing. A few more Quartz implementations were in the very early stages. By April 2005 more than 40 installations or implementations of Quartz were in progress. An example of Quartz implementation (i.e. customisation of Quartz for a specific customer) is shown in Figure 6.2.

The typical methodology adopted by TCS for Quartz product development and solution implementation is illustrated in Figure 6.3.

In this case study two Quartz implementation projects are investigated: (1) implementation in Skandia bank in Zurich and (2) in Dresdner bank in San Francisco. Both projects are concerned with the implementation

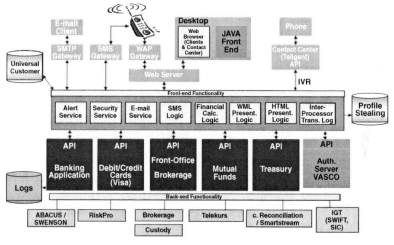

Functionality supported:

- Cash balance forecasting
- Realized P & L calculations
- Integrated Securities broking and trading
- Asset Allocation
- Stock-watch alerts and standing instructions
- Position transfers and electronic payments
- Online Corporate Actions
- Automated e-mail contract ans statement delivery
- Real-time update of settings
- Mobile Access
- Call Center, IVR Support

*Figure 6.2* Technical overview of Quartz implementation (modified example from TKS web site http://www.tks-teknosoft.com/implementation.html)

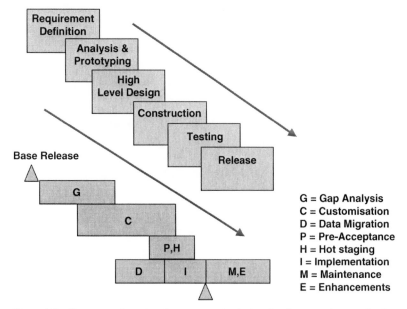

*Figure 6.3*   Quartz product development and solution implementation methodology (adapted from TCS internal documentation)

of Quartz, therefore they are analysed together as one 'embedded' case study.

### Project 1: Skandia

The Skandia project started in October 2000. It involved the development of Apollo, an Internet-based banking platform, and the implementation of this platform in Skandia bank. The Skandia project described in this book is the first implementation of a bigger project (described by Alexandersen et al. 2003) in which Skandia Group, the customer of the Skandia project, aimed to create a so-called 'bank-in-the-box' they could sell in the future to different banks.[1] For the first implementation of this bigger project Skandia Group had chosen its own bank, Skandia bank. Figure 6.4 illustrates the 'bank-in-the-box' Apollo platform and its implementation in different banks.

As shown in Figure 6.4, at the heart of the Apollo platform is the Quartz banking platform. The original Quartz served as a back-office: it

---

[1]Alexandersen et al. (2003) described the Skandia project from the strategic perspective of the Skandia Group – a client of TCS. In this case study the Skandia project is described from a TCS perspective, focusing on the development and implementation of the Quartz platform in a globally distributed environment.

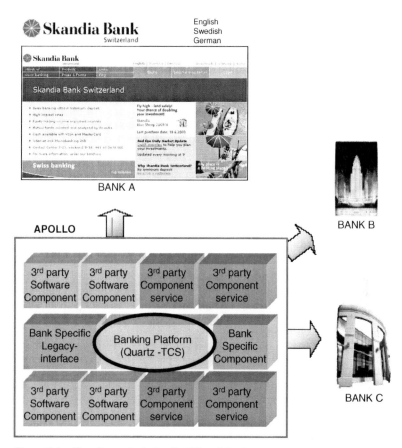

*Figure 6.4*    Skandia project: Apollo CB architecture

was customised and extended to suit the needs of Skandia bank. One of the major extensions was the front-end design that involved design of the users' interface (i.e. what a user sees on a screen when he/she logs into the internet-bank, e.g. a menu with different options of what he/she can do on the screen). The content of the front-end was designed by Mogul, a Swedish company hired by Skandia. The actual programming to implement the content of the front-end was done by a Front-End group of TCS, located in Bombay.

In addition to the Quartz implementation, TCS was responsible for establishing a data and recovery centre, a physical centre to support business operations of an Internet bank: this included the management of vendors delivering third-party components, such as operating systems, hardware and service providers.[2] In total, more than 25 vendors located in many different countries were involved in the project, among them Salomon Smith (broker, UK), Reuters (real-time rate provider, UK), Oracle (database, USA), Sun (servers, USA) and CISCO (networks, USA).

In terms of global distribution, the Skandia project involved three main geographical locations: two offshore TCS teams in Gurgaon and Bombay, and an onsite team at the customer location in Zurich where the physical data and recovery centre had to be established. Furthermore, vendors of third party components were located in different countries.

At the time of data collection, the offshore Quartz team in Gurgaon involved six people, the offshore Front-End team in Bombay had five people, and the onsite team in Zurich included 12 people from TCS (seven people from the Quartz team and five people from the Front-End team).

### Project 2: Dresdner

The Dresdner project involved the implementation of Quartz at the Dresdner RCM Global Investors bank in San Francisco, which specialises in investment and e-commerce. Implementation of Quartz at the Dresd-

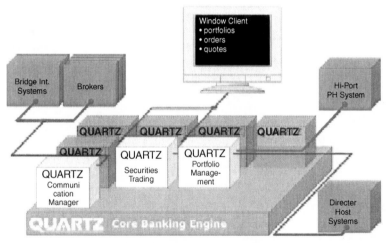

*Figure 6.5*   Dresdner project: Investment and e-commerce bank (from TKS report http://www.tks-teknosoft.com/references/tbs/DresdnerNEW.pdf)

---

[2]For Skandia Group, TCS was a vendor providing the major component (i.e. Quartz as a banking platform); furthermore, it was managing all other vendors delivering components that needed to be integrated in the Apollo.

ner bank started in July 2001. This project included implementation of Quartz as a front-office, integration with the local system and the development of several new components, such as securities trading, portfolio management, and communication manager, as illustrated at Figure 6.5.

In terms of global distribution, the Dresdner project involved people from the Quartz group based in Gurgaon (offshore) and the customer site in San Francisco (onsite). At the time of data collection the offshore Quartz team in Gurgaon involved six people and the onsite team in San Francisco included eight people who had relocated from Gurgaon.

## Background of the software team

### Working experience in a globally distributed environment

From the first implementation in 1998, all implementations of Quartz took place in a globally distributed environment that included at least two locations: a customer site and the main development site of TCS in Gurgaon, where Quartz was customised (existing components were modified and new ones developed) to satisfy the requirements of a specific customer. Therefore, people in the Quartz group were used to working in a globally distributed environment.

### Organisational structure of the software team

The typical project organisation of a Quartz implementation consists of an *onsite* team at the customer location and *offshore* teams at the development centres of TCS. A typical organizational structure of a Quartz implementation project is presented in Figure 6.6.

#### Interactions with a customer

It is important to note that onsite and offshore teams consist of people from TCS only; they work closely with customer's representatives. In general, interactions between a Quartz implementation team and a client are formal to a great extent. Customer's representatives usually interact with an onsite team: in particular, the gap analysis stage and final user acceptance testing (see Figure 6.3) require many interactions. Furthermore, customer's representatives fly to Gurgaon to participate in pre-acceptance tests which are done offshore.

TCS has formal procedures in place that help to capture a customer's requirements and to achieve mutual understanding and agreement (between TCS and the customer) regarding the scope of a Quartz implementation project. For example, technical, security and infrastructure

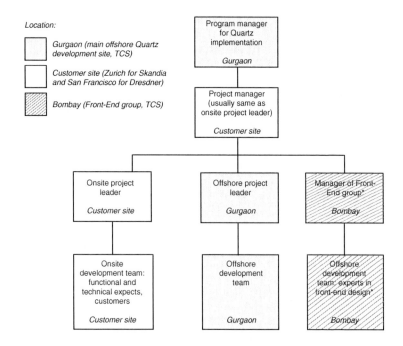

*Figure 6.6*  Typical organisational structure of the Quartz implementation project: Skandia and Dresdner projects

requirements are agreed upon with the customer to avoid ambiguity in the future: 'one way is that the customer should have our high level design, standards and templates reviewed in the beginning and signed off' (Kumar Krishna, Manager of the Front-End group).

### How TCS organises and manages GD CBD: analysis and results

In the TCS case 20 managerial practices were identified as contributing for success in GD CBD. These practices were grouped under the four areas presented earlier plus the *components management* aspect which emerged from our interviews.

We also found evidence for success in these projects by means of (i) *product success*; personal satisfaction which is represented by two sub-categories (ii) *less communication effort* and (iii) *healthy environment;* successful collaboration which is represented by two sub-categories (iv) *effective coordination* and (v) *effective communications*; and (vi) *bridged gaps*. We can conclude that there has been a high degree of similarity between the TCS case and the LeCroy and SAP cases.

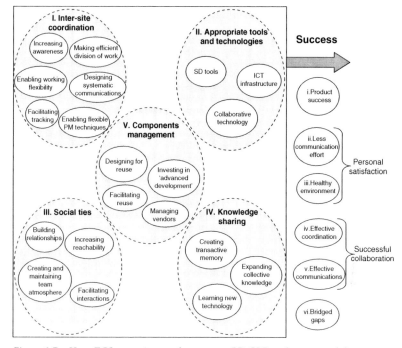

*Figure 6.7* How TCS organises and manages GD CBD to be successful

In the following sections, the contribution of the five factors and corresponding managerial practices to success in GD CBD in SAP is illustrated and discussed using three types of data presentation (explained in 'Within-case display' in Section 4.5.1 and in Section 4.7).

### Managerial practices that contribute to success

Managerial practices linked by interviewees with success are presented in Table 6.1. We indicate in the table only the practice that was most frequently mentioned in connection to a particular factor (marked by X in the table).

From Table 6.1 it follows that managerial practices that were most often explicitly connected to success by interviewees are inter-site coordination practices, in particular *increasing awareness* by ensuring continuous information flows between dispersed teams, and *designing systematic communications*; and knowledge sharing practices, such as *creating transactive memory* and *expanding collective knowledge*. These practices contributed to the majority of categories of success. Furthermore, *managing vendors* was important to achieve effective coordination and product success.

*Table 6.1* Contribution of managerial practices to success at TCS

| Managerial practices | Product success | Less communication effort | Healthy environment | Effective coordinat. | Effective communic. | Bridged gaps |
|---|---|---|---|---|---|---|
| | | Personal satisfaction | | Success. collabor. | | |
| **I) Inter-site coordination** | | | | | | |
| 1 Increasing awareness | X | | | X | | |
| 2 Making efficient division of work | X | | | X | X | |
| 3 Enabling working flexibility | X | | | | X | X |
| 4 Facilitating tracking of bugs and dev. tasks | | | | X | | |
| 5 Enabling flexible PM techniques | X | | | X | | X |
| 6 Designing systematic communications | X | | | X | | |
| **II) Appropriate tools and technologies** | | | | | | |
| 7 Software Development tools | X | | | X | | |
| 8 ICT infrastructure | X | | | X | | |
| 9 Collaborative technology | | | | | | |
| **III) Social ties** | | | | | | |
| 10 Building relationships | X | X | X | X | | |
| 11 Increasing reachability | X | | | | | |
| 12 Creating and maintaining team atmosphere | X | | | X | | |
| 13 Facilitating interactions | X | | | X | | |
| **IV) Knowledge sharing** | | | | | | |
| 14 Creating transactive memory among teams | X | | | X | | |
| 15 Expanding collective knowledge of the team | X | X | | X | X | X |
| 16 Learning new technology | | | | | | |
| **V) Components management** | | | | | | |
| 17 Designing for reuse | X | | | | | |
| 18 Investing in 'advanced development' | | | | | | |
| 19 Facilitating reuse | | | | | | |
| 20 Managing vendors | X | | | X | | |

## Managerial practices: description and evidence

In this section managerial practices perceived by interviewees as important for success in GD CBD are described and illustrated using statements from interviews.

### Inter-site coordination in GD CBD: managerial practices

Interviewees stressed the need for inter-site coordination between onsite and offshore teams. This included the following practices:

#### *Increasing awareness*

The interviewees indicated that increasing awareness of (i) what is going on in the project at the remote location, and (ii) what everybody is working on, are important for success.

(i) Interviewees mentioned that it is important for offshore locations (Gurgaon and Mumbai) to be aware of what is going on at an onsite location, about the development environment and technical infrastructure at the onsite location, to be able to visualise what is happening when a problem occurs, and to solve the problem. For example:

- The manager of the Front-End team recognised that a structured approach is needed to manage globally distributed teams. He summarised lessons learnt from his experience in distributed development projects and created a document entitled 'Lessons Learnt' to serve as a guidelines for such projects. Some of the lessons learnt relate to the need to increase awareness, for example:

   The critical tasks should be graphically displayed in a chart for everybody to see. [...] There should be transparency of the processes, issues and problems faced in the development with the client.

- Another manager explained: 'When a project is being established, proper ground work includes that everything should be conveyed and project information shared among team members'.

(ii) Furthermore, it is important to build awareness of tasks that other team members are doing. The quality assurance manager said:

   It's not that only one person can do a job, otherwise, if one person doesn't come in, we won't be able to work without him/her. So we try to overcome this by making each and every team member aware of nearly all the things which are happening.

Building awareness expands the collective knowledge of a dispersed team.

### Making efficient division of work

Efficient division of work is important: it involves principles that software managers follow to divide work between onsite and offshore locations, and to divide specific assignments (tasks) and responsibilities between individual teams at each location.

(i) Division of work between onsite and offshore teams, and the number of people at onsite and offshore locations, varies at different stages of a Quartz implementation project. Usually, there are more people onsite in the earlier stages of the project, when close interactions with customers are required, and in the later stages during final integration and end-user testing. During the design and construction stages some people from the onsite team relocate to offshore locations to work on the development of new components and modification of core Quartz components (i.e. people from Quartz group go back to Gurgaon and people from Front-End group go back to Mumbai). For example, the number of people at the offshore location in Gurgaon during the design and construction stage of the Skandia project was about 35 people, which was reduced to six people during the final stages.

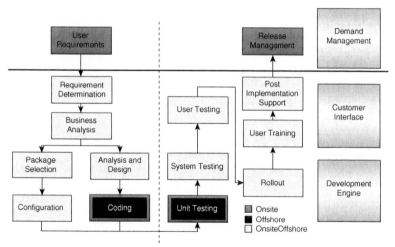

*Figure 6.8*  Skandia project: Onsite-offshore delivery model (adapted from Alexandersen et al. 2003)

Figure 6.8 illustrates the Skandia onsite-offshore delivery model adopted by TCS, which combines steps conducted onsite, offshore, and a combination of onsite and offshore. Transferring some steps to offshore allowed TCS to take advantage of cost, quality, and advanced delivery capabilities infrastructure (Alexandersen et al. 2003).[3]

The main strategy of TCS is: 'to maximize work to be done offshore: keep onsite as few people as possible because this will reduce costs. Typically, an onsite team sends requirements offshore because the expertise and major source code are in Gurgaon, and mainly because of the expertise, it is quicker and easier to work in India' (senior manager, India).

(ii) Moreover, role continuity and project ownership are important for successful implementation of Quartz. Role continuity implies that people who are doing gap analysis (between requirements and available components) are also doing the development, because they understand the requirements. For example, in the Dresdner project:

> The person who had done the requirement study there [onsite, in San Francisco] for the trading system came back [to Gurgaon], and he started leading the trading system development team, three people came back with him (project lead, Germany).

Despite the fact that the project is transferred between onsite and offshore locations at different project stages, ownership of the project stays with the same team: team members are transferred between onsite and offshore together with the project, and work continuously on the same project/components. This setting helps to ensure that customer requirements are understood, captured and implemented in the product. One manager elaborates on roles and responsibilities:

- 'Roles and responsibilities of a team need to be clearly specified. Proper back-up is needed for each responsibility, to accommodate release and movement of personnel across geographies'.
- 'Decentralisation and proper delegation of work are needed to avoid bottlenecks and time lags'.

(iii) Furthermore, the composition of the remote teams is important, in particular of the onsite team. The onsite team is composed of experts

---

[3]The onsite-offshore delivery model is explained in greater detail above.

who provide expertise in areas required at a customer location, and involves technical, functional and support roles:

> Technical people look at technical and architectural issues, functional people look at the functionality and the development of the functionality. Support people handle the configuration management, the groupware, the other various tools which are being used by the team (senior manager).

The onsite team has technical responsibilities and is responsible for implementation of customer requirements. This team provides technical support for teams in the main Quartz development centre in Gurgaon and the Front-End development centre in Bombay.

(iv) Additionally, the division of work between team members at dispersed locations is done according to their skills (expertise):

> Between us [offshore] and our onsite team we say 'we'll do this portion of the job because we have more competent people here who can look at this part, and you can look at that portion of the job'. It's mutual communication (project lead).

### Enabling working flexibility

The interviewees suggested that working flexibility, in terms of providing flexible working conditions, such as mobile phones and computers that allow working from home early and late in a day, and providing flexible working hours, is important for success.

Having flexible working hours (e.g. starting earlier in Zurich and later in Gurgaon) makes it possible to increase the overlap in working hours between locations so that remote teams can collaborate in real-time. Sometimes, in particular during end-user testing when customers are closely involved in the implementation process, team members at the offshore location in Gurgaon stay in the office until late to be able to provide support to the onsite team that is working closely with the customer.

Out of working hours, remote team members can contact each other at home by (mobile) phone, as often happens in the Dresdner project.

### Facilitating tracking of bugs and development tasks

Interviewees at TCS suggested the importance of tracking bugs and development tasks.

- *Tracking of development tasks*
  It is very important to be able to track development tasks during an ongoing project, in particular while working around-the-clock. The offshore and onsite project leads of the Dresdner project explained that during the late stages of a project they often work around-the-clock by sending tasks back and forth between Gurgaon and San Francisco (some of these tasks are fixing bugs). For tracking they use Excel spreadsheets that they update every day, and email an updated file to each other in turns.

  Interviewees mentioned that for each component there is a need to know who developed it, because if the component needs to be modified, typically, there is a need to consult with the developer who originally wrote a particular code of the component; or even delegate the modification to him/her, if possible. Therefore, specifications of each component should include the name of a person who developed it.

- *Tracking of bugs*
  The Quartz group uses a PVCS Tracker software tool to support the tracking of bugs. However, during the last stages of Quartz implementation, when bugs need to be fixed very quickly, often team members avoid the procedure of reporting bugs in the system and use the help of remote counterparts in a non-official manner.

### Enabling flexible Project Management (PM) techniques

Interviewees suggested that flexible PM techniques are important to accommodate complexity and everyday dynamics. They include:

- On a macro level: Planning of major project phases.
  One manager stated that there is a need for a 'unified project plan at a reasonable detailed level and not merely at a higher level, clearly stating the dependencies; clear milestones need to be marked'.
- On a micro level: Flexible and not too detailed planning.

There is a need for flexibility in accommodating changes:

Distinction between clarifications/corrections and changes should be made and agreed upon. Changes can never be avoided. If every change is evaluated and postponed for future implementation the final product will not satisfy users' expectations. One should know where to draw a line (project lead).

### Designing systematic communications

Systematic communications are considered important for success. Design of systematic communications includes:

(i) Scheduling systematic and frequent communications, such as regular teleconferences between software managers in dispersed locations. One programme manager described the situation as follows:

> Project and Program managers have to regularly meet with the personnel to appraise the status of the project, to share management views where applicable, to discuss processes and why and how they are impacting the work, to discuss revision of plans, besides to motivate the team. This forum can also be used to address grievances. This should be a regular practice at the site where the team members are located and this should be percolated to the different geographies through various team leads to their members. Mails are not sufficient.

Typically, onsite and offshore leaders communicate by phone at least twice (and sometimes three or four times) a day:

- For the Skandia project it happens (1) when the team in Gurgaon starts their working day (which is midday in Zurich), and (2) before the team in Zurich leave home (which is midday in Gurgaon).
- For the Dresdner project the first teleconference takes place when the offshore team starts its day (at that time the onsite team in San Francisco is about to leave home), and the second teleconference takes place at the end of the day for the Gurgaon team (when the team in San Francisco starts their day). Usually, not only onsite and offshore project leaders but also team members participate in the teleconferences. We attended one of the teleconferences as an observer. Issues discussed during that conference covered progress update, handover of work from one team finishing their working day to another team starting their working day, and clarifications.

(ii) Communicating directly to reach an appropriate person, i.e. avoiding hierarchy in communications. For example, one software engineer stated: 'Proper communication at all levels through appropriate means, including regular telecons, update of statuses, is key to success'.

## Appropriate tools and technologies in GD CBD: managerial practices

Managerial practices related to tools and technologies identified in TCS as important in GD CBD are as follows:

### *Software Development (SD) tools*

Software development tools include tools for the development and management of components, configuration and version management tools, and tools for testing and tracking bugs, such as:[4]

- Master Craft Tool set
  - ADEX – Repository
  - QDE-IF Process framework
  - Generators and translators
- MS-Access for Issues registration & resolution
- SQA Robot – for regression testing
- PVCS Tracker – for defect logging, tracking & analysis
- PVCS Version Manager – for configuration control
- RoboHELP – for Help and user manual
- SQL Lab, TOAD for SQL Analysis & Optimisation
- Other in-house tools for Performance modeling, Costing etc.

Furthermore, the following tools are used for project management and Quartz documentation:

- MS project, Excel – for Project planning & monitoring
- MS Office – for documents, Lotus Notes for email and internal communication

In order to support CBD in a globally distributed environment SD tools need to provide the following capabilities.

| | |
|---|---|
| **Standardisation of tools across locations** | At TCS, methods and tools are standardised across locations in two ways. |

---

[4]Based on TCS internal documents.

First, all development teams working on Quartz use the same tools and methods and follow same processes: this helps to ensure quality of processes.

Second, for each implementation of Quartz, customer-specific methods, tools and processes are standardised across globally distributed onsite and offshore teams.

Quartz is concerned with banking, where a lot of data and information are confidential, thus TCS cannot have access to the client's actual system for the final (end-user) testing. To overcome this problem, the offshore development team (in Gurgaon) creates a development environment that replicates the one at the customer site. This way, onsite and offshore development teams work together: the onsite team at the customer site working in a real-life environment can delegate work (in particular, bug fixing during testing) by sending the actual code to the offshore team in Gurgaon which can continue working in the replicated environment.

**Centralisation of tools**

There is one central repository, a central server in the main development centre in Gurgaon, where the source code is maintained; therefore, if the onsite team changes source code, the team send the source code to the headquarters where it is integrated into the main repository.

However it is difficult to work in two development environments in parallel because the source code needs to be coordinated manually. In a single development environment the code is coordinated automatically by a 'baseline' mechanism that makes it possible to check code out and in, so that a chunk of code can be checked out only once, and it is considered as 'frozen'; and until it is checked back in, nobody can work on the same chunk of code. However, when there are two development environments, onsite and offshore, the 'baseline' needs to be maintained manually. Furthermore, documentation needs to be centralised, as one senior manager stated:

> Multiple documentation should be strictly avoided. Every additional work/change in scope should be coming in as Change Request Specification (CRS). All clarifications, interpretations should be documented in a common place. Too much information should not be cluttered.

**Standardisation of methods across locations**

Standard procedures are developed to ensure that specifications written by the onsite team are understood correctly by the offshore team. As the quality manager explained:

> We have set procedures for defining the requirements. If people follow the procedures, then the things become very easy to interpret or understand.

However, standard procedures are not always followed. He continued:

> Usually people take shortcuts and explain over the phone, instead of writing a complete specification and

emailing them to offshore, and it is a bit dangerous. Because, for example, after six months the specification document becomes very important, but people who did the change are not there, they should have given specifications when they did the change.

---

**Creating guides that explain procedures and methods, and project template documentation**

TCS has a set of standards and guidelines for the various phases and deliverables for all project lifecycle activities for Quartz implementation. It includes:

– Procedural standards that provide the team with a set of practical tools and techniques with guidelines on when and how to use them

– Documentation standards that provide the team with means of preparing the identified tangible deliverables.

For example, procedural standards include the Quartz Implementation Methodology, and a Program Development Process for Quartz system. During data collection in Gurgaon we obtained access to these documents: however, they cannot be included in the book for confidentiality reasons.

Documentation standards contain different templates for Quartz implementation projects. A standard Quartz documentation set includes the following templates (based on TCS internal documents):

• Project Documentation Set
    – Business Requirements Overview (BRO)

- Business Requirements
  Specifications (BRS)
- High Level Design Document
- DB Design Document
- Module Test Specifications
- Product Acceptance Testing
  Specifications
• User Documentation Set
  - Online Help
  - User's Manual
  - Installation Manual
  - Operations Manual

For specific Quartz implementation project these template documents are filled in and, if necessary, modified.

---

**Developing tools in-house**   In TCS, the majority of SD tools are built in-house. Some of these in-house developed tools are available on the market as off-the-shelf software packages, e.g. the Integrated Project Management System, which is used for project management.

---

### ICT infrastructure

ICT infrastructure needs to support the following capabilities:

---

**Quick and easy connectivity across locations**   Quick and easy connectivity between locations is necessary to send the source code back and forth between onsite and offshore locations. TCS uses a ftp server to transfer the code. One manager explained: 'we don't have any problems, we can send anything via the ftp server'.

---

**Web access**   Web access is needed for version and configuration management, because version control on the Web would solve the problem of manual checking in and out of source code.

Furthermore, some software engineers suggested that the Excel spreadsheets they use to coordinate transfer of tasks between remote teams in a follow-the-sun manner, needs to be Web-based.

### *Collaborative technology*

The following are collaborative technologies used by TCS team to collaborate successfully over distance:

| | |
|---|---|
| **Phone and teleconferencing** | A phone is used on a regular basis for onsite-offshore coordination: for example, onsite and offshore project leaders and managers use phone for updates, clarifications, and resolving issues. |
| **Application Sharing** | Application sharing is used often for bug fixes, for example to show conditions of a system failure. As mentioned earlier, for security reasons, typically, the offshore team does not have access to a customer system. Therefore, the use of application sharing between onsite and offshore teams is limited. In some cases, instead of using application sharing, the onsite team needs to send a source code to the offshore team and/or describe the problem or bug by phone or email. |
| **Videoconference** | Videoconferencing is used mainly between executive managers and with customers, less often between project leaders and managers. |

| | |
|---|---|
| **Email** | Email supports low priority tasks and issues, and tasks that cannot be completed in real-time because of time-zone differences. Email is sometimes used for sending changes in source code. |
| **Intranet** | The Quartz group has access to TCS Intranet, which has a repository for Quartz group where internal documents and other relevant information are posted. |

## Social ties in GD CBD: managerial practices

Our observations confirm that rapport and trust have contributed to success.

In the Quartz group, trust and rapport between members of onsite and offshore teams were developed to some extent because the majority of them have worked together in a co-located environment on the development of Quartz and/or knew each other before re-locating to a customer location (Zurich for Skandia and San Francisco for Dresdner). Following are the managerial practices identified as important to further develop trust and rapport between remote counterparts.

### *Building relationships*

Interviewees consider having good relationships between remote counterparts very important for success. One project lead told us the following:

> In the last few days you've been here and you have seen the environment that we are working in [time pressure, customer-driven: every day new tasks and changes coming from the onsite team]. In such an environment, I think, the most important person is the actual person who does the work, I am just a facilitator here. The day we started the project we agreed – and it was a conscious and unconscious decision – that everybody has to work together to make this project successful, and they have to know some portion of what other team members are working on. If there is friction between team members, it cannot work. So I tried to make that situation correct between each of these people.

### Increasing reach-ability

Increasing reach-ability, i.e. being able to reach the right people at a remote location, is important for successful Quartz implementation. Usually, members of the Quartz group know whom to contact at a remote location: they know the area of expertise of each other from working on previous projects, and because the majority of members of the onsite team spend some time at the offshore location during design and construction stages.

The main difficulties in reaching the right people are caused by time-zone differences, in particular in the case of the Dresdner project, where regular working hours of onsite and offshore teams do not overlap because of a 13.5 hours time-zone difference. To deal with time-zone differences, members of Quartz group have mobile phones and can reach each other by mobile or home phone when their working hours do not overlap. Furthermore, if a counterpart from an onsite/offshore team is needed during his night-time, sometimes Quartz team members call an expert involved in a different project with whom working hours do overlap.

Interviewees suggested that, because the Quartz team members can easily contact each other at any time of a day, they can work faster and utilise time-zone differences to work around-the-clock. While working with clients and vendors (suppliers of third-party components and services to TCS), with whom reach-ability is limited to formal contacts during official working hours, completing the work takes longer. One senior manager explained:

> With other companies which are working with us, our vendors, we have to be very formal in the sense that we can contact them only during office hours and/or they can contact only the official support people. They go from one professional service to another professional service and, therefore, it takes a long time for them to actually arrange for people to be available to solve a problem. Within Quartz we can actually call up anybody whom we know at any point in time to get some assistance, even if we don't know somebody, if he's recommended by someone else, then we can call up and get assistance immediately. It is a very considerable difference.

In general, in the Indian culture it is considered normal that one can approach one's counterpart outside working hours, as opposed to many European cultures, e.g. Dutch, Swiss, German, where it is not common to contact somebody about work outside of his/her working hours. For example, as this senior manager explained:

> If I am facing some problem in my project with respect to a particular area, I can go back home at 10 o'clock at night and knock on the door of a person who might be able to help and just ask him to help me out.

### Creating and maintaining team atmosphere

Creating and maintaining a team atmosphere among onsite and offshore teams is important for success. In TCS, people involved in the Quartz development and all Quartz implementations consider themselves as the 'Quartz family' with their own 'Quartz culture', and 'Quartz language'. People involved in Quartz implementation talk about themselves as 'our own people': they do not distinguish between dispersed onsite and offshore teams 'we' versus 'they'.

One senior manager emphasised the importance of the team members, team atmosphere and motivation for success:

- 'Members are the key to the success. They should be well treated, accommodated, well informed on the schedules and plans for each task. Tasks and schedules should not be committed to a client without acknowledgment from the team responsible for development'.
- 'Members should not be expected to work over weekends/holidays. They should be given proper intimation if they are needed to. The schedule should take this into consideration'.

### Facilitating interactions

Facilitating interactions between people at remote locations is important. In TCS members of onsite and offshore teams interact frequently. First, onsite and offshore project leaders work very closely and interact on a daily basis (as described earlier in the 'design systematic communications' practice). Second, members of onsite and offshore teams have an opportunity to meet in person during the design and construction stages when most of the onsite team members come back to join the offshore team. Furthermore, some of them have interacted during earlier projects and/or the Quartz training program that is compulsory for anybody joining the Quartz group.

### Knowledge sharing in GD CBD: managerial practices

Interviewees consider knowledge sharing as contributing to success: in particular, building up collective knowledge through shared experiences, and creating transactive memory among team members at dispersed locations (Zurich, Bombay and Gurgaon for the Skandia project, and San Francisco and Gurgaon for the Dresdner project).

In the global software team of TCS, transactive memory and collective knowledge were developed before the project started. In particular, the collective knowledge is very broad, because all team members have the same cultural background (developers in Gurgaon, Bombay, Zurich and San Francisco are all Indian), and collective knowledge to a great extent is based on national culture (Baumard 1999). Furthermore, in TCS team members also had collective technical knowledge about Quartz from Quartz-related training and their own experience in Quartz development and implementation.

The following are managerial practices seen as important for knowledge sharing between remote team members, supported by quotations from interviews.

#### *Creating transactive memory among dispersed team members*

Creating transactive memory among team members located onsite and offshore, and among people involved in Quartz group (which includes all Quartz implementation projects TCS is involved in) is considered important for success.

In the Quartz group there are a number of activities, such as training programs, that facilitate interactions among members of Quartz group through which team members get to know each other and create transactive memory.

The following statements illustrate the existence of transactive memory at the studied team:

- 'I am involved since the start, so I know each team member and everything which has been done' (software developer).

- On-site manager said about the offshore team: 'I know team members very well, know their strengths'.

#### *Expanding collective knowledge of the dispersed team*

Expanding collective knowledge of the dispersed team is important for success. In addition to the knowledge of national culture that all team members possess, team members need to have collective knowledge of the overall product (beyond a specific area an individual team member is working on), which includes (i) cross-functional knowledge, (ii) understanding of logic (changes) in the evolving product, and (iii) common language/terminology.

(i) Cross-functional knowledge provides the team with flexibility to accommodate everyday dynamics and uncertainties by reducing dependencies on specific team members. For example, if needed, team members can 'replace' each other. One project lead explained:

> Each and every team member is aware of nearly all the things which are happening, the whole team has a basic knowledge about everything. Usually they work on their own specific code areas, and only in circumstances when the other person is not available, they would work on the other areas. But to make it easier for them to work on the other areas, they have to have the basic understanding of that area.

(ii) People in TCS are convinced that it is important to understand the logic behind the code and changes which have been made in the code. For example, Sunil Singh explained that when his team in Gurgaon and onsite team in San Francisco work around-the-clock by sending code back and forth, they also send descriptions of the changes so that the onsite team understand the changes and don't have to spend time understanding what changes we have made. Describing changes made by remote counterparts helps to expand the collective knowledge of the dispersed team members, sharing understanding of the evolving product.

Furthermore, one manager explained that it is important to describe the logic behind the code so that in case a component is handed over from one developer to another to continue working on it, or a component would need to be modified in the future, anybody (and not just the person who wrote the original code) can continue working on and/or modify the component. Thus, by documenting the logic behind components the Quartz group externalise the tacit knowledge of individual team members and convert it into explicit knowledge (Nonaka and Takeuchi 1995) available for the whole Quartz group, for any Quartz implementation projects.

(iii) Furthermore, collective knowledge includes the use of common language/terminology between remote team members. As one software developer described it:

> We all speak Quartz language. It is a loss for us if somebody leaves Quartz because for somebody new it will take time to learn Quartz.

To utilise the collective knowledge of the people involved in Quartz, this person explained: 'people rotate within Quartz, not out of Quartz'.

### Learning new technology

Interviewees from TCS consider the learning of a new technology important for success.

In TCS, learning new technology is concerned with (i) learning the programming language and tools used for developing Quartz (e.g. the Master Craft Tools, described earlier in 'SD tools' practice), and (ii) learning theoretical principles and different business (financial/banking) functions included in the Quartz platform.

For the learning of Quartz and technologies used to develop it, TCS organises intensive courses in which team members from globally dispersed location all gather at one location, a training center at Trivandrum. For anybody joining the Quartz team attending this training program is compulsory.

### Components management in GD CBD: managerial practices

In addition to the four factors suggested in the theoretical lens, *components management* emerged from the TCS data as a factor contributing to success.

The following are the managerial practices seen as important to ensure successful management of components. These practices are important in co-located CBD as well; however, they become more critical in a globally distributed environment.

### Designing for reuse

Interviewees consider that applying a design-for-reuse strategy is important for success. In TCS, the main advantage anticipated from the CB Quartz architecture is to be able to reuse it in the long term for a number of clients. In order to maximise reuse across different Quartz implementations for different clients all over the globe, jointly with TKS, the TCS team invested time and resources to identify the most common requirements for banking and financial services. The analysis addressed issues such as (i) what components to develop (what functionalities are required that are common for all/a majority of potential clients), and (ii) what should be the granularity of components.

In each Quartz implementation, the majority of components included in the Core Quartz platform are reused. However, since all projects are somewhat different, for each implementation some additional functionality has been developed. For example, in the Dresdner project Quartz was integrated with the client's system as a back-end system (while originally Quartz was developed as a front-end system). One senior manager explained:

> We used a distinct structure of parts, which was already present: we just made minor variations to that, I can say 50–60% were reusable.

Furthermore, TCS exploits customer-specific components by adding them to the Quartz package so that they can be reused in future Quartz implementations. Following this approach, with each new Quartz implementation TCS increases the variety of components/functionalities that TCS can offer to potential clients. For example, TCS implemented Quartz at Royal Skandia UK,[5] an insurance company, where Quartz was implemented as an investment engine. Quartz, originally developed as a banking application, had never been implemented in an insurance company before. One product architect explained about the changes that were made to Quartz:

> A lot of changes were made to the basic Quartz system just to be able to integrate it with the insurance business. We had to build in a lot of things that deal with policy administration and policy distribution, which are not particularly bank products. This way typical insurance products were added to Quartz: they were released as the next version of Quartz.

The use of a CB architecture facilitated reuse of components across different Quartz implementations at different geographical locations.

### Investing in 'advanced development'

Investing in advanced development was considered important by interviewees at TCS. Advanced development in TCS included cooperation with TKS: it was based on integrating core capabilities and knowledge of the two companies – the technical knowledge in developing advanced software products of TCS, and the business knowledge of financial processes, regulations and clients in Europe of TKS.

### Facilitating reuse

Interviewees from TCS indicated that facilitating reuse of knowledge and components across different Quartz implementations is important

---

[5]Royal Skandia UK is a different company from the Skandia Bank Switzeraland discussed in this book in the context of the Skandia project.

for success in GD CBD. There is a central role, *Quartz program manager*, who is coordinating all Quartz implementation projects across all dispersed locations. The Quartz program manager has an overview of all projects, i.e. he is aware of new components being developed for a specific customer and can facilitate the reuse of these components across different implementation projects.

Furthermore, to facilitate reuse of knowledge and components in a globally distributed environment people are rotated between onsite and offshore locations to bridge knowledge gaps between the two sites.

Moreover, by being involved in several functional or technical areas, people develop and extend their expertise. They develop cross-functional knowledge in these areas, and can apply this knowledge later when they move to other (subsequent) implementation projects.

### Managing vendors

Typically, Quartz implementation involves integration of Quartz components with the client system and third-party components (as described on pages 126–131). Therefore, it is important to manage vendors providing third-party components: selecting vendors, agreeing on specifications of the components (e.g. functionality and interfaces), deadlines for components' delivery. In particular, vendor management was very important for the Skandia project, where more than 25 vendors were involved in delivering components. In TCS, it is the responsibility of the Quartz program manager to guide and coordinate work between all parties involved in the implementation project: onsite and offshore teams, and vendors of third-party components. One offshore manager explained:

> Vendor management is needed when you have software vendors: for example, buying security software from someone, or buying hardware from someone. So the Quartz program manager will not only look at what onsite and offshore teams are doing, but he will also look at what vendors are doing and coordinating between the activities of all the vendors, all the interested parties.

## Success in GD CBD: evidence

This section presents evidence collected in interviews about the success achieved in the studied case. The evidence is presented according to the categories of success illustrated in the TCS concept map.

## Product success

The Quartz project was highly successful. In 2002 Quartz was recognised by the International Banking Systems (IBS) Journal as being among the best-selling banking systems. The IBS newsletter (March 2003) states:

> Quartz from Tata Consultancy Services/TKS-Teknosoft did well. This is now sold across a relatively broad range of activities, including asset management. It took a fair while to make it to market but now looks proven and well rounded.

Since 2002, according to annual 2003 and 2004 IBS reports,[6] Quartz has remained among the top 25 best-selling banking systems.

Furthermore, as intended by Quartz development group, the CB Quartz platform was reused for a number of clients.

## Personal satisfaction

### Healthy environment

The offshore project leader of the Dresdner project described the team atmosphere in the Dresdner project:

> Over a period of time (I have known them for around 6–7 months), I know what they feel and what they don't feel. And if somebody has problems at home and he wants to take leave, I try to go ahead and look for other people who can do his job. These things are managed very well within our team.

### Less communication effort

Talking about his remote counterparts one on-site software developer said:

> They know Quartz and I know Quartz, so little things are easy to explain: 'you go there and you do this' – it's not difficult to explain.

## Successful collaboration

### Effective coordination

One of the most important issues in Quartz is ensuring that third-party components are delivered on time and according to specifications.

---

[6]The IBS Annual Sales League Tables are available from the web-site: http://www.ibspublishing.com/sales_league_tables/league_tables.htm

Thus, the program manager facilitates the building of individual plans for participating vendors. One software developer explained:

> so that they deliver components when you need them, that one component of the software is delivered on time for the next component, e.g. the hardware is delivered on time for the software.

*Effective communications*

The following statement made by one functional manager illustrates that a division of work based on expertise of dispersed team members improves efficiency of work:

> There are two areas in which we are working: trading and portfolio management. We have clearly-defined jobs: some people would be working only on trading and other people would be working only on portfolio management. They are very familiar with their area, with each and every line of the product, because they are writing it, they have developed the product, so they are very clever, they know what is there. So once we tell them 'this thing has to be changed', it doesn't take much time for them to understand and change it.

**Bridged geographical, time-zone and cultural gaps**

*Geographical distance* is not perceived as a problem:

> For onsite and offshore teams, geographical distance causes limited inconvenience, i.e. when the help of the offshore team is needed to fix bugs during end-user testing at the customer location. In such a situation the offshore team cannot access the customer system from a remote location for security reasons. However on a regular basis, team members communicate remotely using different types of communication media.

*Time differences* cause some problems, but usually is used as an advantage:

> TCS employees explained that despite the fact that a time difference such as 13.5 hours (in the Dresdner project) is causing some difficulties (e.g. onsite project manager is often contacted during late hours in the evening when he is at home), onsite and offshore teams can work faster and utilise time-zone differences working around-the-clock.
>
> For example, when it is night-time in Gurgaon, instead of contacting offshore team members at night, the team in Zurich can get

help from people involved in different Quartz implementation projects but whose working hours overlap with Zurich.

*No cultural differences* within the Quartz group:

Team members in all locations have the same cultural background: they are all Indian.

## Conclusions

In this chapter, the analysis and results of the TCS case study were presented and discussed. Managerial practices and quotations from interviews illustrating these managerial practices and their contribution to success were presented.

The results of the case study illustrate that interviewees considered four factors suggested in the theoretical lens, and the fifth factor (components management) that emerged from the data, as contributing to success in GD CBD.

In terms of managerial practices, *inter-site coordination* between onsite and offshore teams was effective and efficient: first, the main strategy that TCS followed to divide work was to do maximum work offshore and minimise work onsite; work was divided based on expertise. Second, in order to increase awareness and keep remote teams updated all the time, systematic communications were organised between onsite and offshore managers and developers. Moreover, ownerships of the work packages stayed with the same team: team members were transferred between onsite and offshore locations together with the work packages (components) they were working on.

In relation to *appropriate tools and technologies*, methods, tools and processes were standardised across globally distributed onsite and offshore teams. However full standardisation and centralisation of tools was not possible, as Quartz is concerned with banking, where much data and information is confidential. To overcome this problem, the offshore development team in Gurgaon created a development environment that replicated the one at the customer site.

Regarding *social ties*, in TCS trust and rapport between remote counterparts were developed before the projects started, because the majority of team members have worked together and knew each other before re-locating to onsite locations. Furthermore, the team atmosphere in Quartz group is remarkable: onsite and offshore teams consider themselves as the 'Quartz family' with their own 'Quartz culture' and 'Quartz language'.

Moreover, the Quartz team members could work faster and utilise time-zone differences to work around-the-clock, because they could easily contact each other at any time of a day (approaching one's counterparts out of working hours is considered normal in Indian culture, as opposed to many European cultures, where work-related communications are limited to working hours only).

Concerning *knowledge sharing*, in TCS, global team transactive memory and collective knowledge were developed before the projects started because all team members have the same cultural and technical backgrounds, and because the majority of team members knew each other. To facilitate knowledge sharing Quartz managers rotated people between onsite and offshore teams.

It is important to acknowledge how effective the *components management* was organised in TCS: first, in the Skandia project in which more then 25 vendors of third-party components were involved, coordination of all dispersed parties – onsite and offshore teams, and vendors – was centralised under the supervision of the Quartz program manager. Second, in order to maximise reuse across different Quartz implementations for different clients, jointly with TKS, the TCS team invested time and resources to identify the most common requirements for banking and financial services.

# 7
# The Case of Baan: How Not to Manage Global Teams

*Technology comes to our rescue in working in a distributed environment.*

(Product Manager, Baan)

But is technology alone enough to succeed in a globally distributed environment? Probably not, as we can learn from the unsuccessful Baan E-Enterprise case where technology was in place but the rest, inter-site coordination, social ties and knowledge sharing, were lacking.

## Background of Baan global organisation

The Baan Corporation was created in 1978 by Jan Baan to provide financial and administrative consultancy services. A few years later his brother, Paul Baan, joined the company. Baan started to develop software packages, and in the mid 90s, with the emergence of the Enterprise Resource Planning (ERP) industry, Baan became one of the market leaders and biggest vendors of ERP software, competing with SAP, PeopleSoft and Oracle. In the mid 90s, Baan opened several development centres in different countries: the main sites were in Hyderabad (India), Quebec (Canada), and the headquarters in Barneveld (The Netherlands).

In the 90s, Baan was considered the largest family software firm in Dutch history.[1] However, by the end of the 90s Baan had run into

---

[1]The history of Baan Corporation is based on internet sources (Google search for 'Baan history').

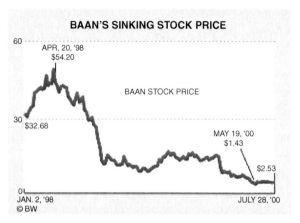

*Figure 7.1*   Baan stock prices (adapted from Baker et al. 2000)

*Table 7.1*   The rise & fall of Baan Co. (adapted from Baker et al. 2000)

| | |
|---|---|
| **1978** | Jan Baan, a high school drop-out and former clerk at a slaughterhouse, founded a software company in his rural hometown of Barneveld, the Netherlands. |
| **1993** | Seeing a bright future for enterprise software, Connecticut's General Atlantic Partners invests $21 million in Baan, buying one-third of the company. |
| **1994** | Jan Baan sells the software system to Boeing. The breakthrough contract raises Baan's profile and prepares it for an IPO. |
| **1995** | Before Baan lists its shares on Nasdaq and the Amsterdam exchange, the Baan brothers put control of company in the hands of their charitable foundation. In the next three years, the stock soars to 13 times its previous value. |
| **1996** | Buoyed by strong stock, Baan goes on a buying spree, snapping up nine different software companies over two years, including Aurum – a rival of Siebel Systems. |
| **1997** | With demand for back-office software at an all-time high, Baan revenue soars 91%. |
| **1998** | In April, the company's share price peaks at $54. Then it adjusts first-quarter 1998 sales by $43 million, explaining that many of the sales were made to its own distribution company. Investors sell down shares 15% in two days. |
| **July '98** | The Baan brothers withdraw from the company. Tom Tinsley, a former McKinsey & Co. consultant who joined Baan in 1995, takes over the CEO position. As the Baan stock falls, banks that were holding the Baan brothers' stock as loan collateral unload 8% of the company. |

*Table 7.1* The rise & fall of Baan Co. (adapted from Baker et al. 2000)
*– continued*

| | |
|---|---|
| Nov. '98 | President Mary Coleman, formerly of Aurum, leads the move to cut 1,200 jobs. |
| May '99 | Tinsley quits, taking a job at General Atlantic Partners, the same VC firm that put Baan on the map. He is replaced by Mary Coleman. |
| June '99 | The Baan brothers' Vanenburg Ventures investment firm, which holds 20% of Baan stock, quietly sells more than half of it by the end of the year. |
| Jan. '00 | With finances plummeting, Mary Coleman quits. New CEO Pierre Everaert searches for a buyer. |
| May '00 | Britain's Invensys announces $700 million offer for Baan, pricing shares at $2.85. Aug. 1: Deal goes through. |
| Late 2000 | Two of Vanenburg's new software companies are scheduled for IPOs on the Nasdaq. This includes Top Tier,[2] a key software supplier to longtime Baan rival SAP. |

some financial troubles. Figure 7.1 shows how the Baan stock price changed between January 1998 and July 2000.

The main events in the history of Baan Corporation are summarised in Table 7.1, as described in *Business Week* (Baker et al. 2000).

Since 2000, Baan has changed owners twice. In 2000, Baan was acquired for about $700 million by Invensys (a global automation, controls and process solutions group that offers products and services to improve resource productivity[3]). Three years later, in 2003 Invensys sold Baan Corporation for $135 million to two USA private equity firms.

A recent update to the story of Baan and the Baan brothers is that, after Baan was sold in 2000, Jan Baan started a new company called Cordys, as a part of Vanenburg Ventures. According to the Cordys web site (www.cordys.com), it is developing 'a Collaborative Real-Time Enterprise Technology platform and 'beyond ERP' collaborative Lean Enterprise applications'.[4]

---

[2]Top Tier was sold to SAP: as a result, some of the teams from Top Tier became part of KM Collaboration group that was the focus of the SAP case study, as described in Chapter 5.
[3]From Invensys web site (http://www.invensys.com/us/eng/aboutus/whoweare/whoweare.htm)
[4]Read more about Cordys and Jan Baan in the media release from June 25 2004 on www.IT-director.com

The case study described in this book focuses on the development of an E-Enterprise suite that consists of several products. The case study was conducted in early 2002, when two globally distributed locations – Hyderabad (India) and Barneveld (The Netherlands) – were involved in developing software. At that time Baan was part of Invensys. As mentioned on page 67, in June 2002, when we planned to interview people in the Barneveld office, Baan started re-organising its development centres and activities. As a result, in July 2002 development of the E-Enterprise was stopped in The Netherlands, and the Baan facility in Barneveld was closed. Although the Baan case study does not fit the unit of analysis and case selection criteria, including it in this book gives an opportunity to compare managerial practices from the successful projects of LeCroy, SAP and TCS with practices that were, or, more importantly, *were not* in place in the unsuccessful project of Baan.

## Background of the project and product

The project investigated in this case study concerns the development of an E-Enterprise suite designed to let users extend their Baan manufacturing, financial, and distribution software on the Web to allow them to collaborate better with customers, suppliers, and partners. According to the *Information Week* of April 26, 1999, Baan then released a first version of the E-Enterprise suite, which included E-Sales, E-Procurement, and E-Collaboration:[5]

> *E-Sales* lets users set up an online storefront that Baan says will be integrated with its back-office enterprise resource planning applications. Also included is E-Config, a self-service product configurator that works over the Web.

> *E-Procurement* lets companies quickly and easily purchase office supplies and production materials. It also sits on top of the traditional Baan ERP applications and pulls out the operations and business information needed to execute a transaction.

> *E-Collaboration* is a lower-cost alternative to electronic data interchange. It lets supply-chain partners share information such as

---

[5]Extract from the *Information Week* of April 26 1999, available on http://www.informationweek.com/731/baan.htm

contracts, purchase orders, and material forecasts over the Web. Data generated within the Baan ERP applications, such as a master production schedules or manufacturing diagrams, can be posted on a common site.

By early 2002, when the data collection took place, the content of the E-Enterprise suite had been extended to include more products. As the interviewees explained, products included in the E-Enterprise suite were developed to be stand-alone as well as to be integrated with the ERP package developed by Baan. In March 2002, the E-Enterprise suite consisted of seven products that were all based on one platform called E-Enterprise Server (previously called E-Common):[6]

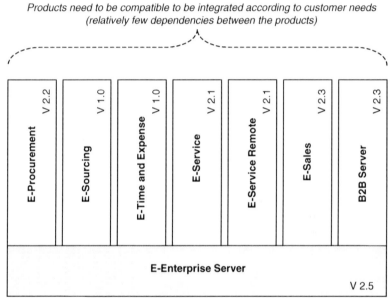

*Products need to be compatible to be integrated according to customer needs (relatively few dependencies between the products)*

| E-Procurement V 2.2 | E-Sourcing V 1.0 | E-Time and Expense V 1.0 | E-Service V 2.1 | E-Service Remote V 2.1 | E-Sales V 2.3 | B2B Server V 2.3 |
|---|---|---|---|---|---|---|

**E-Enterprise Server**

V 2.5

*Platform common for all product of E-Enterprise (many dependencies between products and the platform)*

*Figure 7.2*   Products included in the E-Enterprise suite

---

[6]From the empirical data it seems that the E-Collaboration module was renamed as B2B Server, while in the documents old names are still used (E-Common instead of E-Enterprise Server and E-Collaboration instead of B2B Server).

The E-Enterprise Server included several products that could provide customers with solutions to their business problems. As the Product Manager E-Service and E-Service Remote explained:

> Customers are not concerned about products but the solutions to their business problems. It could be a combination of products, not only products but also certain builds, like customisation. Basically, the solution is a bundle of products, where products are something like assembling parts.

However, from the development group perspective, products cannot simply be 'assembled'. One development manager explained: 'products are not so independent. That kind of plug-and-play scenario is not there yet'.

True Component-Based products can be 'assembled' in a plug-and-play manner; however, the *structure of E-Enterprise was not Component-Based*. The General Manager of E-Enterprise and E-Enterprise India explained:

> In Component-Based development, every business function can grow on its own, it need not be dependent on the other functions. Today, if I want to grow in one function, it is dependent on the other functions so that I cannot release this function, unless the other functions are also released. Today, if you ask me whether these are components, E-Enterprise is not componentised. Slowly we are moving towards componentisation, but we are not there yet.

The software architecture of the E-Enterprise suite was modular: each product included in the E-Enterprise suite was a module, which was dependent on the other modules.

## Background of the software team

### Working experience in a globally distributed environment

E-Enterprise group was relatively young: the first E-Enterprise products were released in 1999. Some people in Hyderabad had been working in a globally distributed environment on other projects: many of them had visited remote locations and worked with some people at a remote site before joining the E-Enterprise group. However, because of a general Baan policy to reduce travel expenses, and because the E-Enterprise organisational structure had changed several times since the group was established (as discussed further in detail in the case), the vast majority of interviewees in Hyderabad hardly knew people involved in E-Enterprise at the remote site.

## Organisational structure of the software team

Development of the E-Enterprise suite was organised by feature/ product function (different functions of the E-Enterprise suite are treated as products). A schematic illustration of the organisational structure of the E-Enterprise group is presented in Figure 7.3.

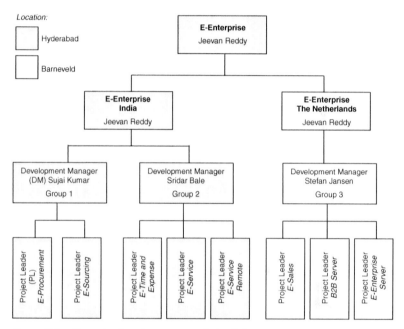

*Figure 7.3*  Organisational structure of the E-Enterprise development group (as of March 2002)

From a geographical perspective, the development group was distributed between two locations (numbers are correct as of March 2002):

1) Barneveld (The Netherlands): headquarters with 35 people involved in E-Enterprise (head of the E-Enterprise group Jeevan Reddy was located in India while the headquarters of Baan, which was

also considered the headquarters of E-Enterprise, was in The Netherlands[7]).
2) Hyderabad (India): 60 people involved in E-Enterprise.

In addition to the E-Enterprise development group, several more groups were involved in the management of the E-Enterprise suite, such as Marketing & Alliances the (M&A) group, and the Project & Process office. In particular, the M&A group had much influence on the E-Enterprise development group. M&A was even considered to be the 'owner' of the E-Enterprise and the ultimate 'customer' of the development group. The product architect of E-Services Remote explained:

> The Product Manager and the Solution Manager [both belong to M&A group], basically are the owners of the product, for us they are end-customers, so whatever they want, we have to do it.

## How Baan organises and manages GDSD teams: problems faced and implications for success factors

In this section, the findings from the E-Enterprise project are analysed and discussed in the light of potential factors contributing to success. We discuss the problems the E-Enterprise project team faced and how these affected the success of this project.

The Baan case is slightly different from the other cases presented in this book, so our conclusions mainly refer to issues pertaining to the management of global teams. However, many of the challenges related below are in fact related to the management of GD CBD projects. We therefore think that the Baan case, though not a pure GD CBD project, adds value to our discussion. We now focus on each area of challenges faced by this project team in the context of the management globally distributed teams.

### Inter-site coordination: problems faced

Interviewees reported a number of problems related to coordination between remote sites. In particular, division of work between the two sites was not efficient: first, ownership of work packages was sequentially switching between teams in The Netherlands and India, which

---

[7]The appointment of Jeevan Reddy (who was located in the Hyderabad office) as a head of the E-Enterprise group was an attempt to transfer the development of the E-Enterprise from The Netherlands to India.

was identified by the interviewees in the Hyderabad office as one of the major problems in the E-Enterprise project (problem 1). Second, too many people were involved in the management of each product in different roles, some of which were overlapping (problem 2). Third, there were many technical dependencies between products included in the E-Enterprise suite, which created knowledge and information dependencies between the dispersed teams (problem 3). In addition, lack of communications between the two teams caused difficulties in the understanding of dependencies between products and plans.

Furthermore, project management techniques adopted by the E-Enterprise group were not efficient: project planning was too detailed (down to 2–20 hour tasks) and could not accommodate the everyday dynamics (problem 4), which reduced the efficiency of the development and increased bureaucracy, because project leaders were busy nearly full-time updating plans and reports, and developers were busy reporting on the work-hours put into tasks. At the same time, there was a lack of proper planning on a high level. Two problems were associated with lack of proper planning on a high level: first, the requirements stage was not defined (problem 5); and second: there were too many changes in many aspects of the Baan organisation and the E-Enterprise project (problem 6).

Problems 1–6 are discussed below and illustrated by empirical evidence from the interviews.

### Problem 1: No clear product/project ownership

Ownership of the project (E-Enterprise) and products comprising it was confusing. Product/project ownership was sequentially switching between India and The Netherlands. The following is the history of the E-Service, illustrating how ownership of the product was switching. One manager described:

> We initiated the project in India in 1999 and developed the initial version. Afterwards we transferred the ownership to The Netherlands because we were busy with another project, E-Service Remote, where we had some customer requirements which were urgent at that stage, so the entire E-Service team concentrated on the E-Service Remote product. Then the actual ownership of the whole product E-Service was shifted to The Netherlands, and the next version (E-Service 2.0) was developed in the Netherlands: they enhanced the version we developed. Once we delivered the E-Service Remote product, we brought E-Service back to India and we developed a service pack called

E-Service 2.0 SP1 (Service Pack 1). That was one which we delivered last June, now we are working on 2.1.

Because the ownership was switching between the teams, there was always a need to understand the product developed by another team (which is often more difficult than to develop a product from scratch), and there was never a complete knowledge of the product and the logic behind it: for example, as one offshore software developer explained:

> It's difficult to visualise the idea when it is not yours. If we have the knowledge of the existing product then we're building on top of it, it's easy. But sometimes it happens that the understanding of the existing architecture is not very good because we are not there from the beginning: the initial product has been transferred from there to here.

Furthermore, there was no feeling of 'our' product, because the product was inherited from another team: 'I expect one of the important things that should happen within E-Enterprise Baan or anywhere is that more ownership must be felt by everybody' (product developer).

### Problem 2: Too many people involved in the management of each product in different roles, some of which are overlapping

It seems that too many people in different roles were involved in the management of each product included in E-Enterprise, so that some responsibilities were overlapping. Combined with other circumstances (e.g. the sequentially changing ownership discussed above), a situation was created where *everybody* was involved but *nobody* was responsible. Figure 7.4 illustrates the different roles (people) involved in the management of each of the eight products comprising E-Enterprise. Figure 7.4 is based on descriptions of the different roles as explained by interviewees (the descriptions follow Figure 7.4). From the descriptions it follows that sometimes people had different views on what they or their colleagues were supposed to do.

There are two *Product Managers: in-bound* and *out-bound*. As the in-bound Product Manager of E-Service and E-Service Remote explained:

> Actually, the in-bound and out-bound is more like an internal arrangement. I would say that the in-bound is more product development oriented, whereas out-bound is more product marketing oriented. Basically, instead of one person taking care of the entire product issues,

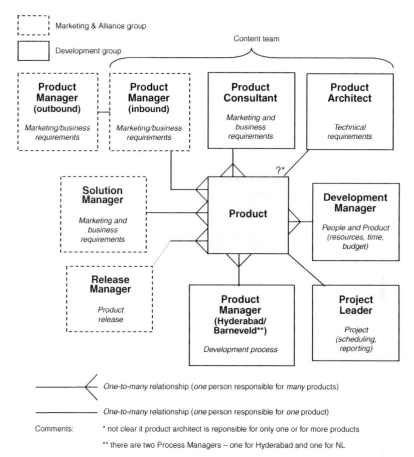

*Figure 7.4*   Roles (people) involved in the management of each of the eight products comprising E-Enterprise

it is split into two roles: Product Marketer [out-bound PM] and Product Manager [in-bound PM]. The Product Marketer takes care of marketing of the product and also getting the inputs. Getting the inputs is not the primary goal of a Product Marketer, whereas getting the inputs is the primary aim of the Product Manager, and the Product Manager is in the picture of how the product evolves and gets mature as a marketable product. Once it is a marketable product, then from there the Product Marketer takes over.

The in-bound Product Manager is part of a content team.

As the General Manager of E-Enterprise explained:

> A *content team* [see Figure 7.3] consists of Product Manager, Pro-duct Consultant and Product Architect. Each product will have one Product Manager, one Product Consultant and one Pro-duct Architect. Some of these people are in The Nether-lands: for different products different people sit in different locations. These people are part of the team here, and similarly part of the team in The Netherlands as well. So this is a generic model.

Within the content team the work and responsibilities are divided in the following way. The Product Architect of E-Service Remote explained:

> The Product Manager gives a product definition in which he gives a brief requirement of what exactly he wants, and the Product Con-sultant will write a conceptual solution on the requirement: a doc-ument outlining what exactly is the business process, and he will explain the requirement in more detail. In the conceptual solution the Architect also will come into the picture and he will explain how this functionality will actually be built into the product, from a technical perspective.

One senior manager explained his role of *Product Architect*:

> As an Architect I will be writing the functional and technical designs that include product definition, version definition and con-ception solution. These two documents are taken as input for the developers. Then the Development Manager starts writing the project plan.

Another product architect of E-Service said:

> when a requirement comes to me I say, 'this requirement needs this much solution time, this much design time, this much real-isation'. Then comes the Project Leader who extrapolates this.

The role of Development Manager seemed to be controversial to some extent. People in different roles had different opinions on what were the responsibilities of the Development Manager, as illustrated by the following quotes:

*Opinion of Product Architects*:

> The Development Manager will be making the project plan. Once the requirements are clear and we have a version definition ready, he will start making the project plan. But since the requirements are changing he has to again change the plans: sometimes it becomes impossible to change the plan every day because requirements change so frequently.

Furthermore, as the product architect of E-Procurement said: 'The Development Manager has the prime responsibility for delivering the product and he is the one who takes care of all the resource allocation'.

*Opinion of Development Manager* (himself)

The Development Manager of Group 1 explained his perspective:

> My involvement is about the decision-making mostly, to see basically how does this [planning] match with the capacity we have. But on the technical decisions or functional decisions, normally we leave it to functional Consultant as well as the Architect.

*Opinion of Product Manager*:

> The Development Manager is taking care of the schedule of the project, the quality of the project and the people. It was becoming too complex for one person to handle, so in E-Enterprise they created a Project Leader and a Development Manager. There is still a gap there. Still the Development Manager is the one who is supposed to take care of schedule as well as quality (product manager and Consultant of E-Time and Expense).

*Opinion of the General Manager of E-Enterprise*:

> The Development Manager is responsible for product and people. Overall, the Development Manager still takes the lead in the projects, he is a people-manager. A *Project Leader* is only planning and tracking the progress of the project. And he will work closely with the Development Manager for any resource management, any issues

which need to be covered (General Manager of E-Enterprise and E-Enterprise Hyderabad).

The *Solution Manager*, who is part of the M&A group, is also involved in the management of E-Enterprise. His involvement is associated with some problems, in particular:

> We have another person called the Solution Manager, who is actually a boss of the Product Manager, he is sitting in The Netherlands and this causes a lot of problems. The way we see it, in our organisation, the way it should work is the Product Manager is representing the marketing team discussions, and here the Product Consultant and the Product Architect will represent the development. So that means that it is assumed that the Solution Manager and the Product Manager work together. But sometimes it does not work, because they are in different locations. So it causes a lot of confusion, because lots of times the Product Manager says 'I will convince him [Solution Manager] to do it the way you are doing it', then later Solution Manager comes into the picture and he says 'no I don't like this' [...] Sometimes we feel it is better to talk to the Solution Manager, because he's the ultimate boss. What happened in one of the products: the Solution Manager himself said 'I want this change', and the Product Manager said 'No I don't think we should do it'. But still the Solution Manager forced everyone to do it (product architect of E-Service Remote).

There is also a *Release Manager.* This was his opinion:

> The Release Manager is the person who is part of the M&A organisation. He is basically responsible for releasing the product. He is involved right from the project initiation stage and he'll drive the entire project until it is released to the market. He's the guy who has to be in touch with the sales people, who has to get in touch with the customers, with Baan development: Project Leaders and Development Managers, with M&A: in-bound and out-bound Product Managers. The Release Managers of different products should interact as well.

In terms of location, one manager explained: 'we worked with The Netherlands Release Manager, but now we got one Release Manager here, so now basically the transition is taking place'.

There are two *Process Managers*, one located in The Netherlands and one in India. These two Process Managers work closely together on a process plan to improve the software engineering and development process, guided by the CMMI (Capability Maturity Model Integration) framework. The Process Manager in India is responsible for the group in India, and the Process Manager in The Netherlands works closely with the group in the Barneveld office and is responsible for processes in both locations. As the Process Manager in Hyderabad, explained:

> We are not specialised in any one area – we are close to the teams and we are intermediaries between specialists and teams. We try to arrange a plan and we try to implement, bring some change, these are the kinds of actions that we do.

### Problem 3: Dependency of all products on the common platform (E-Enterprise Server) and dependencies between products

There was a strong dependency between the E-Enterprise Server (earlier versions called E-Common) and everything else, and some dependencies between other products included in the E-Enterprise suite (see Figure 7.2); these dependencies existed because combinations of products had to work together. For example, as one process manager described:

> E-Procurement and E-Sourcing are two applications which use E-Common. Both of them are independent, they can be released to the market, but we need to synchronise them because, if there is a customer who buys both applications, they should work together. So products are dependent because if there is a customer that buys several products, he wants to see an integrated solution. Then features have to be integrated, or some kind of adjustment has to be made, in such a way that they both work together.

In the first place there were technical dependencies on the E-Enterprise Server. This caused knowledge and information dependencies between the dispersed teams:

*Technical dependencies on the E-Enterprise Server*

One solution manager explained:

> This particular component [E-Enterprise Server], which is also a product, becomes a common or a dependency component for all

the products. So you cannot release any product unless the E-Enterprise Server is available. This is a dependency. Because of this product, dependency between Hyderabad and The Netherlands exists.

Technical dependencies on the E-Enterprise Server cause two problems: (1) specifications and (2) schedules across products needed to be synchronised:

> When they start working on E-Common, we need to view what is required in this for us [Group 2] at this moment of time. That means we need to already see what is the time-frame, what are the features they are going to incorporate into this particular area (product architect).

Similarly, another product architect stressed that 'coordinating requirements [specifications] between different products is a problematic area'. In order to synchronise schedule and specifications, 'coordination and a lot of communication is required', said one process manager; he explained that:

> Somebody needs to moderate the discussion because everybody independently looks at their product. Collectively we have to find a solution, then comes the sharing of the ways of doing things, so a lot of discussion and co-ordination is required for this. It is expected that the people who are owning E-Common have to be more careful and have to consider all the applications, but in that they are independent.

### Knowledge and information dependencies

The technical dependencies of all products on the E-Enterprise Server created more dependencies and problems, as one product developer explained:

> The dependency on NL is causing problems. Dependency on information, dependency on knowledge (even in terms of simple design documents, for example, functional designs, or technical designs, they are not complete), dependency on requirements, because everything is centralised in Holland and then that has to be shared with us so that we can proceed. The problem is ultimately

extended schedules, they were not able to complete the projects in time.

Taking into account the numerous dependencies discussed above, *there was no structured approach to identify and coordinate these dependencies*:

> One thing that is missing right now in E-Enterprise is that at any time you can't look into any document to see what are the exact dependencies involved. Right now they're coming with something like a dependency matrix. But so far we didn't have that. So it's generally, like if you want to know tomorrow whatever dependency with another product, you have to actually talk to the team members or the Architect or the Consultant. There is no central store or central repository (product architect of E-Sourcing).

### Problem 4: Very detailed planning (down to 2–20 hours tasks) and a fast-changing situation do not work together

As mentioned earlier, the situation at the Baan E-Enterprise group was changing very fast: requirements for products were changing, causing changes in dependencies between products; processes were changing; people and their roles were changing; ownership of products was changing between the teams. At the same time, Baan required very detailed planning: the Project Leaders were busy planning short (2–20 hours) tasks. It seems that Baan put too much effort into planning and controlling whether the work is effective and efficient, so that it became too detailed and not capable of catching up with changes. Thus the effort and resources (man/hours) put into planning, in practice reduced the efficiency of the development and increased bureaucracy, because the Project Leaders were busy almost full-time updating plans and reports, and developers were busy reporting on the work-hours they put into tasks.

### Problem 5: The requirements stage is not clear and requirements are not frozen; a power game as a management approach to manage requirements

The requirements stage (in terms of procedure) was not defined:

> The requirements stage is not very clear, so it happens that even if the Product Manager is sitting in Hyderabad, even if we sit together and discuss the way we'll be doing our product, at later stage a lot of changes and things come into the picture. Product Manager

again gets some new ideas and says what we should do (product manager).

Furthermore, requirements were changing continuously, causing (i) difficulties in the planning and management of development for specific products, and (ii) tensions between people involved in marketing, development and across teams developing dependent products. One Process Manager explained the reason why requirements were not frozen:

> The marketing takes the lead, so that means whatever the marketing says the development has to do it. Because they say ultimately the marketing team is responsible for selling the product. They will bring the revenues. So that's why development takes a back stage, development has to listen to what they say. It is good if they are really clear what exactly they want, what is the vision, what is the roadmap and things don't change very frequently, but if on their side it is not clear, then it causes a lot of confusion. There is no guarantee the requirements will not change. That's the biggest problem we have.

One Product Architect elaborated on the problem:

> For example, if we want to start coding, we need to have a clearly-frozen functional design, and many times that is not possible because it keeps changing. It's a document that keeps improving from one day to another, whenever you have new ideas, new thoughts. And the changes that take place are also not coming through immediately.

It seems to be either the general approach at Baan that requirements cannot be frozen, or the personal approach of the Solution Manager. One manager explained:

> The Solution Manager gives us a lot of changes, even if the project is going on. He believes that the product should always be open. The requirements cannot be frozen. So we should be in a position to give him whatever requirement he wants. He is that kind of person. Other colleagues [for other E-Enterprise products and Baan ERP] experience the same. The requirements are never frozen.

Interviewees also reported that typically there was a 'power game' between individual people involved (Solution Manager, Product Manager, Architect, Development Manager). It means that the person who is the most powerful (in terms of character or personality) is the one who sets up 'rules of the game': if requirements can be changed, how often and to what extent. This is how one Solution Manager described the 'power game':

> If requirements are changing depends on who is more powerful. Basically from the organisation point of view it should not happen, but a difference of how much influence he [Solution Manager] can put on the development. If he feels that the development team is not really strong he will request a lot of changes.
>
> For example, Baan Service [ERP group] usually takes the lead role over Solution Manager, he doesn't change a lot of things there, because they [Baan Service group] are more powerful. It is more about the character of the person. The line manager, product architect, they feel that the Solution Manager can't do just whatever he wants. Once he has given requirements, that's it, he cannot change them whenever he wants. The way they do it, once Product Manager or Solution Manager requests for a change, they [Baan Service group] will say, 'OK we will take this', and they will say that it will take long to make the change: 'it will take six months or one year'. So if you start projecting that much time, the Solution Manager will never come back with a change, because he knows that they will always say another thing.

### Problem 6: Too many changes in many aspects of organisation and project

The E-Enterprise project and the Baan organisation were continuously changing: people, their roles, products, product's requirements, processes, ownership and physical location of tasks – all was changing very fast. Everything seemed to be in a transition and unstable. This situation reduced morale in the organisation and increased tensions between Indian and Dutch group members. Every interviewee mentioned several aspects that had changed recently, for example:

- *Change in product: from E-Common to E-Enterprise Sever*: One Product Manager explained: 'there was always migration from E-Common to E-Enterprise Server going on. So when we started with our project, that is E-Source, we started with E-Common, then E-Enterprise Server took over from E-Common'.

- *Changing ownership: moving tasks between India and The Netherlands*: as described earlier (problem 1).

- *Organizational structure was changing:* for example, the role of the Solution Manager had been changed. One Solution Manager explained: 'The actual solution manager for the product manager has moved out. Previously we had a concept for solutions, so they said for the time being we will remove that concept'.

It seems that there was no clarity about the changes within Baan: for example, one manager defined the new role of the former Solution Manager differently:

> Actually the Solution Manager has been re-presented as Group Manager now. What happened was, there was some confusion about the term 'solution', so they dropped the term 'solution', but still you have a name called Group Manager. But the Group Manager, if you want to look at it practically, it is nothing but a Solution Manager.

This gave the impression that people were used to changes (and expected more changes) in the organisational structure.

- *Processes were changing:* One process manager explained: 'earlier we had BDM (Baan Development Method), now we have D-method. It advocates certain ways of finding requirements, we also have been advised to do that kind of finding of requirements'.

Problems 1–6 discussed above can emerge in co-located as well as in globally distributed software development projects. However, these problems become more critical and more difficult to solve in a globally distributed environment where teams cannot meet face-to-face but need to collaborate and solve problems over distance.

### Inter-site coordination: implications for success factors

Three main critical success factors related to inter-site coordination were mentioned by interviewees: (i) communications between key people, (ii) clearly defined ownership, and (iii) a centralised plan that includes all dependencies. The following quotations illustrate the importance of each of these factors.

### *Communications between key people*

- One critical success factor is communication between people who are supposed to be involved very closely in the development: communications between Product Manager and Development Manager, communications between Product Consultant and the development teams, communication between the Consultants because there are so many dependencies between products.

- Another manager reflected on this issue: 'The bottleneck that I see here is communication and understanding. These two are very important. Definitely a visit to the other country is going to give a lot of added value in understanding people. Personal understanding, definitely, and building up personal relations'.

However, visiting the other country was difficult for people involved in the E-Enterprise group because Baan was 'trying to make cost-cutting measures, and they tried to shift everything to one location to reduce the communication costs' (senior manager, India).

### Ownership clearly defined

- One senior manager from India reflected on this matter: 'Involvement of the people and clear ownership is important. It has impact on people, their commitment and motivation. If people working on the product do not feel this ownership, then they are not motivated and not committed. They do not get involved. They do not understand the various dependencies and they'll not work towards the target goal'.

### One centralised plan with a clear requirements matrix and a dependency matrix for coordination and control

- Based on a successful project related to Baan ERP in which one product architect was involved before he started working on E-Enterprise, he explained:

> Initially the broad rule is that there will be one plan, not two plans, and the plan has the requirements matrix clearly defined. We know that there are 170 requirements to be done: for each requirement there is a spreadsheet made especially for it – which area it goes into, and who is the owner, who is the consultant, and who is the technical owner for this development matrix. The requirements matrix clearly defines where all the ownership lies and who is the contact. For a period of time that has become the key factor for controlling the whole thing.

### Appropriate tools and technologies: problems faced

The E-Enterprise group was well equipped with tools and technologies required to enable working in a globally distributed environment.

There was only one problem reported in regard to tools and technologies: lack of configuration management tools and methods. In particular, there was lack of compatibility between versions of different products (problem 7). This problem is discussed below and illustrated by empirical evidence from interviews.

### Problem 7: Lack of compatibility between versions of different products

It is important to ensure that whenever a product is changed and a new version is released, it should be backward compatible. Backward compatibility means that the new product (version) should recognise and work with all previous versions of other products of the E-Enterprise suite (the same as a new version on MS Word would recognise Word files created in earlier versions of Word). One product manger gave an example:

> If today we go into the market with E-Source 1.0 version. Then, during some time B2B Server would have released 3 versions. Now the customer should be in such a position that with E-Source 1.0 he should be able to buy any of these three versions of B2B Server.

However, in practice products included in E-Enterprise were not backward compatible, and this created additional dependencies between products because only specific versions of specific products could work together. Therefore, 'for each product we need to know specific properties, for example, in a product scenario [combination of products] which versions

| Applications running with which E-Common version 1) | |
| --- | --- |
| E-Sales 2.0 | E-Common 2.0 |
| E-Collaboration 2.0 | E-Common 2.0 |
| E-Procurement 2.0 | E-Common 2.1 |
| E-Sales 2.1 | E-Common 2.2 |
| E-Collaboration 2.1 | E-Common 2.2 |
| E-Procurement 2.1 | E-Common 2.3.0 |
| E-Service 2.0 | E-Common 2.3.1 |
| E-Service Remote 2.0 | E-Common 2.3.1 |
| E-Sales 2.2 LA | E-Common 2.3.1 |
| E-Sales 2.2 GA | E-Common 2.3.1 SP1 |
| E-Sales 2.2 SP1 | E-Common 2.3.1 SP2 |
| E-Collaboration 2.2 | E-Common 2.3.1 SP2 |
| E-Procurement 2.1 SP1 | E-Common 2.3.1 SP3 |

1) Applications which are running on the same E-Common version are able to run together on one server.

2) Applications which are running on E-Common 2.2 or higher are able run together on one server.

*Figure 7.5*   Compatibility between versions of different products (extract from Baan product compatibility matrix)

are in, which release works with which version of E-Common' (release manager). As versions of products were not backward compatible, compatibility was managed manually by creating lists of compatible product versions, for example by listing versions of E-Enterprise Server compatible with other products and by documenting connectivity packs.

Management of multiple versions of different products without proper configuration management tools is difficult even in a co-located environment. In a globally distributed environment management of multiple versions manually would require seamless coordination between dispersed sites and complete awareness of what is happening at the remote site. Otherwise it is impossible to manage multiple versions manually across dispersed locations (as happened in the E-Enterprise project).

### Appropriate tools and technologies: implications for success factors

Tools and technologies were considered very important: 'this is actually one of the most important things: technology comes to our rescue in working in a distributed environment' (process manager). Different tools were used to save on travel costs between The Netherlands and India, as one process manager explained:

> Quite some time back, before all of these tools came into practice, we used to travel to The Netherlands and they used to travel here in order to meet us, especially at the start of a new release or to share some important needs that stretch over a long time. Even for small purposes people used to travel. That was becoming expensive and they [Baan] had to think of alternatives, then all of these media came in the picture. Then the Videoconference was immediately applied. We started using VC, and we don't have to go to The Netherlands: we are saving a lot of dollars.

Interviewees mentioned several attributes of software development tools that are important for working in a globally distributed environment. Furthermore, we asked them what collaborative technologies they use and how they choose media for different purposes. Software development and collaborative tools used in E-Enterprise are described below:

### *Software Development tools*

In order to support GDSD, interviewees identified the following capabilities that need to be supported by SD tools (described in Table 7.2).

*Table 7.2*   Capabilities of SD tools at Baan

| **Standardisation of tools and methods across locations** | Baan tried to standardise development methods and processes: |
| --- | --- |
| | We want to have common processes across the locations. We try to achieve a uniform standard for all these. So that is a basic aim of this. Though we have not reached it in all the areas, but in certain areas we are making steps (process manger). |
| **Centralisation of tools** | There was an attempt to have a central requirements database; however requirements were changing so quickly that the database was not up to date. |
| **Synchronisation of code** | Code was synchronised via synchronisation of databases at two locations. One product developer explained how it works: |
| | Generally we have what we call 'sources' [source code], we have other sources that are shared. For modules that we have ownership of, whatever files are modified under this particular module they are the sources that are present in the Indian server. They are the leading sources. Then we have a synchronisation mechanism wherein we synchronise both the databases at the same time. |

### Collaborative technology

The following are collaborative technologies that were used by the E-Enterprise team to collaborate over distance (described in Table 7.3).

*Table 7.3*   Collaborative technologies used in Baan

| **Online chat** | The Hyderabad group could use AOL for chat. However, it seemed that chat was used very seldom for communications between The Netherlands and India, if at all (only one interviewee mentioned the existence of chat). |
| --- | --- |
| **Phone and teleconferencing** | As interviewees explained, the phone was used in the following situations: |
| | Telephone usually involved when a lot of emails have exchanged and certainly we feel that everyone is talking differently and it is taking too much time and no one is coming to any conclusions, then we start organising a telephone call (product developer). |
| | Furthermore, 'sometimes when the issue is very urgent and you need to get a reply very fast, then also we use phone' (product developer). |

*Table 7.3*    Collaborative technologies used in Baan  – *continued*

| | |
|---|---|
| | This person continued: |
| | If it is complicated or I feel mailing would really be inadequate at that stage, then what we do is we simply call them. |
| | The attitude of some interviewed towards the use of phone can be described as 'we try to minimise the way we have to talk over the telephone as far as possible. One reason is it being expensive'. |
| **Email** | There were different opinions about the use of email, in particular regarding preferences between email and phone. For example, one manager prefers to use emails: |
| | If I require some quick queries I generally use the mail, because there is no point in phoning them up. But when there is an issue, then I would actually prefer to send a mail even in that case, because the other person is not aware of the full background, so I try to prepare a document for detailing some of these concerns. If we are unable to sort out the issue via mail, we try to have a conference call. By mails you can express things more clearly because when you are on a telephone you can't just go on elaborating the things which you want to solve, but explain in a mail so that the other person has time to read, contemplate and then prepare his responses. So better have a telephone conference only at that point and with a fixed agenda. |
| | Another manager has different opinion: |
| | Telephone clears lots of things much better than if you contact by mail. Mail I think is not the right medium for high-level discussing requirements or something like that, because you are never clear what the other person understands. |
| **Application Sharing** | Net Meeting and Webex (a Web-based conferencing tool) were often used for meetings between sites and with customers. In particular Webex was convenient: |
| | If you want to talk to a customer, for example, if you want to give a knowledge transfer in something like 1–2 hours, I call a Webex meeting then ask all the parties to log in to that meeting at a given point of time. As a chairman, once you start the meeting and you see people logging in, you can use the telephone for conferencing. Then you start sharing the application or you start sharing the presentation (senior manager). |

*Table 7.3* Collaborative technologies used in Baan – *continued*

| | |
|---|---|
| **Videoconference** | On the one hand, 'videoconferences are fairly heavy in equipment, heavy in the sense that it uses a lot of performance. It needs a fairly big network. You can use a videoconference from point to point' (senior manager). |
| | On the other hand, videoconference was considered important because it allowed people to see each other and see each other's emotions: |
| | To bring everybody in synch, we had many people participating in a telephone conference. But then we realised that we were not able to see each other's emotions, we were taking decisions and sometimes arguments used to be a little bit heated. Heated in the sense that sometimes I don't agree with what they say and vice versa. We were getting too emotional, and it also became a bit of a fight. Then we realised why not use the VC?! We have a centralised videoconference room, one in India, one in Holland. We decided to stop Net Meeting and go for VC. Then we fixed up a lot of videoconferencing, twice to three times a week almost (senior manager). |

## Social ties in GDSD: problems faced

Interviewees reported a number of problems related to social and human aspects. In particular, there was a lack of team atmosphere between teams in Hyderabad and Barneveld: from interviewing members of both teams, tensions between the teams became evident, and teams were not motivated to work together (problem 8). Furthermore, many of the people interviewed did not know in person their remote counterparts: Baan tried to reduce project costs by reducing travel costs, thus reducing the opportunity of remote team members to meet in person.

Problem 8 is discussed below and illustrated by empirical evidence from interviews.

### Problem 8: Tensions between Indian and Dutch groups

We observed and were also told about tensions between the Indian and Dutch groups. The following statements show the tension existing between the groups:

- When *we* gained a lot of knowledge (for example myself: being consultant, I knew the product in and out), *we* realised that *we in India* could take the ownership of the entire product, one module at least, and create everything from scratch. So then *we* really had a huge problem with *Holland* to take ownership. *We* wanted to build a product in India without any influence from Holland, but *they* were not willing to give (manager based in India).

- The major issue is that people don't perceive that on the other side, *they*'re not reciprocating our needs: what *we* want, during which time, what priority *we* have. *They* don't see the same priority as *our* people see, and vice versa. So there is always a gap (manager based in India).

This problem is not unique to GDSD projects: each nation has its own unique characteristics (Hofstede 1993) that may lead to misunderstandings and conflicts between people with different cultural backgrounds involved in a GDSD project, as it happened in the E-Enterprise project.

### Social ties in GDSD: implications for success factors

To learn about the importance of social ties in globally distributed software development we asked interviewees if it was important for them to know personally their remote counterparts; and if so, what had changed after they met face-to-face. All interviewees considered that knowing personally and building relationships with remote counterparts was very important for success. Following are quotations illustrating the importance of rapport and trust, and the importance of face-to-face interaction for creating rapport and trust.

### *Importance of rapport*

*Rapport may reduce the need to travel in the future*

- Talking about his colleague in The Netherlands with whom this product developer worked earlier on Baan ERP:

  We have established such rapport that we don't need to visit each other anymore. Whatever he says I understand, whatever I say he understands. Even when you send a mail, the meaning of the mail, the way the sentences are formed and the meaning out of it is extremely easy to gather.

*Good relationships between individuals may reduce problems between remote sites*

- If the marketing people, Solution Manager or the Product Manager, are on good terms with the development team, the Product Architect and the Consultants, things will go on smoothly. We don't need any process and any rules. But if they're not on good terms, like if a lot of things are changing every time from the Solution Manager, Product Manager, then definitely it will be all this kind of problems. Things are managed built on relations (product developer, India).

### Importance of trust

*Trust (confidence, mutual respect) makes it easier to collaborate over distance (easier to approach somebody, easier to understand, easier to reach an agreement)*

- Asking interviewees at Baan about the importance of knowing their remote colleagues personally, we were told that:

  It [knowing remote colleagues personally] builds the confidence. Confidence in the sense that now I can depend on him, because now we understand each other. Even if I go to him, then whether it is right or wrong, he will give me advice or he will give his opinion. I'm building a confidence in me to go to him. So some kind of a mutual respect comes. Then there is a higher transaction, then you can further collaborate much more easily (product architect).

- Talking about his former counterpart in The Netherlands with whom this solution manager worked in a successful Baan ERP project:

  I got to know more about the person and about the value-system that he has, then I realised what kind of person he is. He can be uncomfortable (he can straightaway say that what you say is absolutely wrong and not acceptable), a little bit harsh, straightforward and direct, but then this is in his nature, that's what I realised. So after that experience it was so good and so pleasant to interact with him, and it just went off so smoothly.

- Regarding relationships with remote colleagues, we were told:

  If your personal relationship is not good, the issue will either die down or it will be just casually taken. If the relation is good, you have mutual interactions, then he might go out of his way. If the confidence and trust are built, he'll stretch himself to a greater extent. That may not happen if that is not there (senior manager).

## *Importance of face-to-face meetings*

*Meeting in person improves understanding between remote counterparts, makes it easier to communicate*, as illustrated by the following quotes:

- After going through face-to-face discussions and started understanding each other I could see a lot of change in the way we deal with things. Issues are still issues, but now the issues are tackled differently. How is he responding to my need and how I am responding to his needs. There is a change. During face-to-face we shared with each other what are the issues and discussed each other's wishes. So some kind of empathising is coming in. Understanding each other. To some extent yes, it helps (product manager).
- Personally I feel meeting the people would help you resolve the tasks more quickly, because you can really think and feel the person when you are actually talking. For example, assume two people, one has never come to India and the other has never gone to Holland. If they are interacting, there would be some gaps. But if they had an interaction at a personal level at some point in time, then the interaction would really be better, the response will be generally quicker (product manager).
- Until you have face-to-face relation, it's very difficult to really judge how that other person is and what techniques I can use for convincing. So it's really important that I know you personally and you know me personally. That is my strong feeling on that. Then you will be successful and we will have an effective communication in place (solution manager).

## Knowledge sharing in GDSD: problems faced

Despite the fact that the E-Enterprise group had been established several years before this research was conducted, the constantly changing organisational structure and ownership of products (discussed in problem 6) resulted in a situation where the majority of team members at dispersed locations were either new or had moved from another group (e.g. the ERP group that worked on a Baan ERP product, very different from E-Enterprise). Thus, team members did not have a history of working together: the majority of them did not know each other and did not know the composition of the dispersed team. Therefore, in Baan transactive memory among dispersed team members was not developed.

Furthermore, team members in The Netherlands and India had different cultural backgrounds in terms of national culture (Dutch and

Indian), and organisational culture (newcomers and people from Baan ERP group), and did not have a common technical background: there was a gap in common understanding of the technology and the processes team members were supposed to follow (problem 9). Moreover, it was reported that often people in the Hyderabad office were not aware of what was happening in the Barneveld office: they were not updated about changes in requirements and dependencies between the products, and not aware of product and technology roadmaps. Consequently, there was no (or very limited) collective knowledge shared between the two dispersed teams in Baan (problem 10).

Problems 9 and 10 are discussed below and illustrated by empirical evidence from interviews.

### Problem 9: Cultural gaps between people in terms of national culture (Indian vs. Dutch) and organisational culture (Baan culture vs. newcomers)

People involved in the E-Enterprise experience two types of cultural differences: in national and organisational cultures. One product manager expressed his opinion on cultural differences:

> In the current scenario there's a lot of gap in the culture. Let me tell you the difference between earlier and now. When we were working in ERP, ERP was understood very well; also the Dutch culture, the Dutch people, because there was continuity in the people, they understood each other very well. But now in E-Enterprise the major difference is because E-Enterprise is a new set of people, even in The Netherlands it's a new set of people. Most of the people have not met face-to-face, except some key people. It is my perspective, I might be wrong, E-Enterprise overall (both The Netherlands and India) is not part of the ERP culture. Especially in E-Enterprise Hyderabad, you find two sets of people, you clearly see the difference when you start interacting.

He explained that people involved in E-Enterprise could be divided into two 'sets of people' who are different in cultural aspects:

1) *People working in Baan for a long time:*

> 'people who have come from an ERP background or worked for 3–4 years on ERP, and moved into E-Enterprise. They appreciate the processes, they understand the issues because they have also

gone through them in the past, they also understand how the Dutch culture is.'

2) *Newcomers:*

> 'people who have come directly from outside and started working on E-Enterprise products. They have not undergone the process of maturity, they have not understood the Baan culture very well. They are not exposed to the Dutch culture, they are not exposed to the ERP processes. [...] What we found is that it is too much to tell them that they need to follow the process, because the people are just dragged from outside in a multi-national company and, provided need to deal with the Dutch culture, they are not digesting.'

### Problem 10: Gaps in understanding products, processes and technology

There were problems related to the understanding of products (requirements and architecture of the E-Enterprise suite and individual products), of development processes, and of technology that the products are based on. The gaps were caused to a great extent by the combination of two factors. First, products, processes and technology were not established and were changing all the time. Second, even what was decided upon and established was often not communicated, and therefore not known to the remote team in Hyderabad.

**Product:** *people were not clear about a roadmap for E-Enterprise and individual products*   For example, one manager from Holland said: 'in some cases when the product belongs to The Netherlands, we want to know what exactly they are looking ahead: we want to know what exactly they're doing, what is their approach, how they are going about it'.

One manager from India said that, according to the M&A group, there is a product roadmap. He gave very strong opinion about this existing roadmap:

> It is very vague in terms of what exactly it should contain, this they don't say. Maybe the product roadmap is saying that this year, or this quarter we will be delivering a new product, but it is not clearly specifying exactly what will be the requirements, it is very vague. It [the product roadmap] is there just for the name's sake, just for the profit of it. What it means is that M&A have returned a roadmap

just because someone said that they should have it, not because it is their responsibility or it is the result of something.

Another manager from India suggested that because the vision of the product was not defined, requirements were not clear and were changing all the time.

The vast majority of interviewees said that often product requirements were not clear. One reason that interviewees gave to explain why requirements are not clear was: because for some products a Product Manager who provides the development team with product requirements is at a remote location. As one manager put it:

> We had a Product Manager who was our boss at that time, he was sitting in The Netherlands and there was a lot of time gap: he will send the requirements, we will try to understand it, there were a lot of email exchanges, telephone calls, what exactly he wants or the way we think. It causes problems – if we are not sitting in one location it is a big problem.

Another manager from India expressed similar opinion:

> We started thinking now that Product Managers should be in a place where the development takes place. We find it more logical if these people are here [in Hyderabad], that is from the experience we have seen, because then communication goes very well.

*Technology: new technology was not established, people were not clear about the technology roadmap for E-Enterprise*   As one product developer from India explained:

> Our suite of products in the E-Enterprise is a fast-changing scene. In the case of E-Enterprise, where we work with Microsoft technology right now, probably we move to another technology, but I don't know, it depends on some kind of feasibility study being conducted now. Microsoft itself is changing its platform from time to time: you can see it might be as frequent as 3–4 years. First of all your technological basis is changing, probably changing for better, but we have to adapt to the changing scenarios there. So obviously we can't have a roadmap that would stretch for more than 1–1½ years.

***Processes:*** *gap in common understanding of processes and resistance to following them*   A process manager explained:

> The processes are not really defined well, so still you find some gaps in having a common understanding on the processes. Slowly, slowly that is getting reduced, but still I can see an issue over that.

Furthermore, there was internal resistance to following the processes, in particular among newcomers. He continued:

> Whenever we start on a project, we will say that these are the processes which we need to follow. But still we find some people are not very keen, they think that 'what advantage do we get if we follow this process?' So some kind of a one-to-one counselling or coaching takes place. It's a slow process. We have to tell them that they have to follow the processes, but even if they follow the processes, the effectiveness will not be there. So I strongly believe the person himself has to be aware, rather than pushed.

Problems 9 and 10 discussed above are unique to GDSD projects: people from different countries experience differences in national and, sometimes, organisational cultures, and often they have different technical backgrounds. Moreover, breakdowns in coordination between globally distributed teams lead to gaps in common understanding of products, processes and technology between dispersed team members.

### Knowledge sharing in GDSD: implications for success factors

Interviewees considered that knowledge sharing is important for success, as the following quotes illustrate:

#### *Common knowledge of an architecture/product is required*

- We have an existing architecture and we need to build future products based on this architecture, so understanding the existing architecture is most important in that case, to be able to build on top of it (product architecture).
- We have completed our realisation from our side and E-Enterprise Server has also completed their realisation. But now we need to integrate these two: E-Enterprise Server to our applications. So for that we need a lot of knowledge of that product, E-Enterprise Server 2.5 (product manager).

### Common understanding between key people is necessary

- I think one of the important features in a collaborative framework is the understanding between the key people, the main stakeholders who are architects and consultants and probably lead engineers. If you are working on a distributed ownership, you need that the key software engineers know each other and understand each other. That really helps (product developer).

### Common knowledge about culture is needed

- Common knowledge includes understanding of a culture. For example, the Process Manager for Baan Hyderabad explained that understanding of cultural differences helps to define better processes that would be acceptable for Dutch and Indian cultures:

   When we write the process plan there are a lot of cultural issues that come into the picture. How to deal with this particular area? I can give you an example on quality assurance – a critical area. In the Indian culture, quality assurance is an important topic – people don't mind someone checking the work they do, but if you compare with our counterpart: in The Netherlands sometimes people don't like this. Because the counterpart The Netherlands team have a different culture – individualistic. So there will be some resistance on that front sometimes. Once we understand this and appreciate the cultural factors, then we can define that better plan.

## Possible impact of the adoption of CBD on the success of the E-Enterprise project: discussion

Taking into account that E-Enterprise was not CB, the question arises: **would adoption of CBD help to avoid the problems experienced by the E-Enterprise group?**

In our opinion some of the problems discussed above could have been avoided if E-Enterprise (the products comprising it) had had a CB structure. The possible impact of the adoption of CBD on the success of E-Enterprise project is discussed in Table 7.4.

It follows from Table 7.4 that it is likely that the adoption of CBD could have helped to avoid some of the problems discussed above, in particular problems caused by the existence of dependencies between

*Table 7.4*   Would adoption of CBD help to avoid the problems: Discussion

| Problem | Would adoption of CBD help to avoid the problem? |
| --- | --- |
| 1. No clear product/ project ownership | **Probably not,** because there would still be a need to understand a product developed by another team. |
| 2. Too many people involved in management of each product in different roles, some of which are overlapping | **Probably not,** because management would still be confusing. |
| 3. Dependency of all products on the common platform (E-Enterprise Server) and dependencies between products | **Probably yes** <br> Technical dependencies between products would be reduced to (standard) interfaces between (business) components (if each product is treated as a business component). This would reduce the problem of synchronising specifications/ requirements. However if some functionality is missed out and not included in any product, the problem of lacking component(s) can appear. This means that there would still be a need for synchronisation of requirements but on a conceptual (not very detailed) level. <br> However, CBD also requires careful management of technical dependencies (e.g. as in the LeCroy case), in particular in a globally distributed environment. <br> Knowledge and information dependencies will be reduced. |
| 4. Very detailed planning (2–20 hours tasks) and fast changing situation do not work together | **Probably yes** <br> Planning can become simpler if done per business component. |
| 5. The requirements stage is not clear and requirements are not frozen | **Probably not,** as long as the requirements stage is not clearly defined. Furthermore, if requirements are not frozen, they would influence the functional requirements for each component. |
| 6. Too many changes in many aspect of organisation and project | **Probably not,** if organisational structure, people and ownership are still changing. |
| 7. Lack of compatibility between versions of different products | **YES** <br> If interfaces are standard and not changing, it would be easier to maintain compatibility between versions of different products. |

*Table 7.4*   Would adoption of CBD help to avoid the problems: Discussion –
*continued*

| Problem | Would adoption of CBD help to avoid the problem? |
| --- | --- |
| 8. Tensions between Indian and Dutch groups | **Probably yes, to some extent**<br>To a great extent tensions are caused by dependencies between products developed in different countries (e.g. E-Enterprise Server not being released on time, lack of information and knowledge about dependencies). Thus, reducing these dependencies, possibly, would reduce tensions between the two groups (however it also depends on division of work, e.g. if teams are given full ownership or not). |
| 9. Cultural gaps between people in terms of national culture (Indian vs. Dutch) and organisational culture (Baan culture vs. newcomers) | **Maybe yes, to some extent**<br>Possibly, adoption of CBD would introduce a new (CB) culture to the organisation.<br>Thus, differences in organisational culture would be reduced as everybody would be at the same level (new) in this new CB culture (as opposed to the current ERP culture vs. non ERP culture). |
| 10. Gaps in understanding products, processes and technology | **Probably yes, to some extent**<br>CBD methodology includes component technologies and processes. Therefore, adoption of CBD (specific component technology and related processes) would give some clarity to the group regarding processes and technology. However it would not give clarity regarding products that need to be developed, if the marketing team does not clarify it. |

products developed at remote locations: i.e it would have been easier to coordinate and control these dependencies, and tensions between remote groups would have been reduced.

For example, one development manager in India explained the difficulties his group was facing because of the current (non-CB) software architecture. He also mentioned the advantages they would have had if the software architecture had been CB:

> Originally, when we planned these products [E-Procurement and E-Sourcing], we didn't have a full view of how the products should

be and how they have to grow. So as the products have been designed, they are not very componentised, not modularised. When we started adding features, we didn't think about a lot of complexities intervening, so we didn't think about modularising at that point. Things started growing, the core started growing and it became really huge. Now we feel that we should have narrowed it down. So for both products we have the same issue – modularisation.

To improve the product technically we need to change some of the architecture in order to modularise it. Then it will become easy for us to maintain it in the future: instead of modifying a big, huge program, it's easy to handle modules. We could change the modules very easily, and the impact of that component [E-Enterprise Server] on other parts would also be very much lower.

## Conclusions

In this chapter, the E-Enterprise project was analysed and discussed in the light of potential factors contributing to success suggested in the theoretical lens.

First, the problems faced by the globally distributed E-Enterprise group at Baan were presented and illustrated by empirical evidence from interviews. These problems, reported in March 2002, gave an indication of unsuccessful collaboration in the E-Enterprise project. Based on these findings we suggest that the problems faced by the globally distributed E-Enterprise group at Baan might have had an influence on the failure of Baan to develop software in a globally distributed environment.

Furthermore, critical success factors considered by interviewees as important to make a globally distributed development successful were assessed. Some of these success factors were mentioned because they were lacking in the E-Enterprise project, and other factors were mentioned based on the experience interviewees had had in other globally distributed projects of Baan that were successful. Interviewees considered four factors suggested in the theoretical lens as contributing to success in GDSD.

In terms of managerial practices, *coordination* between India and Hyderabad was not efficient: first, division of work between the two sites was not efficient; second, there was lack of communications between the team in The Netherlands and India; third, often people in the Hyderabad office were not aware of plans and changes in products and technology originated by the Barneveld office; fourth, project management techniques adopted by the E-Enterprise group were not efficient.

In relation to *appropriate tools and technologies,* Baan tried to standardise development methods and processes across locations. There was an attempt to have a central requirements database: however, requirements were changing so quickly that the database was not up to date. Code was synchronised via synchronisation of databases at two locations.

Regarding *social ties,* Baan did not have managerial practices aiming to build up social ties between dispersed team members. As a result, there was a lack of team atmosphere between teams in Hyderabad and Barneveld. Furthermore, many of the people interviewed did not know in person their remote counterparts: Baan tried to reduce project costs by reducing travel costs, thus reducing the opportunity of remote team members to meet in person.

Concerning *knowledge sharing,* in the E-Enterprise group, there was lack of managerial practices aimed to develop transactive memory and extend collective knowledge of dispersed team members. Moreover, there was no managerial practice in place that would aim to educate dispersed team members in new technologies. As a result, there was a gap in common understanding between dispersed team members of the technology and the processes they were supposed to follow.

In terms of software architecture the E-Enterprise suite was not designed to support reuse. On the contrary, versions of products included in the E-Enterprise suite were not compatible (as described in problem 7), thus creating obstacles to reusing them in new releases.

The E-Enterprise suite and products included in it were developed in an atmosphere of continuous change of technologies and requirements.

---

The results of this case study show that the interviewees considered four factors suggested in the theoretical lens as contributing to success in GDSD.

It is important to note that out of four potential success factors identified in the theoretical lens, only one – *tools and technologies* – was present at the studied E-Enterprise project. The other three – *inter-site coordination, social ties* and *knowledge sharing* – were lacking. This leads to the question: *is technology alone enough to succeed in a globally distributed environment? Probably not, as we can learn from the unsuccessful Baan E-Enterprise case.*

Development of the E-Enterprise suite at Baan was undertaken without proper investigation of the available technologies and generic products' requirements. As a result, technologies, requirements and interdependencies between the products included in the suite and their versions were constantly changing, thus reducing the efficiency and effectiveness of the ongoing development project. It is possible that adoption of CBD would help to avoid some of the problems experienced by the E-Enterprise group.

# Part III

# Component-Based Development in Global Teams: Learnt Lessons

# 8
# What Can Be Learnt From These Cases?

## Similarities and differences between the studied cases

In many ways the projects we studied are similar. Firstly, three out of the four cases (LeCroy, SAP and TCS) comply with the two criteria that we set up for this research, namely:

(1) CBD projects are globally distributed between at least two locations of a single organisation;
(2) The projects are successful.

Baan case serves as a counter-case to compare successful managerial practices with managerial practices that were lacking in the unsuccessful Baan case.

We can also say that all four projects satisfy our secondary requirements:

(a) The projects were concerned with new product development. They were interested in long-term collaboration (as opposed to one-time outsourcing projects);
(b) The overall sizes of the project teams were comparable (25–35 people).

However, there are some differences between the four studied cases, mainly contextual, such as the different countries involved and, consequently, different cultures and different time-zone differences; different types (and granularity) of components; and different histories (number of years) of the remote teams working together. These differences could explain the differences in results across the cases. We bring these similarities and differences together in Table 8.1.

*Table 8.1* Similarities and differences between the studied cases

| | LeCroy | SAP | TCS | Baan |
|---|---|---|---|---|
| **Distribution between continents** (countries and locations) | **Europe-USA** Switzerland (Geneva) and USA (NY and Maine) | **India-Europe-USA** India (Bangalore), Germany (Walldorf) and USA (Palo Alto) | **India-Europe-USA** India (Gurgaon and Bombay), Switzerland (Zurich) and USA (San Francisco) | **India-Europe** India (Hyderabad) and The Netherlands (Barneveld) |
| **Cultures** | **American and Swiss** to a great extent: both teams have multiple nationalities | **Indian, German and American** to a great extent: the team in Palo Alto has multiple nationalities | **Indian** – all team members are Indian | **Indian and Dutch** |
| **Time-zone differences** | **6 hours** between Geneva and USA East coast (NY and Maine) | **3½–13½ hours** 3½–4½ hours between Bangalore and Walldorf (summer–winter) 9 hours between Walldorf and Palo Alto 12½–13½ hours between Bangalore and Palo Alto | **3½–13½ hours** 3½–4½ hours between India (Gurgaon and Bombay) and Zurich 12½–13½ hours between India and San Francisco | **3½–4½ hours** between Hyderabad and Barneveld (summer–winter) |
| **Project duration and Stage of project** (at the time when last interviews were taken) | **4.5 years Final stage** Two weeks before release of the first version of the product | **10 months Final stage** A few weeks before release of the second version of the product | **1½ years** (Skandia) **8 months** (Dresdner) **Both final stage** A few weeks before release of the first version of the product (before 'going live') | **3+ years Close to completion** A few months before release of a new version of (some modules of) the product |

*Table 8.1* Similarities and differences between the studied cases – *continued*

| | LeCroy | SAP | TCS | Baan |
|---|---|---|---|---|
| **History of collaboration between remote teams** (before the studied project) | **15 years** From mid 80s teams in NY and Geneva worked closely together, team members know each other and have long history of collaboration | **No history** Teams were merged into one group for the Collaborative tools project, team members never worked together before | **2–3 years** Most team members worked together in India on development of Quartz and knew each other before the project started | **Very limited history** Most team members never worked together before: some of them were new, the others were moved from other groups/projects |
| **Project type** | **New product development**, for large market of potential customers | **New product development**, for a large market of potential customers | **New product development and implementation**, for a specific customer | **New product development**, for a large market of potential customers |
| **Intended duration of collaboration** | **Long-term collaboration** between teams in Geneva and NY | **Long-term collaboration** between teams in Walldorf, Bangalore and Palo Alto | **Long-term collaboration** between people on future implementations of Quartz, team members can be rotated between different projects | **Long-term collaboration** between teams in Hyderabad and Barneveld |
| **Type of components in the product** (and granularity) | **Technical components** Fine-grained | **Technical components** Fine-grained | **Business components** Large-grained | **N/A** business modules that are interdependent (as opposed to components that are independent) |

## Managerial practices important for success in GD CBD

In total 22 managerial practices are important for GD CBD. They spread across the five areas identified in this book and contribute to the success of teams in various ways. Some managerial practices were more dominant than others in supporting success; however, our view is that each of these practices is needed in order to improve coordination, knowledge sharing,

*Table 8.2*  Managerial practices: comparison of results across cases

| Managerial practices | LeCroy | SAP | TCS | Baan |
|---|---|---|---|---|
| **I) Inter-site coordination** | | | | |
| 1 Increasing awareness | + | + | + | –/need |
| 2 Making efficient division of work | + | + | + | –/need |
| 3 Enabling working flexibility | + | + | + | |
| 4 Facilitating tracking of bugs and development tasks | + | | + | |
| 5 Enabling flexible PM techniques | + | + | + | – |
| 6 Designing systematic communications | + | + | + | –/need |
| **II) Appropriate tools and technologies** | | | | |
| 7 Software Development tools | + | + | + | + |
| 8 ICT infrastructure | + | + | + | + |
| 9 Collaborative technology | + | + | + | + |
| **III) Social ties** | | | | |
| 10 Building relationships | + | + | + | –/need |
| 11 Increasing reachability | + | | + | |
| 12 Creating and maintaining team atmosphere | + | + | + | –/need |
| 13 Facilitating interactions | + | + | + | –/need |
| 14 Facilitating cross-pollination | + | + | | – |
| **IV) Knowledge sharing** | | | | |
| 15 Creating transactive memory among team members | + | + | + | –/need |
| 16 Expanding collective knowledge of dispersed team | + | + | + | –/need |
| 17 Managing 'by intuition' | | + | | |
| 18 Learning new technology | + | | + | –/need |
| **V) Components management** | | | | |
| 19 Designing for reuse | + | | + | –/need |
| 20 Investing in 'advanced development' | + | | + | – |
| 21 Facilitating reuse | | + | + | – |
| 22 Managing vendors | N/A | N/A | + | N/A |

'+' – indicated as important, '–' – lacking, '–/need' – lacking but mentioned as needed, 'NA' – not applicable

social aspects, the use of appropriate tools and the management of components. These managerial practices are listed in Table 8.2 and their contribution to success is indicated per each firm studied. On the other hand, the Baan case, which serves as a counter-case, is providing an opportunity to assess which managerial practices were missing and how they could negatively affect the success of globally distributed teams. We discuss each managerial practice in detail in the following sections.

### (I) Inter-site coordination in GD CBD: managerial practices

The following is a comparison across the four cases of managerial practices that deal with inter-site coordination in GD CBD.

### 1. *Increasing awareness*

Increasing awareness of *what is going on in the company and the project* was identified in the three successful case studies. It is particularly important for offshore locations, which are Geneva for LeCroy, Bangalore and Palo Alto for SAP, and Gurgaon, San Francisco and Bombay for TCS. As one manager from SAP explained: 'Staying here [in Bangalore], often we lose out a lot of information, because people don't have time to write every small information in a mail and send it across, or they just forget'.

Furthermore, increasing awareness of the *remote team members* was important in SAP because teams in India, USA and Germany had not worked together before, and many of the team members were not familiar with the culture of their counterparts. In LeCroy and TCS, increasing awareness of remote team members was less important, because the majority of the remote team members knew each other and had worked together either in a co-located environment (in TCS, while developing Quartz) or over distance (in LeCroy).

Moreover in the three successful cases the importance of increasing awareness of *the environment at a remote site* was identified; it helps to visualise what is happening when a problem occurs and to understand how to solve the problem.

The significance of this practice can be further underlined by the results from the Baan case, where the team members in Hyderabad office reported about lack of awareness of products, processes and technology as one of the main problems in the E-Enterprise project.

Based on the research findings the following proposition can be formulated:

> **P1:** *Increasing awareness of what is going on at dispersed locations and about remote team(s) will reduce the possibility of misunderstanding, conflicts and coordination breakdowns.*

This proposition is relevant for CB and also for traditional GDSD projects. With regard to CB projects, this proposition suggests that, despite the expectations that the adoption of CBD in globally distributed projects will allow remote teams to work more independently, in GD CBD projects the efficiency of dispersed teams is likely to be greater in the teams which are aware of what their remote counterparts are doing, than in the teams that work independently.

### 2. Making efficient division of work

Interviewees in the three successful projects indicated the importance of efficient division of work for success. The strategies to divide work that managers follow differ somewhat between the projects studied, in particular:

(i) In SAP, the *work is divided feature-wise, providing full ownership and responsibility for each team*: i.e. each of the four teams has full responsibility for an entire block of functionality. There are two reasons why SAP gives full ownership to each of the remote teams. First, because the Collaborative tools were developed from scratch: when the project started, teams did not have knowledge about the product. Second, because teams had just merged, they did not have a history of working together. Thus, giving full ownership to each of the remote teams reduced dependencies and therefore, the need for coordination between the teams.

Different from the SAP case, in LeCroy and TCS, team members had worked together before, and expertise in different areas of the product was already developed. Therefore, in LeCroy and TCS, work is divided according to *where technical or functional expertise is located*. In TCS the expertise is usually at the main development centre in Gurgaon: thus, a main strategy that TCS follows to divide work is to do maximum work offshore and minimise work onsite.

(ii) In SAP and TCS, there is a *division of technical and 'social' responsibilities* that includes establishing reporting channels across the globe.

In SAP and TCS, local development managers (in TCS referred to as on-site and offshore managers) are responsible for the division of specific assignments (tasks) between team members and resolving social issues, because they are aware of the local context and circumstances of the team members. In SAP, the second reason to give 'social' responsibilities to local managers is because they belong to the same culture as team members, which makes it easier for them to understand and deal with team members.

Technical responsibilities in SAP and TCS are centralised in the main development centre (Walldorf for SAP and Gurgaon for TCS):

- In SAP, design of the overall product architecture and quality of the product are centralised in headquarters (Walldorf): two architects located in Walldorf provide technical supervision to teams in Bangalore and Palo Alto.
- In TCS, the offshore team in Gurgaon has technical responsibilities. This team provides technical support for the onsite team that is responsible for implementation of Quartz. This is in line with the main strategy of TCS to do maximum work offshore.

In LeCroy, the product architects of the Geneva and NY teams combine both technical and 'social' responsibilities; they work closely together (and with the architect in Maine) developing and coordinating the overall product architecture between Geneva, NY and Maine. The reason that in LeCroy there is no need to divide technical and 'social' responsibilities might be because product architects have worked together for more than 15 years, and each of them visit the remote locations 5–6 times a year. Therefore they can work closely and coordinate the development successfully without a need to centralise technical responsibilities at one location.

(iii) Furthermore, the importance of *role continuity and ownership of work* was emphasised by interviewees from TCS and SAP. In SAP, for example, teams at dispersed locations have full ownership of a product functionality they are expected to deliver. In TCS, although a project is transferred between onsite and offshore locations, ownership of the work packages stays with the same team: team members are transferred between onsite and offshore locations together with the work packages (components) they are working on. LeCroy also support role continuity and ownership of work packages despite physical location: for example, similarly to the TCS approach, one product developer continued working on the same functional area of Maui from NY where he was relocated for one year, as he had worked in Geneva.

The importance of role continuity and ownership of work packages can be further underlined by the example of the unsuccessful E-Enterprise project of Baan, where ownership of work packages was continuously changing between teams in The Netherlands and India, which was identified by interviewees from Baan as one of the major problems in the studied project.

The findings of this research lead to the following proposition:

> **P2:** *If globally distributed teams have tightened relationships and experience of working together, then a skills-based division of work between dispersed team members will be positively related to project outcomes to a greater extent than a division of work by product feature.* (Skill-based division of work can be based on technical or functional/domain skills).

Proposition P2 is unique to GD CBD projects. It will not be relevant for traditional GDSD projects, where a skilled-based division of work will create a great deal of dependencies on the source-code level that will need to be managed over distance; while in GD CBD the dependencies will be limited to interfaces between components and service components.

> **P3:** *Changing ownership of a module / component between dispersed teams throughout the project will be negatively related to the product success and to the motivation of dispersed team members to collaborate (work together) in the future.*

According to the proposition P3, the more the ownership of a module/component is shifted between dispersed teams during a product life cycle, the higher the chances of losing sight of or misunderstanding the original product requirements: (i.e. each switch in the ownership of development is a potential risk for missing out some information and/or misunderstanding product requirements).

In the first place, proposition P3 is relevant in the case of traditional GDSD as it is based on a comparison of findings between the three CB cases and one non-CB case (Baan). It might be that in CB projects changing process or component ownership throughout the project will have less severe impact on success than in traditional GDSD projects. This leads to the following proposition:

> **P3a:** *Changing ownership of work packages between dispersed teams throughout the project will be negatively related to the product success and to the motivation of dispersed team members to collaborate to a greater extent in traditional GDSD, than in CB projects.*

### 3. Enabling working flexibility

The interviewees from the LeCroy, SAP and TCS projects suggested that working flexibility, in terms of (i) providing flexible working conditions, e.g. working from home, and (ii) flexible working hours, is important for success. Flexible working hours help to increase the overlap in working hours between locations so that teams can collaborate in real time:

- in LeCroy: early start in NY and late start in Geneva
- in SAP: early start in Walldorf and late start in Bangalore
- in TCS: early start in Zurich and late start in Gurgaon.

Interviewees from Baan did not mention working flexibility as important for success; however, we do not have evidence that would indicate a lack of this practice in Baan.

### 4. Facilitating tracking of bugs and development tasks

*Tracking development tasks*

- In LeCroy and TCS the need to track development tasks was mentioned for specific, critical tasks that need to be completed quickly (e.g. for tasks on which onsite and offshore teams work around-the-clock by sending them back and forth, as was described in the Dresdner project of TCS).
- In SAP the tracking of development tasks is done within local teams. The overall system functionality is managed by technical architects from Walldorf.

*Tracking and tracing of bugs*

- In LeCroy and TCS the tracking and tracing of bugs is particularly important, because for each single bug being reported, several aspects need to be managed, such as:
  o the source of the bug needs to be tracked: it can have originated from one of the customers, or from an internal development team;
  o all components in which code that contains the bug is reused need to be traced, because a bug reported in one product needs to be fixed in all other products that reuse the same code/component.
- Interviewees at SAP did not mention a need for tracking bugs. The interviewees said that bug fixing can be passed from one time-zone

to another time-zone, but did not mention the need for specific mechanisms and/or tools for bug tracking.

Interviewees from Baan did not mention the need to track bugs and development tasks as important for success; however, we do not have evidence that would indicate a lack of this practice in Baan.

### 5. Enabling flexible Project Management (PM) techniques

Interviewees from LeCroy, SAP and TCS pointed out that flexible PM techniques are important in large-scale new product development projects, such as the ones investigated in this research. Flexible PM techniques help to accommodate everyday dynamics, and include:

- On a macro level: planning of major project phases (in SAP this included setting up clear objectives for each team; in LeCroy and TCS, teams work jointly on the same objective).

- On a micro level: flexible and not too detailed planning (2–3 week milestones).

The significance of this practice can be further underlined by the evidence from the Baan case, in which very detailed planning (down to 2–20 hour tasks) could not accommodate the everyday dynamics, which reduced the efficiency of the development and increased bureaucracy, because project leaders were busy, nearly full-time, updating plans and reports, and developers were busy reporting on the work-hours put into tasks.

These finding lead to the following propositions, which are complementary:

> **P4a:** *Flexible and not too detailed planning on a micro level by weekly milestones will accommodate everyday dynamics and will allow control to a greater extent than too detailed planning of hourly or daily tasks.*

> **P4b:** *Planning of major project phases with clear objectives for each dispersed team will be positively related to success in the delivery of project objectives.*

The propositions P4a and P4b are relevant for CB and also traditional GDSD projects.

## 6. Designing systematic communications

Interviewees from all four companies mentioned the importance of systematic communications for success. However, only in the three successful cases was this practice in place, and in the Baan case this practice was lacking: interviewees from Baan reported problems caused by a lack of communications between key people.

This practice includes organising frequent communications and designing rules aiming to make communications more effective, in particular:

(i)   Scheduling systematic and frequent communications, such as regular teleconferences between software managers in dispersed locations; transatlantic videoconferences with all team members every one or two months (mentioned as important by interviewees from all four companies, but lacking in the Baan case).

(ii)  Communicating directly to reach an appropriate person. i.e. no hierarchy in communications (mentioned as important by interviewees from the three successful cases).

(iii) Improving the style and content of communications, which helps to reduce the misunderstandings and confusions that typically happen as a result of different cultural backgrounds. Therefore, improving style and content of communications were considered very important in the LeCroy and SAP cases, where people from different cultures collaborate over distance. In TCS it was not important, as all team members are originally from India and have the same cultural background.

The significance of this practice can be further underlined by observations from the Baan case, in which a lack of communications caused difficulties in the understanding of dependencies between products and plans. Interviewees from Baan stressed the importance of this practice for success.

Based on the research findings the following proposition is formulated:

---

**P5:** *When/If people with different national culture backgrounds collaborate over distance, paying attention to the style and content of communications, agreeing on rules regarding the style and frequency of communications, will reduce the possibility of misunderstandings and conflicts, and will be positively related to the effectiveness of dispersed communications and to personal satisfaction.*

---

This proposition is relevant for CB and also for traditional GDSD projects.

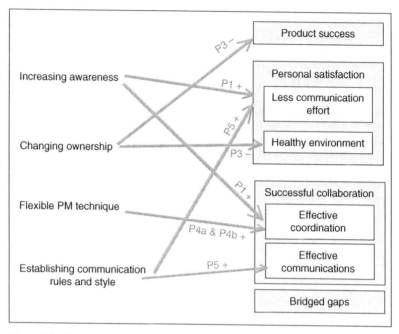

*Figure 8.1*  Inter-site coordination: Propositions

Figure 8.1 illustrates the relationships between propositions associated with inter-site coordination and the categories of success.

### (II)  Appropriate tools and technologies in GD CBD: managerial practices

Following is a comparison across the four cases of managerial practices related to tools and technologies that are important in GD CBD.

### 7.  Software Development (SD) tools

In order to support CBD in a globally distributed environment SD tools need to provide capabilities described in Table 8.3, which compares the results of the four projects studied ('+'- indicated as important, 'N/M' – not mentioned, 'N/A' – not applicable).

*Table 8.3* Capabilities of SD tools: Comparison of results across cases

| Capabilities of SD tools | LeCroy | SAP | TCS | Baan |
|---|---|---|---|---|
| **Automated management of interdependencies between components and related files**<br>– supports rapid update of changes by automatically (four times a day) building components that have changed, thus enables the utilisation of time-zone differences (LeCroy). | + | N/M | N/M | N/A |
| **Automated testing of components** | + | N/M | + | N/A |
| **Standardisation of the tools and methods across locations**<br>– using similar tools and methods across locations (LeCroy, SAP, TCS)<br>– replicated development environment of a customer at offshore site (TCS)<br>– in Baan there was an attempt to standardise development methods and processes across locations | + | + | + | + |
| **Centralisation of tools**<br>– Web access (LeCroy, SAP)<br>– replicated databases (LeCroy, Baan)<br>– single development environment (LeCroy and SAP)<br>– central repository (LeCroy, TCS)<br>– in Baan there was an attempt to have a central requirements database | + | + | + | + |
| **Creating a Guide that explains how to use tools and methods**<br>– documentation about standard tools and methods available on SAPNet (SAP) | + | + | N/M | N/M |
| **Developing tools in-house** | + | N/M | + | N/M |

Results reported in this research lead to the following proposition:

**P6**: *Standardisations of tools across locations and centralisations of tools in a single development platform/environment will be positively related to greater reuse rate (number of components being reused across different projects/products).*

This proposition is unique to GD CBD.

## 8. ICT infrastructure

Interviewees from the three successful cases suggested that a reliable and high bandwidth ICT infrastructure is required to ensure connectivity between remote sites and make coordination between sites more effective and efficient. For example, the vice president of information systems at LeCroy outlined:

> The role of the WAN, server and applications pool, how file shares are set up, conferencing tools, and just plain network speed are of very high importance [...] and no firm trying to execute GD CBD successfully can do so without the right infrastructure.

Furthermore, appropriate ICT infrastructure needs to support security requirements:

> Security is paramount these days, and the internet (plus Microsoft issues) have raised it to a top tier concern. The correct choice of technologies, correct placement of firewalls, correct balance of 'locks', 'police', and 'public awareness' is essential to reduce security risks, while not snuffing out collaboration.

Interviewees from Baan did not mention the importance of the ICT infrastructure, but from our observations (during video- and tele-conferences we attended) we assume that the ICT infrastructure was sufficient to

*Table 8.4*   Requirement for ICT infrastructure: Comparison of results across cases

| Requirements for ICT infrastructure | LeCroy | SAP | TCS | Baan |
|---|---|---|---|---|
| **Quick access to the network** | + | + | + | N/M |
| **Shared resources**<br>– shared databases (LeCroy)<br>– shared server and project repository (SAP, TCS) | + | + | + | N/M |
| **Web access**<br>– constant replication of databases over the Web (LeCroy)<br>– centralised access to tools over the Web (SAP) | + | + | – | N/M |
| **Quick and easy connectivity across locations**<br>– use collaborative tools (all four cases)<br>– e.g. dial 5-digit number across the globe (SAP) | + | + | + | + |

provide appropriate connectivity between dispersed locations. Table 8.4 illustrates the requirement for ICT infrastructure and compares the results of the four cases ('+'- indicated as important, '–' – lacking, 'N/M' – not mentioned, 'N/A' – not applicable).

Based on the results of this research, the following proposition can be formulated:

> **P7:** *If the ICT infrastructure provides identical ICT facilities (i.e. similar network speed, server, applications) for teams at dispersed locations as for co-located teams, then the ability of a dispersed team to collaborate effectively and efficiently and the success of project outcomes will be greater, than if the ICT infrastructure provides fewer facilities to dispersed teams than to co-located ones.*

This proposition is relevant for CB and also traditional GDSD projects.

### 9. Collaborative technology

In all four case studies remote team members used collaborative technology extensively. Table 8.5 illustrates the collaborative technologies that are important for collaboration between remote teams and compares the results of the four cases ('+'- indicated as important, 'N/M' – not mentioned, 'N/U' – not used):

*Table 8.5*   Collaborative technologies: Comparison of results across cases

| Collaborative technologies | LeCroy | SAP | TCS | Baan |
|---|---|---|---|---|
| **Online chat**<br>– short and/or urgent questions (LeCroy)<br>– in Baan online chat is available for Hyderabad group, but it is not used to communicate with the remote team in The Netherlands<br>– in SAP remote teams do not use online chat; furthermore, need for online chat was not mentioned in SAP | + | N/U | N/M | N/U |
| **Phone and teleconferencing**<br>– urgent matters (all four cases)<br>– update between managers (all four cases)<br>– resolve misunderstandings and conflicts (all four cases)<br>– help in bug fixing (LeCroy) | + | + | + | + |

*Table 8.5*   Collaborative technologies: Comparison of results across cases
– *continued*

| Collaborative technologies | LeCroy | SAP | TCS | Baan |
|---|---|---|---|---|
| **Application Sharing**<br>– help in fixing bugs (e.g. show conditions of failure (LeCroy, SAP, TCS)<br>– knowledge sharing (e.g. show slides) (LeCroy, SAP, Baan) | + | + | + | + |
| **Videoconference**<br>– progress meetings between managers (LeCroy, SAP, Baan)<br>– major design reviews (SAP) | + | + | N/M | + |
| **Email**<br>– low priority tasks (all four cases)<br>– sending source code for small changes (TCS)<br>– sending requirements (Baan)<br>– clarifications (all four cases) | + | + | + | + |
| **Intranet**<br>– post internal documents (LeCroy, SAP, TCS) | + | + | + | N/M |

Results reported in this research lead to the following propositions:

**P8:** *Providing a wide range of collaborative technologies for members of globally dispersed teams is more likely to increase the effectiveness of communications and personal satisfaction than imposing specific types of collaborative technologies to be used.*

**P9:** *Teams/team members who have rapport already developed will use online chat to communicate more often than teams/team members that do not have such rapport.*

These propositions are relevant for CB and also traditional GDSD projects.

Figure 8.2 illustrates the relationships between propositions associated with tools and technologies and the categories of success.

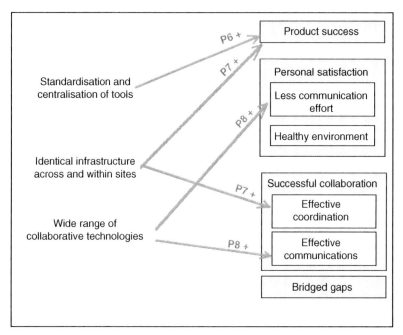

*Figure 8.2*   Appropriate tools and technologies: Propositions

## (III)  Social ties in GD CBD: managerial practices

Interviewees from all companies indicated the contribution of trust and rapport to success. In LeCroy and TCS, trust and rapport between remote counterparts were developed to some extent because (i) at LeCroy the software team has a long history of collaborating over distance, and (ii) at TCS the majority of team members have worked together in a co-located environments on the development of Quartz and knew each other before re-locating to onsite locations (customer sites in Zurich and San Francisco). However, in SAP three teams were merged into one group in the beginning of the project studied, and they had to build trust and rapport from scratch.

In the E-Enterprise project of the Baan, the majority of team members in Hyderabad and Barneveld did not know each other; thus, similar to the SAP teams, they had to build up rapport and trust from scratch. However, in contrast to SAP, who invested in building up social ties, in the Baan case the importance of social ties was ignored, which, in turn, led to problems and tensions between teams caused by lack of rapport and trust. These results from the Baan case further underline the significance of social ties in globally distributed teams.

Interviewees from the unsuccessful Baan case emphasised the importance of rapport and trust for success, basing their arguments mainly on their experience in earlier, successful projects, and problems caused by lack of rapport and trust between remote counterparts involved in the E-Enterprise project.

Following is a comparison across the four cases of managerial practices suggested to develop social ties between remote counterparts.

### 10.  Building relationships

Building relationships involves building rapport and trust between remote team members: it was considered very important for success in all four cases. Interviewees indicated that the best way to build relationships is to meet face-to-face. In LeCroy and SAP, team-building exercises were organised to give developers and key players an opportunity to meet in person in an informal environment. In TCS, the majority of team members had met in person on different occasions (e.g. earlier projects, training).

This practice was lacking in the Baan case; however, interviewees from Baan stressed the importance of building relationships between remote counterparts for success, which further emphasises the significance of this practice.

### 11.  Increasing reachability

The importance of increasing reachability was identified by interviewees at LeCroy and TCS: in particular, (i) knowing whom to contact (in LeCroy and TCS), and (ii) knowing who is available on the given day and time (in LeCroy).

Knowing whom to contact is related to the transactive memory of a dispersed team, because when team members know areas of expertise of their remote counterparts, they will know whom to contact.

Interviewees from TCS suggested that because Quartz team members can easily contact each other at any time of the day, they could work faster and utilise time-zone differences to work around-the-clock.

Furthermore, in some cultures, e.g. Indian culture, it is considered normal that one can approach one's counterparts out of working hours, as opposed to many European cultures, e.g. Dutch, Swiss, German, where it is not common to contact somebody about work out of one's working hours. Therefore, the ability to reach somebody out of working hours depends to some extent on the characteristics of a national culture.

Interviewees from SAP and Baan did not mention this managerial practice.

The results of this research lead to the following propositions:

> **P10:** *Creating a transactive memory among dispersed team members is positively related to the ability to reach the right people at a remote location.*

> **P11:** *Increasing reachability between remote team members is likely to reduce the length of the project.*

> **P12:** *The ability to reach the right people at dispersed locations is higher in the cultures with less personal distance or that are more informal (e.g. in collectivist cultures, according to the Hofstede cultural dimensions).*

These propositions are relevant for CB and also traditional GDSD projects.

### 12. Creating and maintaining team atmosphere

Maintaining team atmosphere was considered important by interviewees from all four companies. In particular, it was important for offshore team members: the team in Geneva (in LeCroy), teams in Bangalore and Palo Alto (in SAP) and the team in Hyderabad (in Baan), because some information/news from the headquarters does not reach remote locations, causing a remote team to feel 'unplugged' from the rest of the company, as happened in Baan where the team in Hyderabad felt isolated.

As opposed to LeCroy, SAP and Baan, in each of which major decisions and updated information typically originated from a headquarters office, in TCS there was more balance between onsite and offshore teams in terms of information flows: while offshore teams at the main development centre in Gurgaon were most updated on the technical side of Quartz, the onsite teams (in Zurich for Skandia project and in San Francisco for Dresdner project) had the most updated information regarding customer requirements and progress. In TCS onsite and offshore teams consider themselves as the 'Quartz family'.

In the Baan case, there was a lack of team atmosphere between teams in Hyderabad and Barneveld; furthermore, from interviewing members of both teams, tensions between the teams became evident, and teams were not motivated to work together. This further emphasises the significance of this practice for success.

This leads to the following proposition:

---

**P13:** *Creating and maintaining team atmosphere between dispersed teams is positively related to personal satisfaction and motivation to collaborate in the future, and will reduce the possibility of coordination breakdowns and conflicts between the teams.*

---

This proposition is relevant for CB and also traditional GDSD projects.

### 13. Facilitating interactions

Facilitating interactions between people at remote locations is considered important in all four cases. This includes (i) facilitating personal face-to-face interactions and (ii) organising regular and frequent interactions over distance.

Interviewees from SAP and LeCroy indicated that personal face-to-face interactions were particularly important in the beginning of a new collaboration, as in the SAP case when several teams were merged into one group, and in the LeCroy case when a team-building exercise was organised in the early stages of the Maui project.

Face-to-face interactions facilitate sharing of knowledge with each other and building relationships. It is an occasion to learn about communication styles; in SAP it was also used to set up rules of communications for future collaboration over distance.

As described earlier, in TCS the majority of team members had an opportunity to meet face-to-face. Therefore, for TCS a major effort in facilitating interactions was put into organising interactions over distance between onsite and offshore project leaders and team members. For example, in the Dresdner project onsite and offshore project leaders had to adjust their working hours to be able to communicate in real time, bridging 13.5 hour time differences.

In the Baan case, interviewees stressed the importance of meeting in person and suggested that this improves understanding between remote counterparts and makes it easier to communicate. However, this practice was lacking in the Baan case, because Baan tried to reduce project costs by reducing travel costs, thus reducing the opportunity of remote team members to meet in person. Lack of this practice in the unsuccessful E-Enterprise project of Baan further underlines the importance of facilitating interaction for success.

These findings lead to the following propositions:

---

**P14a:** *Facilitating interactions is positively related to building up rapport and trust between dispersed team members.*

**P14b:** *Face-to-face meeting will improve understanding between remote counterparts and increase effectiveness of communications over distance.*

**P14c:** *Rapport and trust (confidence, mutual respect) between remote team members will improve understanding between remote counterparts and increase efficiency of communications over distance.*

---

These propositions are relevant for CB and also traditional GDSD projects.

### 14. Facilitating cross-pollination

Interviewees at LeCroy and SAP considered cross-pollination (i.e. that people from the one group spend a significant amount of time in the remote group and vice versa) to be important for success. In particular, in the SAP case it was helpful in dealing with cultural differences between German and Indian cultures.

Interviewees from TCS did not mention the importance of cross-pollination. This difference between the TCS case and the LeCroy and SAP cases, in which cross-pollination was considered important, can be explained by the fact that all team members of TCS are Indian, thus they do not need to learn about cultural differences.

Cross-pollination was lacking in the unsuccessful Baan case, which further underlines the significance of this practice for success.

Based on the findings of this research the following proposition can be formulated:

---

**P15:** *Facilitating cross-pollination will reduce the cultural gaps between team members.*

---

This proposition is relevant for CB and also traditional GDSD projects.

Furthermore, based on all the practices that facilitate development of social ties (i.e. practices 10–15), the following propositions can be suggested:

**P16**: *Globally distributed teams in which social ties such as rapport and trust are developed will be more effective and efficient in achieving collaborative project outcomes than teams where social ties are not developed.*

**P17**: *If dispersed teams belong to different national cultures, more efforts by managers, and more investment in terms of time and money, are required to build up rapport and trust.*

These propositions are relevant for CB and also traditional GDSD projects.

Figure 8.3 illustrates the relationships between the propositions associated with social ties and the categories of success.

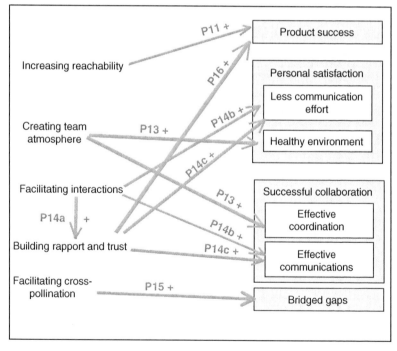

*Figure 8.3*  Social ties: Propositions

## (IV) Knowledge sharing in GD CBD: managerial practices

Interviewees from all four cases consider knowledge sharing as contributing to success. Following is a comparison across the four cases of managerial practices suggested to develop transactive memory and collective knowledge in globally distributed teams.

### 15. *Creating transactive memory among dispersed team members*

Interviewees from all four companies considered creating transactive memory among team members located at remote locations as important for success.

Transactive memory of a globally distributed team implies that team members know the composition of a remote team (who people are, their roles) and know the areas of expertise of their remote counterparts.

In LeCroy, SAP and TCS, a number of activities that facilitate interactions among dispersed team members were organised through which team members could get to know each other and create transactive memory. Examples of such activities are: training programs organised in LeCroy and TCS, and team-building exercises organised in SAP; visits to remote locations (in LeCroy and SAP), and rotating people between onsite and offshore teams (in TCS).

Interviewees from LeCroy, SAP and TCS suggested that knowing who knows what at a remote location enables the organisation to reduce development life cycle because some tasks such as bug fixes can be delegated in an around-the-clock manner (in LeCroy and TCS), and response is quicker when team members know whom to contact for a specific problem (in SAP).

In LeCroy and TCS, team members had a history of working together, and many of the dispersed team members had an opportunity to meet in person (the majority in TCS and some in LeCroy), therefore in these two companies transactive memory was developed to some extent (greater in TCS, less in LeCroy) before the case project started, and was also facilitated throughout the project.

In SAP, the globally distributed teams in Walldorf, Bangalore and Palo Alto did not have a history of working together before they were merged into the KM Collaboration group. Thus, in this group transactive memory was created from scratch in the early stages of the project through activities such as visits and team-building exercises.

In Baan, despite the fact that the E-Enterprise group had been established several years before this research was conducted, the constantly changing organisational structure and ownership of products resulted in a situation where the majority of team members at dispersed locations were either new or had moved from another groups. Thus, team members did not have a history of working together; the majority of them did not know each other and did not know the composition of the dispersed team. Therefore, in Baan transactive memory among dispersed team members was not developed. Consequently, the lack of this practice, and the fact that team members in Baan identified the importance of knowing the composition of the dispersed team and areas of expertise of remote counterparts further underlines the significance of this practice.

Based on the results of this research the following proposition can be formulated:

> **P18:** *Creating transactive memory among dispersed team members is positively related to collaborative project outcomes (e.g. it will reduce project life cycle).*

This proposition is relevant for CB and also traditional GDSD projects.

### 16. *Expanding collective knowledge of the dispersed team*

Interviewees from all four companies emphasised the importance of collective knowledge shared between members of dispersed teams for success.

Typically collective knowledge is created through shared experiences. In the context of globally distributed teams this means the creating of shared experiences of dispersed team members. Thus, in LeCroy and TCS, collective knowledge of dispersed teams had developed before the project started, from the past experience of working together. In particular, in LeCroy and TCS team members also had collective technical knowledge of the Maui platform (for LeCroy) and of Quartz (for TCS). Furthermore, in TCS collective knowledge is very broad, because all team members have the same cultural background (the developers in Zurich and San Francisco are Indian).

However, in SAP dispersed teams (in Walldorf, Bangalore and Palo Alto) did not have a history of working together. Therefore, in this group collective knowledge of these dispersed team had been developing since the start of the project.

In Baan, because of continuous changes in the organisational structure and ownership of products, members of the E-Enterprise group did not have a history of working together. They had different cultural backgrounds in terms of national culture (Dutch and Indian) and organisational culture (newcomers and people from Baan ERP group), and did not have a common technical background. Consequently, there was no collective knowledge shared between the two dispersed teams in Baan. The lack of this practice, and the fact that team members in Baan identified the importance of common understanding between key people, common knowledge of a product architecture and knowledge about the culture of counterparts further underlines the significance of this practice.

Results reported in this research lead to the following propositions:

---

**P19:** *Expanding collective knowledge of a dispersed (project) team is positively related to collaborative project outcomes (e.g. will reduce a possibility of misunderstandings and conflicts and reduce project life cycle).*

In particular (propositions P19a and P19b are complementary):

**P19a:** *Expanding common knowledge about national and organisational cultures is (i) positively related to personal satisfaction and effectiveness of communications over distance, and (ii) will reduce the possibility of misunderstandings and conflicts.*

**P19b:** *Expanding collective knowledge related to product architecture and achieving common understanding between key people are likely to reduce project life cycle.*

---

These propositions are relevant for CB and also traditional GDSD projects.

### 17. Managing 'by intuition'

In SAP, the ability to manage 'by intuition' is important for success. Management 'by intuition' is based on catching signals and sensing that something is working or not working properly. To be able to manage 'by intuition' extensive experience in the management of software development in general and globally distributed projects in particular is required.

In LeCroy and TCS, this practice has not been reported. However, there is some evidence that implies the possibility that management 'by intuition' is taking place in LeCroy and TCS as well. For example, during our visit to the NY office of LeCroy we observed how senior managers communicate with each other and with software engineers. We observed that they have an intuitive awareness of the situation (environment), of each other and of other people. Similarly, during our visit to the TCS office in Gurgaon, we observed that the offshore managers of Dresdner and Skandia have intuitive awareness of members of their team and about the situations at remote locations.

The importance of management 'by intuition' was mentioned during our visit to the SAP office in Walldorf. Therefore, we did not have an opportunity to ask managers at LeCroy and TCS if they relied on intuition, and if so, to what extent (i.e. how important is intuition for managing GD CBD). The need to investigate more in depth the role of management 'by intuition' can be suggested for future research.

Interviewees from Baan did not discuss the importance of management 'by intuition'.

Based on the results of this research the following complementary propositions can be formulated:

---

**P20a:** *Rapport with remote team members and awareness of what is going on at dispersed locations are positively related to the ability of a manager of a globally distributed team to manage 'by intuition'.*

**P20b:** *The ability of a manager of a globally distributed team to manage 'by intuition' (i.e. catch signals, sense that something is working or not working properly) will reduce the possibility of coordination breakdowns and increase the effectiveness and efficiency of a globally dispersed team.*

---

These propositions are relevant for CB and also traditional GDSD.

### 18. Learning new technology

Interviewees from LeCroy and TCS considered learning of a new technology important for success. In both companies this practice included (i) learning a specific component technology used for developing a CB product, and (ii) learning of the CB product, the principles and logic that it is based upon. Learning the design principles and logic was important to make sure that newcomers can understand the product that has been developed already, and will then work following the same principles and logic.

In LeCroy, learning new technology involved (i) learning new Microsoft COM technology, and (ii) learning the Maui principles.

In TCS, it was concerned with (i) learning the programming language and tools used for developing Quartz, and (ii) learning the theoretical principles and different financial modules included in the Quartz platform.

In both companies intensive courses for learning new technologies were organised.

Interviewees from SAP did not mention this practice. A possible explanation could be that development of Collaborative tools in SAP did not involve the use of a new technology; therefore, team members were familiar with the technology from their experience in previous projects in SAP.

In the Baan case, this managerial practice was lacking: as reported in the Baan case, there was a gap in common understanding of the technology and the processes team members were supposed to follow.

The lack of this practice in the unsuccessful E-Enterprise project of Baan further underlines the significance of this practice, which was identified as important in the successful projects of LeCroy and TCS.

Based on the results reported in this research the following proposition can be formulated:

---

**P21**: *If globally distributed team members learn new technology in a co-located environment, they will develop more extensive collective knowledge and transactive memory than if training is organised for each dispersed location separately.*

---

This proposition is relevant for CB and also for traditional GDSD projects.

Figure 8.4 illustrates the relationships between the propositions associated with knowledge sharing and the categories of success.

### (V) Components management in GD CBD: managerial practices

In addition to the four factors suggested in the theoretical lens, *components management* emerged from the data as a factor contributing to success.

Following is a comparison across the four cases of managerial practices seen as important to ensure successful components management in a GD CBD.

### 19. Designing for reuse

Interviewees in LeCroy and TCS consider that applying a design-for-reuse strategy is important for success.

In both companies (LeCroy and TCS) the main advantage anticipated from developing a CB product was to be able to reuse components in a number of products in the future. Both cases (LeCroy and

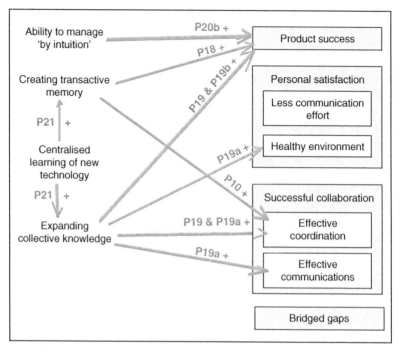

*Figure 8.4*   Knowledge sharing: Propositions

TCS) aimed to develop a platform that could be extended for a product family (the WaveMaster family at LeCroy and Quartz financial services platform at TCS). In order to maximise reuse across products, software teams of both companies invested time and resources in analysis aimed at identifying the most common functionalities for product families they intended to develop. The analysis addressed the following issues: (i) what components to develop (what functionality is common to all/ a majority of products), and (ii) what should be the granularity of the components.

Applying a design-for-reuse strategy in the early stages of a project helped LeCroy and TCS to achieve the benefits of reuse and be more efficient in developing new products based on the Maui platform (for LeCroy) and different implementations of the Quartz platform for different clients (for TCS).

Interviewees from SAP did not mention this practice. However, they mentioned the importance of facilitating reuse (discussed further in this section, managerial practice 21), which emphasises the importance of facilitating reuse in ongoing projects, while a design-for-reuse strategy emphasises the importance of reuse during the planning stage of a project, before the actual development has started.

In the Baan case, this managerial practice was lacking: the E-Enterprise suite was not designed to support reuse. On the contrary, as described in the Baan case, versions of products included in the E-Enterprise suite were not compatible, which created obstacles to reuse products included in the E-Enterprise suite.

The lack of this practice in the unsuccessful E-Enterprise project of Baan further underlines the significance of this practice, which was identified as important in the successful projects of LeCroy and TCS.

The results reported in this research lead to the following propositions:

---

**P22**: *In CBD applying a design-for-reuse strategy in the development of a product family will reduce significantly development costs and life cycle in the long run.*

In particular:

**P22a**: *In CBD applying a design-for-reuse strategy in the development of a product family is likely to increase development costs and life cycle of a first product and reduce development costs and life cycle with every new release (of products of the product family).*

---

These propositions are relevant for globally distributed (and also co-located) CBD projects.

### 20. Investing in 'advanced development'

Investing in advanced development was considered important by interviewees of LeCroy and TCS.

In LeCroy, development of the Maui platform was treated not as a typical product development project, when product requirements are defined in the very beginning, but as a research project (referred to by interviewees as 'advanced development'). It included learning about available technologies, and conducting a feasibility study aiming to test whether or not a 'proof of concept' for the product can be achieved by applying available technology(ies).

TCS had a similar approach to the development of the Quartz financial platform. Advanced development in TCS included cooperation with TKS, which was based on integrating core capabilities and knowledge of the two companies – the technical knowledge of developing advanced software products of TCS, and the business knowledge of financial processes, regulations and clients in Europe of TKS.

Interviewees from SAP did not mention this managerial practice.

In the Baan case, this managerial practice was lacking: the E-Enterprise suite and products included in it were developed in an atmosphere of continuous change in terms of technologies and requirements. As opposed to the advanced development (i.e. R&D) approach adopted by LeCroy and TCS, development of the E-Enterprise suite at Baan was undertaken without proper investigation of available technologies and generic products' requirements. As a result, technologies, requirements and interdependencies between the products included in the suite and their versions were constantly changing, thus reducing the efficiency and effectiveness of the ongoing development project.

The lack of this practice in the unsuccessful E-Enterprise project of Baan further underlines the significance of this practice, which was identified as important in the successful projects of LeCroy and TCS.

Based on the results of this research the following proposition can be formulated, related to the propositions P22 and P22a:

---

**P23:** *In CBD, approaching the development of a new product as an R&D project is positively related to the ability to reuse components in future products and will reduce development costs and life cycle in the long run.*

---

This proposition is relevant for globally distributed (and also co-located) CBD projects.

### 21.  Facilitating reuse

Interviewees from SAP and TCS indicated that facilitating the reuse of knowledge and components across locations is important for success.

In SAP, globally dispersed teams organised formal meetings, usually using video-conferencing tools, to discuss what each team had developed and to identify an opportunity to reuse knowledge and/or software components (applications).

In TCS, reuse of knowledge is facilitated on two levels: (i) within one project, when people rotate between onsite and offshore to bridge knowledge gaps between the two sites; (ii) across different Quartz implementation projects, which is facilitated by a central person (Quartz program manager) who coordinates all Quartz implementation projects and is aware of new components being developed for a specific customer.

In LeCroy, this managerial practice was not mentioned. The reason might be that because in SAP remote teams work on different work packages (each team has full ownership of a work package) and in TCS people from the Quartz group are involved in different Quartz implementation projects, they do not have a direct exposure to the work other teams are engaged in. Therefore in SAP, there is a need to have special meetings to learn of what other teams are doing to facilitate reuse across teams; and in TCS, a central role (Quartz program manager) is needed to facilitate reuse of components across different implementation projects. However, at LeCroy dispersed teams are exposed to the work of their remote counterparts, first because work is divided based on expertise (skills) and not location, and second because remote teams work in a single development environment (Maui) where they can see what new components have been developed and whether these components can be reused.

In the Baan case, this managerial practice was lacking. As mentioned in the 'designing for reuse' practice, development of the E-Enterprise did not consider reuse: on the contrary, versions of products included in the E-Enterprise suite were not compatible, thus creating obstacles for reuse in new releases.

The lack of this practice in the unsuccessful E-Enterprise project of Baan further underlines the significance of this practice, which was identified as important in the successful projects of SAP and TCS.

The results of this research lead to the following propositions:

> **P24a:** *GD CBD teams that divide work based on skills will achieve higher reuse rate than teams that divide work based on geographical location (i.e. when dispersed teams work on different parts of the project).*
>
> **P24b:** *In GD, where CBD teams that divide work based on geographical location, if members of dispersed teams do not organise formal meetings to discuss reuse possibilities, it is not likely that they will know about components developed at a remote location that they could reuse.*

These propositions are unique to GD CBD.

## 22. *Managing vendors*

Interviewees from TCS stressed the importance of managing vendors providing third-party components: this includes selecting vendors, agreeing on specifications of the components (e.g. functionality and interfaces) and on deadlines for components' delivery.

In particular, vendor management was very important for the Skandia project in which more than 25 vendors were delivering components. In TCS, coordination of all dispersed parties – onsite and offshore teams, and vendors of third-party components – is centralised under the supervision of one person (Quartz program manager) who is responsible for coordinating the work between all parties involved in a Quartz implementation project.

The importance of managing vendors for success was reported in the TCS case only. This practice is not relevant to the SAP and Baan projects as these projects did not use external vendors: all the work was distributed between dispersed teams within one organisation. Interviewees from LeCroy mentioned one large vendor in Japan who has been working closely with LeCroy already for several years developing acquisition systems. Possibly because LeCroy is working with fewer vendors than TCS, the interviewees of LeCroy did not stress the importance of vendor management. Further investigation of this topic can be recommended for future research.

Based on these results, the following complementary propositions can be formulated:

---

**P25a:** *In GD CBD projects that involve vendors delivering third-party components, centralising coordination of work carried out by all parties involved in the development (internal dispersed development sites and external vendors) will reduce development life cycle.*

**P25b:** *The more vendors are involved in delivering third-party components, the more important is centralisation of coordination of work carried out by all parties involved in the GD CBD project under one function.*

---

These propositions are unique to GD CBD projects.

Figure 8.5 illustrates the relationships between the propositions associated with components management and the categories of success.

In this section, managerial practices were discussed and compared across the cases. The next section will discuss factors perceived as contributing to success and compare results from the four studied projects.

## What factors contribute to success in each firm

We identified five factors that contribute to success in GD CBD: (I) *Inter-site coordination*, (II) *Appropriate tools and technologies*, (III) *Social*

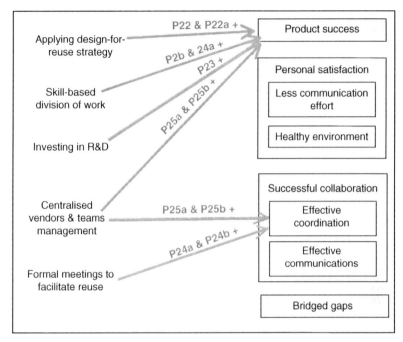

*Figure 8.5*  Components management: Propositions

*ties,* (IV) *Knowledge sharing and* (V) *Components management.* We assess the degree to which each factor affected the various criteria we set up for success in GD CBD projects in Table 8.6 (three rows 'LeCroy', 'SAP' and 'TCS' under each factor (I–V) are rows with the same factor from Tables 4.1, 5.1 and 6.1 respectively).

## Conclusions

In this chapter, we have carefully examined the various cases across the different success factors proposed for GD CBD projects.

First, the similarities and differences between the studied cases were presented. Despite the fact that in many ways the projects studied are similar, there are some differences between the four cases studied, mainly contextual, such as the different countries involved and, consequently, different cultures and different time-zone differences; the different types (and granularity) of components; and different histories (number of years) that remote teams have been working together. These differences between the projects help to explain differences in the results across cases.

*Table 8.6* Factors contributing to success (per success dimension)

| Factors | Product success | Personal satisfaction | | Success. collabor. | | |
|---|---|---|---|---|---|---|
| | Product success | Less communication effort | Healthy environment | Effective coordinat. | Effective communic. | Bridged gaps |
| **I) Inter-site coordination** | | | | | | |
| LeCroy | | X | X | X | X | X |
| SAP | X | X | X | | X | X |
| TCS | X | | | X | X | X |
| **II) Appropriate tools and technologies** | | | | | | |
| LeCroy | X | | | X | X | X |
| SAP | | X | X | | X | X |
| TCS | X | | | X | | |
| **III) Social ties** | | | | | | |
| LeCroy | X | X | X | X | X | X |
| SAP | | X | X | X | X | X |
| TCS | X | X | X | X | | |
| **IV) Knowledge sharing** | | | | | | |
| LeCroy | X | X | X | X | X | X |
| SAP | | X | X | X | X | X |
| TCS | X | X | | X | X | X |
| **V) Components management** | | | | | | |
| LeCroy | X | | | | | |
| SAP | | | | X | | |
| TCS | X | | | X | | |

Second, managerial practices perceived as important for success in GD CBD in the four studied cases were compared, and propositions that suggest relationships between specific managerial practices and categories of success were formulated.

Many of the propositions, in particular propositions regarding inter-site coordination, social ties and knowledge sharing, are not unique to

CB but are also relevant in the context of traditional GDSD projects. In regard to CB projects these propositions suggest that, despite the expectations that adoption of CBD in globally distributed projects will allow remote teams to work independently, GD CBD teams that work closely will be more successful (i.e will achieve better project outcomes: shorter time-to-market, lower costs, higher reuse rate), than teams that work independently and do not communicate on a regular basis.

Furthermore, examples of LeCroy and TCS show that in order to succeed in GD CBD and achieve the benefits of components reuse across products, it is important to invest in R&D and apply a design-for-reuse strategy in the early stages of a project. In LeCroy and TCS, these practices facilitated the development of a flexible product architecture and a large pool of reusable components that were later reused in a large number of products.

Finally, the success factors identified in the companies studied were compared. While in the three successful cases, managerial practices supporting the five factors (four potential factors identified in the theoretical lens, and one factor that emerged from the data) were evident, in the unsuccessful Baan case only appropriate tools and technologies were in place. The lack of practices supporting non-technical aspects, such as social ties, knowledge sharing and inter-site coordination, further underlines the significance of these factors for success.

This chapter presented cross-case analysis and results. In the next chapter the conclusions of this book will be presented.

# 9
# Towards a Framework of Successful Global Distributed CBD

At this juncture we ask: what can be learnt from the insights provided in this book and what tools we can provide academics and practitioners to advance the field of componentisation and global teams.

This journey has led us to believe that our initial framework should be revised. We have come across various factors that we have not considered in our theoretical framework which we believe have had an impact on the success of GD CBD projects. We also observed that some tools were, in particular, critical in some projects. We wish to recap on this aspects and offer managers a tool-set that they can consider in their projects. Finally, we will summarise the theoretical and practical contributions of this research to offer young researchers the opportunity to continue the work we have started.

## Theoretical lens: revisited

The potential factors contributing to success, suggested in the initial theoretical lens, can be revisited based on the results of the four case studies discussed above. As a result, a theoretical framework is proposed: it brings together (i) factors contributing to success in GD CBD and (ii) propositions suggesting relationships between specific managerial practices associated with each factor and success, as is presented in Figure 9.1.

With regard to GD CBD projects, the existing literature is yet very limited. We can clearly see that (I) *Inter-site coordination* and (II) *Tools and technologies* have already been considered as influential factors; however, the relevant literature somehow ignores the contribution of (III) *Social ties* and (IV) *Knowledge sharing* to success of GD CBD projects. Furthermore, the emergence of *Components management* as a critical factor is, in

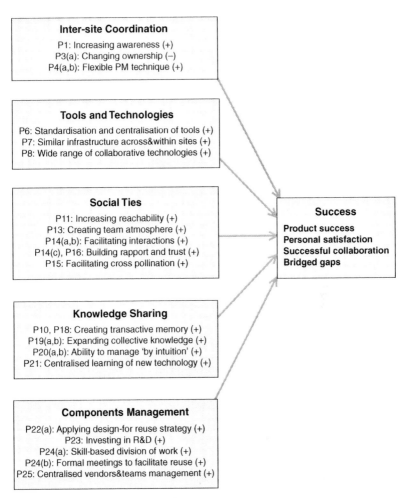

*Figure 9.1*   Theoretical framework

particular, important as it opens up opportunities to broaden the scope of research regarding GD CBD.

## The role of technology: technology alone is not enough

Technology is crucial for globally distributed teams: without ICT, people at dispersed locations would not be able to connect and collaborate. In the IS literature, technology is seen as an enabler and a chief factor that may lead to successful GDSD projects. However, *is having the right technology in place enough for a globally distributed team to succeed in GD CBD?*

The importance of tools and technologies can be assessed and compared with the importance of the other four success factors identified in the theoretical framework by comparing the results of the unsuccessful Baan case, where technology was in place but other factors were lacking, with the results from the three successful cases. Table 9.1 summarises factors that were in place and those that were lacking in all four cases, grouped in successful cases versus unsuccessful case ('+' – in place, '–' – lacking, 'N/A' – not applicable). The number of managerial practices associated with each factor is shown in brackets.

As illustrated in Table 9.1, while in the three successful cases, all five factors identified in the theoretical framework were evident, in the unsuccessful Baan case only appropriate tools and technologies were in place, and three factors – inter-site coordination, social ties and knowledge sharing, were lacking (the fifth factor – components management – is not relevant as the studied E-Enterprise project was not component-based). This illustrates that technology alone is not enough to succeed in a globally distributed environment.

## How companies organise and manage CBD in a globally distributed environment: successful managerial practices

In total, 22 managerial practices perceived as important in GD CBD were identified in the studied cases. These practices were classified into groups that focus on different aspects of the management of GD CBD, in accor-

*Table 9.1*   Factors contributing to success

| Project outcome (per case) | | Factors that contribute to success | | | | |
|---|---|---|---|---|---|---|
| | | Inter-site coordination | Appropriate tools and technologies | Social ties | Knowledge sharing | Components management |
| **Successful:** | LeCroy | + (6) | + (3) | + (5) | + (3) | + (2) |
| | SAP | + (5) | + (3) | + (4) | + (3) | + (1) |
| | TCS | + (6) | + (3) | + (4) | + (3) | + (4) |
| **Unsuccessful:** | Baan | – | + (3) | – | – | N/A |

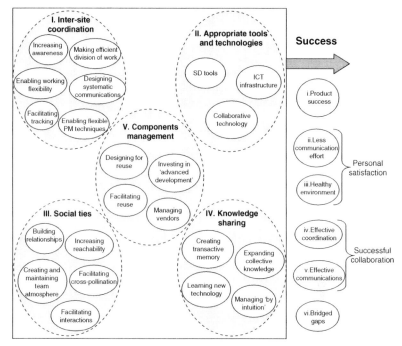

*Figure 9.2*  How companies organise and manage GD CBD to be successful

dance with the five factors included in the proposed theoretical framework, and are presented in the form of the concept map in Figure 9.2. The concept map contains practices identified in all the case studies. The majority of these managerial practices were identified in all successful cases; however, some practices are unique to specific cases, and most of these practices were lacking in the unsuccessful Baan case.

## The role of context in selecting managerial practices: context does matter

In this research, successful managerial practices that show how companies organise and manage GD CBD are identified. These practices are perceived as successful by the interviewees in the companies studied, where application of these managerial practices indeed resulted in successful project outcomes. Nevertheless, would the same managerial practices contribute to success if applied in different companies involved in GD CBD? Not all managerial practices will suit the needs of any GD CBD project. For example, as illustrated in Chapter 8, in all three successful cases, practices of efficient division of work were in place. However, specific practices were different between the three companies: in LeCroy, work was divided on a skills basis, in SAP, by product feature, and in TCS, in order to maximise work offshore. These observations lead to the question: **how does the context of GD CBD project organization matter in selecting managerial practices that will be successful for a specific project?**

Several propositions suggested in the previous chapter illustrate how the context matters when selecting successful managerial practices for different GD CBD projects. In particular, the following contextual characteristics were identified:

- *History of working together* defines what strategy for the division of work will be more successful (proposition P2).

- *Existence of relationships such as rapport and trust* have an impact on the choice of a successful strategy for division of work (proposition P2).

- *National culture* has an impact on the following managerial practices:
  - o The need to improve content and style of communications, if members of dispersed teams have different cultural backgrounds (proposition P5).
  - o The ability to reach the right people varies between cultures, based on the characteristics of a specific culture (proposition P12): for example, in the Indian culture it is usual to contact somebody outside working hours, which is not common in German, Dutch and Swiss cultures.
  - o The effort of managers required to build rapport and trust will be different for different cultures (proposition P17): less effort will be required for socially-open cultures, such as India (e.g. in collectivist cultures, according to the Hofstede cultural dimensions).

Therefore, contextual characteristics need to be taken into account when managers select managerial practices to adopt in GD CBD: practices that are successful for one company will not necessarily be successful in another organisation, if specific contextual characteristics of these organisation are different.

## Theoretical contributions

This research has studied in depth the phenomenon of GD CBD, which is becoming a promising area, as increasing numbers of companies are setting up software development in a globally distributed environment and at the same time adopt a CBD methodology. Thus, being an emerging area, the management practice of GD CBD is evolving primarily on an *ad hoc* basis.

So far, researchers in the IS field have studied only one aspect of the phenomenon: some have focused on the impact of globalisation on the management of traditional (non-CB) software development projects, others have focused on the management of CBD in co-located projects. Research into the management of GD CBD projects that combine these two streams is just emerging and is yet in the early stages. Research on GD CBD has reported that extensive coordination between people working from dispersed locations is required to succeed in GD CBD (Carmel 1999; Alexandersen et al. 2003; Turnlund 2004); other aspects of management were not discussed in this literature. At present, little is known about how to organise and manage GD CBD to be successful. Therefore, the research presented in this book advances our knowledge of the management of GD CBD projects, and suggests a more structured (theory-based) approach to the management of such projects. In particular, this book makes three main theoretical contributions.

First, a theoretical framework that identifies factors contributing to success in GD CBD is proposed (Figure 9.1). It suggests that (I) *Inter-site coordination*, (II) *Appropriate tools and technologies*, (III) *Social ties*, (IV) *Knowledge sharing* and (V) *Components management* contribute to success in GD CBD.

In particular, interviewees stressed the importance of social ties and knowledge sharing for success. The importance of these two factors has not been identified previously in the IS literature. Therefore, identifying the importance of social ties, such as rapport and trust and knowledge sharing, for success in GD CBD is particularly valuable as it gives a new perspective on the phenomenon of GD CBD, the *importance of social and human aspects in managing GD CBD projects*, which needs to be studied further.

Second, 22 managerial practices that illustrate how companies organise and manage CBD in GD environment are offered (Figure 9.2). In terms of a theoretical contribution, these practices suggest a more structured (theory-based) approach to management of GD CBD projects. These practices support the five success factors included in the proposed theoretical framework (Figure 9.1).

Third, within the IS field, this book provides an integrated view which combines three areas of research: (i) IS research on the management of globally distributed development of traditional (non-CB) software;

(ii) IS research on the management of co-located CBD, and (iii) OB research on collaboration in GD teams that examines the importance of social aspects in global collaborations. This book connects findings from these three research areas into one integrated framework to study the phenomenon of GD CBD.

## Practical contributions: implications and lessons for managers

The research presented in this book is of high relevance to management practice: it has the following practical contributions and lessons for managers.

First, 22 successful managerial practices identified in the GD CBD projects studied are of high relevance to managers. Other companies involved in GD CBD can learn from these practices how to organise and manage GD CBD in their organisations: they can use the concept map with 22 managerial practices (Figure 9.2 on page 239) together with the Glossary of Managerial Practices for GD CBD as guidelines.

Second, specific activities that help to implement the above-mentioned successful managerial practices in actual GD CBD projects are proposed.

As explained above, data was analysed on two levels: (i) on a conceptual level, to identify managerial practices; and (ii) on a detailed level, to identify specific activities that helped to implement the managerial practices. Activities identified during detailed analysis are included in the *Checklist for Managers* involved in GD CBD (Table 9.2): they are grouped into two categories (1) *Before face-to-face (f2f) meeting*, and (2) *After f2f meeting*.

We distinguish between these two stages (before f2f meeting and after f2f meeting) because interviewees from all four companies indicated that their perception of and attitude towards remote colleagues changed dramatically after they met in person, even if only for a short while (as captured in the proposition P14b). Therefore, managers should focus on different sets of activities before team members meet in person and after they meet.

Furthermore, a *Guide to Tools and Technologies for GD CBD* (Table 9.3 on page 244) is offered to managers, to help to choose technologies that would match the needs of their organisations. The Guide summarises the main requirements for software development tools and ICT infrastructure, based on the results of all the cases studied. Table 2.1 on page 26), which describes different types of collaborative technologies, can be included in the Guide.

Moreover, a *Communication Protocol Template* (on page 245) is provided for managers and developers, to help to agree on the rules of communications. The protocol offers recommendations regarding use of collaborative technologies in different situations.

*Table 9.2*   Checklist for managers

| Checklist for managers of GD CBD |
| --- |

**1. Before f2f meeting**

**1.1 Planning for introductions** *(tick activities for action)*
- ❑ virtual f2f meeting
- ❑ introduction of new members
- ❑ kick-off meeting
- ❑ short visit to remote site
- ❑ temporary co-location (long-term stay)
- ❑ social activity
- ❑ team-building exercise
- ❑ show people at remote sites that they are as valuable as the main site

**1.2 Design communication processes** *(tick activities for action)*
- ❑ set up mini-teams for different functional/technical areas
- ❑ try to reduce the communication paths
- ❑ subsidise language courses (e.g. English)
- ❑ agree on communication rules
- ❑ appoint a contact person for remote teams
- ❑ distribute internal newsletter (e.g. every month)
- ❑ create template for proposals initiating new ideas (e.g. for new product/ improvement)

**2. After f2f meeting**

**2.1 Organise systematic communications** *(tick activities for action; decide on frequency of communications)*
- ❑ regular (all) managers' meetings, every _____
- ❑ regular (one-to-one) managers' meetings, every _____
- ❑ regular meetings with all teams/team members, every _____
- ❑ regular visits of managers to remote location, every _____
- ❑ regular reflection sessions, every _____

**2.2 Ensure targeted communications** *(tick activities to advise team members)*
- ❑ communicate one-to-one (i.e. direct communication, no hierarchy in communications)
- ❑ distribute information (without being contacted)
- ❑ use synchronous communications

### Collaborative technologies

The following *Communication Protocol Template* is intended for all members of a globally distributed teams (not only managers but developers as well). For different types of collaborative tools, the Protocol lists situations/scenarios in which the tool is suitable.

*Table 9.3*  A guide to tools and technologies for managers of GD CBD

| A Guide to Tools and Technologies for managers of GD CBD |
| --- |

**1. Capabilities of Software Development tools** *(tick required capabilities)*

- ❏ Automated management of interdependencies between components and related files
- ❏ Automated building of components that have changed (e.g. every 6–12 hours)
- ❏ Automated testing of components
- ❏ Standardised tools and methods across locations

Centralised tools *(you may select more than one from the range of options)*:

- ❏ Web access
- ❏ Replicated databases
- ❏ Single development environment
- ❏ Central repository/database
- ❏ A Guide that explains how to use tools and methods (make it available for everybody, e.g. on an Intranet)

**2. ICT Infrastructure** *(tick required capabilities)*

- ❏ Quick access to the network

Shared resources:

- ❏ Shared databases
- ❏ Shared server
- ❏ Shared project repository

Web access

- ❏ Constant replication of databases over the Web
- ❏ Centralised access to tools over the Web

Quick and easy connectivity across locations:

- ❏ Wide range of collaborative technologies available (see different types of collaborative technologies in Table 2.1)
- ❏ Phone connection available and easy to use (e.g. internal phone numbers across the globe)
- ❏ Identical ICT facilities (i.e. network speed, server, applications) for dispersed and co-located teams

*Table 9.3*   A guide to tools and technologies for managers of GD CBD – *continued*

---

**Communication protocol template: recommended use** *(discuss suggested use of collaborative technologies with your remote counterpart(s) to agree on the rules of communications)*

---

**Online chat** (suitable for teams with established rapport)

❏ Short and/or urgent questions

---

**Phone and teleconferencing**

❏ Urgent matters
❏ Updates between managers
❏ Resolve misunderstandings and conflicts
❏ Help in fixing bugs

---

**Application Sharing**

❏ Help in fixing bugs (e.g. show conditions of failure)
❏ Knowledge sharing (e.g. show slides during presentation)

---

**Videoconference**

❏ Progress meetings between managers
❏ Major design reviews

---

**Email**

❏ Low priority tasks
❏ Sending source code for small changes
❏ Clarifications

---

**Intranet**

❏ Post internal documents (e.g. specifications, plans, designs, issues)

---

## Limitations

The conclusions offered in this research are based on an in-depth study of four companies, by applying a qualitative interpretive approach that is often considered as subjective and having limited generalisability (Klein and Myers 1999). Successful managerial practices and factors that contribute to success identified in this research are based to a great extent on the perceptions of interviewees, which may be subjective. To compensate for this subjective source of data, evidence was also collected from internal and external documentation and observations, as suggested by Yin (1994) and Eisenhardt (1989), which are considered to be more objective sources, in particular external reports. Applying additional methodological approaches used in positivist research, such as propositions testing and a quantitative survey, may contribute to a further understanding of the phenomenon of GD CBD.

Furthermore, taking into account the fact that national culture was identified as one of the contextual characteristics that need to be considered when selecting managerial practices that would be successful in a specific organisation, conducting similar case studies that involve different national cultures may reveal new results, unique to the specific cultures. Therefore, conducting more case studies across CBD projects globally distributed across different countries will enable researchers to test the proposed theoretical framework in different cultural settings and will extend the proposed set of managerial practices to include more culture-specific practices.

Finally, it is important to note that many of the successful managerial practices and activities offered to practitioners are expensive (e.g. visits to remote locations, investing in R&D). However, the results of this book indicate that investment in these practices in the early stages of a project pays off and is considered beneficial at later stages of the project (as can be seen from the three successful cases described in this book). By contrast, lack of these 'expensive' practices in Baan led to project closure.

## Suggestions for future research

The results of this research provide an insight into the technical and social aspects of GD CBD projects that can be further studied in future research. A number of topics can be suggested for a future research agenda.

First, future studies can conduct a survey across the IS industry to test the propositions developed in this research.

Second, there is a need to investigate the relative importance of each of the five factors included in the proposed theoretical framework. For example, the Baan case illustrated that technology only is not enough to succeed in GD CBD. More case studies that would offer different combinations of factors that are lacking and factors that are in place will give an opportunity to assess the relative importance of each of the five factors.

Third, the role of social and human aspects in GD CBD can be studied further to investigate the causal relationships between social ties, knowledge sharing and success.

Finally, to study further the phenomenon of GD CBD, exploratory research in different cultural settings and different types of GD CBD, such as Open Source Software development, is needed. Within commercial GD CBD projects, projects that involve more than one company (e.g. outsourcing and joint ventures) need to be explored as well.

# Appendices

**Appendix 1** Replication approach for multiple-case design (adapted from Yin, 1994)

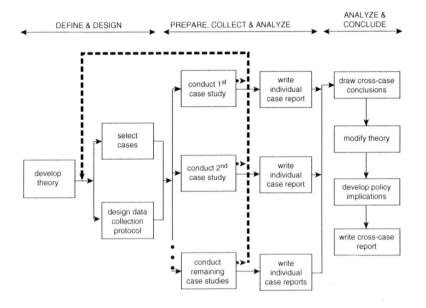

## Appendix 2    Oscilloscopes: general information and products of LeCroy Corporation

'An oscilloscope is a laboratory instrument commonly used to display and analyse the waveform of electronic signals. In effect, the device draws a graph of the instantaneous signal voltage as a function of time'.[1] Oscilloscopes are used extensively for industrial, scientific and medical purposes (e.g. they are much used for design and testing in high-tech industries, and in research labs in universities). Below are digital oscilloscopes produced by LeCroy Corporation: the WaveMaster Series (top) and the WaveRunner Series (bottom).

---

[1]Explanation from www.whatis.com

# Appendix 3    LeCroy Corporation: organisational structure

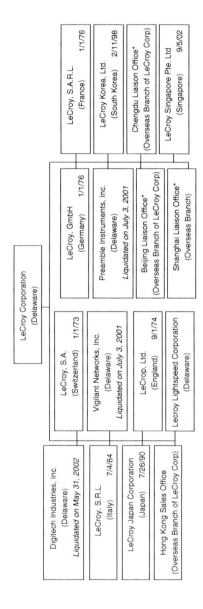

**LeCroy Corporation**
For the Fiscal Year Ending June 30, 2003

LeCroy Corporation
(Delaware)

Digitech Industries, Inc.
(Delaware)
*Liquidated on May 31, 2002*

LeCroy, S.R.L.
(Italy)    7/4/84

LeCroy Japan Corporation
(Japan)    7/26/90

Hong Kong Sales Office
(Overseas Branch of LeCroy Corp)

LeCroy, S.A.
(Switzerland)    1/1/73

Vigilant Networks, Inc.
(Delaware)
*Liquidated on July 3, 2001*

LeCrop. Ltd.
(England)    9/1/74

Lecroy Lightspeed Corporation
(Delaware)

LeCroy, GmbH
(Germany)    1/1/76

Preamble Instruments, Inc.
(Delaware)
*Liquidated on July 3, 2001*

Beijing Liaison Office*
(Overseas Branch of LeCroy Corp)

Shanghai Liaison Office*
(Overseas Branch)

LeCroy, S.A.R.L.
(France)    1/1/76

LeCroy Korea. Ltd.
(South Korea)    2/11/98

Chengdu Liaison Office*
(Overseas Branch of LeCroy Corp)

LeCroy Singapore Pte. Ltd
(Singapore)    9/5/02

* Set up through the Chinese Government's Foreign Enterprise Service Corporation (FESCO). These offices can provide sales, marketing, technical, etc. support to Chinese customers but cannot directly conduct business in China.

Notes:

Parenthesis indicate Jurisdiction of Incorporation.

## Appendix 4    Glossary of Managerial Practices for GD CBD
*(managerial practices organised in alphabetical order)*

### Building relationships

Building relationships involves building rapport and trust between remote team members.

*Rapport* is defined as 'the quality of the relation or connection between interactants, marked by harmony, conformity, accord, and affinity' (Bernieri et al. 1994).

*Trust* is defined as 'the willingness of the one person or group to relate to another in the belief that the other's action will be beneficial rather than detrimental, even though this cannot be guaranteed' Child (2001).

This practice is related to *social ties*.

### Collaborative technology

Collaborative technology covers communication media and collaborative tools. Most commonly used collaborative technologies include email, online chat, phone and teleconferencing, Voice-over-IP (VoIP) application and desktop sharing, videoconferencing facilities and Intranet (see detailed overview of different types of collaborative technologies in Table 2.1).

This practice is related to *appropriate tools and technologies*.

### Creating and maintaining team atmosphere

Creating and maintaining a team atmosphere implies making sure that all remote teams/team members are 'plugged' into the project/company: in particular, it is relevant for members of offshore teams.

This practice is related to *social ties*.

### Creating transactive memory among dispersed team members

Transactive memory is defined as the set of knowledge possessed by group members coupled with an awareness of who knows what (Wegner 1987). Transactive memory of a globally distributed team implies that team members know the composition of a remote team (who the people are, their roles) and know the areas of expertise of their remote counterparts.

This practice is related to *knowledge sharing*.

### Designing for reuse

This practice aims to maximise reuse of software components across a number of products in the long term. This involves analysis and long term planning for future products and product families (i.e. identifying common functionalities), and making strategic decisions about the granularity level of components.

This practice emphasises the reuse during the *planning* stage of a project, before the actual development has started. It is related to *components management*.

### Designing systematic communications

This practice includes organising frequent communications and designing rules aiming to make communications more effective. It includes:

(i) Scheduling systematic and frequent communications, such as regular teleconferences between software managers in dispersed locations; videoconferences with all team members (e.g. every one or two months).
(ii) Communicating directly to reach an appropriate person. i.e. no hierarchy in communications.
(iii) Improving style and content of communications to achieve better understanding (and prevent conflict and misunderstanding) between remote counterparts.

This practice is related to *inter-site coordination*.

### Enabling flexible Project Management (PM) techniques

Flexible PM techniques help to accommodate everyday dynamics. They include:

- On a macro level: planning of major project phases and deliverables, and setting up clear objectives for a dispersed team
- On a micro level: flexible and not too detailed planning (2–3 week milestones).

This practice is related to *inter-site coordination*.

### Enabling working flexibility

Supporting working flexibility implies providing (i) flexible working conditions e.g. working from home, and (ii) flexible working hours, in order to accommodate personal circumstances of team members, to make their working environment more convenient and comfortable.

This practice is related to *inter-site coordination*.

### Expanding collective knowledge of the dispersed team

Collective knowledge comprises elements of knowledge that are common to all members of an organisation (Grant 1996).

In the case of GD CBD projects, the 'organisation' involves all people participating in the globally distributed project from their remote locations. Therefore, the collective knowledge of a dispersed team includes knowledge of the national culture of remote counterparts, collective knowledge of the overall product (beyond a specific area an individual team member is working on) and common technical knowledge.

This practice is related to *knowledge sharing*.

### Facilitating cross-pollination

Cross-pollination implies that people from the one group spend significant amounts of time in the other group (other location) and vice versa.

This practice is related to *social ties*.

### Facilitating interactions

Facilitating interactions between people at remote locations includes:

(i)   facilitating personal face-to-face interactions (in particular between key people for decision-making) and
(ii)  organising regular and frequent interactions over distance.

This practice is related to *social ties*.

### Facilitating reuse

This practice implies facilitating the reuse of knowledge and reuse of components across dispersed locations. It includes identifying an opportunity to reuse knowledge and/or software components (applications) developed by dispersed teams. Reuse can be facilitated on two levels: within one product and across different products of the same product family.

This practice emphasises reuse in *ongoing* projects. It is related to *components management*.

### Facilitating tracking of bugs and development tasks

Tracking possibility means (i) having constantly updated status about the stages in fixing a bug, or progress in a task, and (ii) knowing who is responsible for fixing the bug, or completing the task.

This practice is related to *inter-site coordination*.

## ICT infrastructure

An ICT infrastructure enables connection between all remote sites. It includes Internet, WAN, server and applications pool, how resource shares are set up (i.e. sharing of databases, server, project repository), conferencing tools, and network speed and bandwidth. Furthermore, it includes capabilities aiming to support security requirements, such as firewalls and access rights.

This practice is related to *appropriate tools and technologies*.

## Increasing awareness

This practice involves increasing awareness of (i) what is going on in the company and the project, (ii) progress made by remote teams, (iii) remote team members (the team composition, culture of remote counterparts and cultural differences), and (iv) the environment at a remote site, e.g. ICT and tools available for remote teams.

This practice is related to *inter-site coordination*.

## Increasing reachability

Increasing reachability implies making it easier to reach the right people at a remote location, in particular, (i) knowing whom to contact (i.e. who is the person who has knowledge of a certain domain or issue), and (ii) knowing who is available on the given day and time.

This practice is related to *social ties*.

## Investing in 'advanced development'

Investing in 'advanced development' implies that a development of a new CB product is treated not as a typical product development project, in which product requirements are defined in the very beginning, but as a research (i.e. R&D) project.

'Advanced development' includes learning about available technologies, and conducting a feasibility study aiming to test whether or not a 'proof of concept' for the product can be achieved by applying available technology(ies).

This practice is related to *components management*.

## Learning new technology

Learning a new technology includes (i) learning a specific component technology used for developing a CB product, and (ii) learning of the CB product, the principles and logic that it is based upon.

This practice is related to *knowledge sharing*.

### Making efficient division of work

Efficient division of work involves strategies that software managers follow (i) to divide work between globally distributed teams (e.g. by skills or by product features/components), as well as (ii) to divide specific assignments (tasks) and responsibilities between individual team members at remote locations (e.g. division of technical and 'social' responsibilities that include establishing reporting channels across the globe). This practice also includes the approach regarding ownership of work packages – whether ownership stays with the same teams or is shifted between dispersed teams during a project life cycle.

This practice is related to *inter-site coordination*.

### Managing 'by intuition'

Management 'by intuition' is based on catching signals and sensing that something is working or not working properly. It implies having an intuitive awareness of the situation (environment) and of remote counterparts (in particular, managers of remote teams and key members).

This practice is related to *knowledge sharing*.

### Managing vendors

This practice implies managing vendors providing third-party components: this includes selecting vendors, agreeing on specifications of the components (e.g. functionality and interfaces), and deadlines for components' delivery.

This practice is related to *components management*.

### Software development tools

Software development tools include tools for development and management of components, configuration and version management tools, tools for testing and tracking bugs. This practice also includes software development methods and processes.

This practice is related to *appropriate tools and technologies*.

# Appendix 5 Baan product version compatibility matrix (internal document)

## Baan E-Enterprise product Matrix E-Common

### Web Server Configuration Browsers

|  | IE 4.01 SP1 | IE4.01 SP2 | IE 5.x | IE 6.x | NS 4.72 | NS 6.x | NS 6.0 | NS 6.1 | NS 6.2 | IE 5.0 | IE 5.5 | IE 6.0 |
|---|---|---|---|---|---|---|---|---|---|---|---|---|
| E-Sales 2.0 | Yes 1) | No 2) | No 2) | | | | | | | | | |
| E-Collaboration 2.0 | Yes 1) | No 2) | No 2) | | | | | | | | | |
| E-Procurement 2.0 | Yes 2) | Yes | Yes | | | | | | | | | |
| E-Sales 2.1 | Yes 2) | Yes | Yes | | | | | | | | | |
| E-Collaboration 2.1 | Yes 2) | Yes | Yes | | | | | | | | | |
| E-Procurement 2.1 | Yes 2) | Yes | Yes | | | | | | | | | |
| E-Service 2.0 | Yes 2) | Yes | Yes | | | | | | | | | |
| E-Service Remote 2.0 | No | No | Yes | | | | | | | | | |
| E-Sales 2.2 | Yes 2) | Yes | Yes | | | | | | | | | |
| E-Collaboration 2.2 | Yes 2) | Yes | Yes | | | | | | | | | |

1) This product contains E-Common 2.0 which works only with MDAC 2.0 SP2 (which is part of IE 4.01 SP1)
2) This product contains E-Common 2.1(+) which works only with MDAC 2.1 (which is part of IE 4.01 SP2)
   When used with IE 4.01 SP1 MDAC2.1 needs to be installed manually or MS SQL 7 has to be installed on the webserver (contains MDAC 2.1).

### Web Server Configuration Databases, MS Technology

|  | MS SQL 7.0 | Office2000 | ADSI 2.5 | Frontpage2 | Site Serv.SP2 |
|---|---|---|---|---|---|
| E-Sales 2.0 | No 3) | No | Yes 4) | No | Yes 5) |
| E-Collaboration 2.0 | No 3) | No | Yes 4) | No | Yes 5) |
| E-Procurement 2.0 | Yes | Yes | Yes 4) | No | Yes 5) |
| E-Sales 2.1 | Yes | Yes | Yes 4) | No | Yes 5) |
| E-Collaboration 2.1 | Yes | Yes | Yes 4) | No | Yes 5) |
| E-Procurement 2.1 | Yes | Yes | Yes 4) | No | Yes 5) |
| E-Service 2.0 | Yes | Yes | Yes 4) | No | Yes 5) |
| E-Service Remote 2.0 | Yes | No | Yes 4) | No | Not test |
| E-Sales 2.2 | Yes | Yes | Yes 4) | No | Yes 5) |
| E-Collaboration 2.2 | Yes | Yes | Yes 4) | No | Yes 5) |

3) Because MS SQL 7 instaaalles MDAC 2.1
4) Only allowed in combination with ADSI 2.5

### Web Server Configuration Proprietary technology

|  | OW2.1 | OW2.2 | OW2.2.1 | OW3.0 | BCLM1.0 |
|---|---|---|---|---|---|
| E-Sales 2.0 | | | | | |
| E-Collaboration 2.0 | | | | | |
| E-Procurement 2.0 | | | | | |
| E-Sales 2.1 | | | | | |
| E-Collaboration 2.1 | | | | | |
| E-Procurement 2.1 | yes | | | | |
| E-Service 2.0 | | | | | |
| E-Service Remote 2.0 | | | | | |
| E-Sales 2.2 | | | | | |
| E-Collaboration 2.2 | | | | | |

### Applications and database on the same server

| E-Sales 2.0 | no |
|---|---|
| E-Collaboration 2.0 | no |
| E-Procurement 2.0 | yes |
| E-Sales 2.1 | yes |
| E-Collaboration 2.1 | yes |
| E-Procurement 2.1 | yes |
| E-Service 2.0 | yes |
| E-Service Remote 2.0 | yes |
| E-Sales 2.2 | yes |
| E-Collaboration 2.2 | yes |

### Applications running with which E-Common version 1)

| E-Sales 2.0 | E-Common 2.0 |
|---|---|
| E-Collaboration 2.0 | E-Common 2.0 |
| E-Procurement 2.0 | E-Common 2.1 |
| E-Sales 2.1 | E-Common 2.2 |
| E-Collaboration 2.1 | E-Common 2.2 |
| E-Procurement 2.1 | E-Common 2.3.0 |
| E-Service 2.0 | E-Common 2.3.1 |
| E-Service Remote 2.0 | E-Common 2.3.1 |
| E-Sales 2.2 LA | E-Common 2.3.1 |
| E-Sales 2.2 GA | E-Common 2.3.1 SP1 |
| E-Sales 2.2 SP1 | E-Common 2.3.1 SP2 |
| E-Collaboration 2.2 | E-Common 2.3.1 SP3 |
| E-Procirement 2.1 SP1 | E-Common 2.3.1 SP3 |

1) Applications which are running on the same E-Common version are able to run together on one server.
2) Applications which are running on E-Common 2.2 or higher are able to run together on one server

| Applications running with Extensions | Automotive VRC | Status |
|---|---|---|
| E-Sales 2.1 | NASCAR SCH1 | tested |
| E-Collaboration 2.1 | NASCAR SCH1 | tested |
| E-Procurement 2.1 | NASCAR SCH1 | tested |
| E-Service 2.0 | | |
| E-Service 2.0 Remote | | |
| E-Sales 2.2 LA | NASCAR SCH1 | expected to work, not tested |
| E-Collaboration 2.2 | NASCAR SCH1 | expected to work, not tested |

# Appendix 6   Baan connectivity pack (internal document)

## Connectivity Packs

| Connectivity Pack 2.0.0 | Triton 3.1 | Baan IVb2 | Baan IVc | Baan Vb | Baan Vc |
|---|---|---|---|---|---|
| E-Sales 2.0 | no | yes | yes | no | no |
| E-Collaboration 2.0 | no | yes | yes | no | no |
| E-Procurement 2.0 | no | yes | yes | no | no |
| E-Sales 2.1 | no | no | no | no | no |
| E-Collaboration 2.1 | no | no | no | no | no |
| E-Procurement 2.1 | no | no | no | no | no |
| E-Service 2.1 | no | no | no | no | no |
| E-Service Remote 2.0 | no | no | no | no | no |

| Connectivity Pack 2.1.0 | Triton 3.1 | Baan IVb2 | Baan IVc | Baan Vb | Baan Vc |
|---|---|---|---|---|---|
| E-Sales 2.0 | no | yes | yes | no | no |
| E-Collaboration 2.0 | no | yes | yes | no | no |
| E-Procurement 2.0 | no | yes | yes | no | no |
| E-Sales 2.1 | no | yes | yes | yes | no |
| E-Collaboration 2.1 | no | yes | yes | yes | no |
| E-Procurement 2.1 | no | no | no | no | no |
| E-Service 2.1 | no | no | no | no | no |
| E-Service Remote 2.0 | no | no | no | no | no |

| Connectivity Pack 2.1.1 | Triton 3.1 | Baan IVb2 | Baan IVc | Baan Vb | Baan Vc |
|---|---|---|---|---|---|
| E-Sales 2.0 | no | no | no | no | no |
| E-Collaboration 2.0 | no | no | no | no | no |
| E-Procurement 2.0 | no | no | no | no | no |
| E-Sales 2.1 | no | yes | yes | yes | no |
| E-Collaboration 2.1 | no | yes | yes | yes | no |
| E-Procurement 2.1 | no | yes | yes | yes | no |
| E-Sales 2.2 | no | yes | yes | yes | no |
| E-Service 2.1 | no | no | no | yes | no |
| E-Service Remote 2.0 | no | no | no | yes | no |

**iPack E-Sales 2.2 Sp1 - Vc**

**G2**

| Connectivity Pack 2.1.1 | Triton 3.1 | Baan IVb2 | Baan IVc | Baan Vb | Baan Vc |
|---|---|---|---|---|---|
| E-Sales 2.0 | no | no | no | no | no |
| E-Collaboration 2.0 | no | no | no | no | no |
| E-Procurement 2.0 | no | no | no | no | no |
| E-Sales 2.1 | no | yes | yes | yes | no |
| E-Collaboration 2.1 | no | yes | yes | yes | no |
| E-Procurement 2.1 | no | yes | yes | yes | no |
| E-Sales 2.2 | no | yes | yes | yes | no |
| E-Service 2.1 | no | no | no | yes | no |
| E-Service Remote 2.0 | no | no | no | yes | no |
| E-Collaboration 2.2 | no | yes | yes | yes | no |

# References

Adler, P. S. and B. Borys (1996). 'Two types of bureaucracies: enabling and coercive'. *Administrative Science Quarterly* **41**: 61–89.

Alexandersen, C., K. Kumar and J. Van Hillegersberg (2003). 'Bank-in-a-Box: Skandia 's a Agile and Customizable Financial Services Platform', Society for Information Management (SIM).

Amrit, C. and J. van Hillegersberg (2008). 'Detecting coordination problems in collaborative software development environments'. *Information Systems Management* **25**(1): 57–70.

Andres, H. P. (2002). 'A Comparison of Face-to-face and Virtual Software Development Teams'. *Team Performance Management* **8**($\frac{1}{2}$): 39–48.

Arato, P., Z. A. Mann and A. Orban (2005). 'Extending component-based design with hardware components'. *Science of Computer Programming* **56**(1–2): 23–39.

Arino, A., J. de la Torre and P. S. Ring (2001). 'Relational Quality: Managing Trust in Corporate Alliances'. *California Management Review* **44**(1): 109–131.

Avram, G. (2007). 'Knowledge Work Practices in Global Software Development'. *Electronic Journal of Knowledge Management* **5**(4): 347–356.

Ba, S. (2001). 'Establishing Online Trust Through a Community Responsibility System'. *Decision Support Systems* **31**(3): 323–336.

Baker, S., M. Spiro and S. Hamm (2000). 'The Fall of Baan'. *Business Week*: http://www.businessweek.com/2000/00_33/b3694015.htm.

Bass, L., C. Buhman, S. Comella-Dorda, F. Long, J. Robert, R. Seacord and K. Wallnau (2000). 'Volume I: Market Assessment of Component-Based Software Engineering', Carnegie Mellon Software Engineering Institute (SEI).

Battin, R. D., R. Crocker and J. Kreidler (2001). 'Leveraging Resources in Global Software Development'. *IEEE Software* **18**(2): 70–77.

Baumard, P. (1999). *Tacit Knowledge in Organizations*. London, Sage Publications.

Beath, C. M. and W. Orlikowski (1994). 'The Contradictory Structure of Systems Development Methodologies.' *Information Systems Research* **5**(4): 350–377.

Bechky, B. A. (2003). 'Sharing Meaning Across Occupational Communities: The Transformation of Understanding on a Production Floor'. *Organization Science* **14**(3): 312–330.

Bernieri, F. J., J. M. Davis, R. Rosenthal and C. R. Knee (1994). 'Interactional Synchrony and Rapport: Measuring Synchrony in Displays Devoid of Sound and Facial Affect'. *Personality and Social Psychology Bulletin* **20**: 303–311.

Bertoa, M. F., J. M. Troya and A. Vallecillo (2006). 'Measuring the usability of software components.' *Journal of Systems and Software* **79**(3): 427–439.

Beynon-Davies, P., C. Carne, H. Mackay and D. Tudhope (1999). 'Rapid application development (RAD): An empirical review.' *European Journal of Information Systems* **8**(3): 211–223.

Bracciali, A., A. Brogi and C. Canal (2005). 'A formal approach to component adaptation'. *Journal of Systems and Software* **74**(1): 45–54.

Braga, R. M. M., C. M. L. Werner, M. Mattoso (2006). 'Odyssey-Search: A multi-agent system for component information search and retrieval'. *Journal of Systems and Software* **79**(2): 204–215.

Brenner, D., C. Atkinson, R. Malaka, M. Merdes, B. Paech and D. Suliman (2007). 'Reducing verification effort in component-based software engineering through built-in testing'. *Information Systems Frontiers* **9**(2–3): 151–162.

Brogi, A., C. Canal and E. Pimentel (2006). 'Component adaptation through flexible subservicing'. *Science of Computer Programming* **63**(1): 39–56.

Brooks, F. P. (1987). 'No Silver Bullet'. *Developer Productivity* (November): 39–48.

Brown, H. G, M. S. Poole and T. L. Rodgers (2004). 'Interpersonal traits, complementarity, and trust in virtual collaboration'. *Journal of Management Information Systems* **20**(4): 115–137.

Carmel, E. (1999). *Global Software Teams: Collaborating Across Borders and Time Zones*. Upper Saddle River, NJ, Prentice-Hall P T R.

Carmel, E. (2003a). 'The New Software Exporting Nations: Impacts on National Well Being Resulting from their Software Exporting Industries'. *The Electronic Journal on Information Systems in Developing Countries (EJISDC)* **13** (May).

Carmel, E. (2003b). 'Taxonomy of New Software Exporting Nations'. *The Electronic Journal on Information Systems in Developing Countries (EJISDC)* **13** (May).

Carmel, E. and R. Agarwal (2001). 'Tactical Approaches for Alleviating Distance in Global Software Development'. *IEEE Software* **18**(2): 22–29.

Carmel, E. and R. Agarwal (2002). 'The Maturation of Offshore Sourcing of Information Technology Work'. *MIS Quarterly Executive* **1**(2): 65–77.

Carmel, E., R. Whitaker and J. F. George (1993). 'Participatory Design and Joint Application Design: a transatlantic comparison'. *Communications of the ACM* **36**(6): 40–48.

Cheng, L., C. R. B. De Souza, S. Hupfer, J. Patterson and S. Ross (2004). 'Building Collaboration into IDEs'. *Queue* **1**(9): 40–50.

Child, J. (2001). 'Trust – The Fundamental Bond in Global Collaboration'. *Organizational Dynamics* **29**(4): 274–288.

Colbert, R. O., D. S. Compton, R. L. Hackbarth, J. D. Herbsleb, L. A. Hoadley and G. J. Wills (2001). 'Advanced Services: Changing How We Communicate'. *Bell Labs Technical Journal* **6**(1): 211–228.

Coronato, A., A. d'Acierno and G. De Pietro (2005). 'Automatic implementation of constraints in component based applications'. *Information and Software Technology* **47**(7): 497–509.

Cramton, C. D. (2001). 'The Mutual Knowledge Problem and Its Consequences for Dispersed Collaboration'. *Organization Science* **12**(3): 346–371.

Cramton, C. D. and S. S. Webber (2005). 'Relationships among geographic dispersion, team processes, and effectiveness in software development work teams'. *Journal of Business Research* **58**(6): 758–765.

Crnkovic, I. (2003). 'Component-based software engineering – New challenges in software development'. *25th International Conference on Information Technology Interfaces*: 9–18. Univ Zagreb, Fac Forestry: Cavtat, Croatia.

Crnkovic, I., B. Hnich, T. Jonsson and Z. Kiziltan (2002). 'Specification, Implementation and Deployment of Components'. *Communications of the ACM* **45**(10): 35–10.

Crnkovic, I. and M. Larsson (2002). 'Challenges of Component-Based Development'. *The Journal of Systems and Software* **61**(3): 201–212.

Crnkovic, I., S. Larsson and M. Chaudron (2005). 'Components-Based Development Process and Component Lifecycle'. *Journal of Computing and Information Technology* **13**(4): 321–327.

Crowston, K. and E. E. Kammerer (1998). 'Coordination and collective mind in software requirements development'. *IBM Systems Journal* 37(2): 227–245.

Crowston, K., Q. Li, K. N. Wei, U. Y. Eseryel and J. Howison (2007). 'Self-organization of teams for free/libre open source software development'. *Information and Software Technology* 49(6): 564–575.

Crowston, K. and B. Scozzi (2002). 'Open Source Software Projects as Virtual Organizations: Competency Rallying for Software Development'. *IEE Proceedings Software* 149(1): 3–17.

Cummings, J. N. (2004). 'Work groups, structural diversity, and knowledge sharing in a global organization'. *Management Science* 50(3): 352–364.

D'Souza, D. F. and A. C. Wills (1999). *Objects, Components, and Frameworks with Uml: The Catalysis Approach*. Amsterdam, Addison-Wesley.

Damian, D. (2007). 'Stakeholders in Global Requirements Engineering: Lessons learned from practice'. *IEEE Software* 24(2): 21–27.

Datar, S., C. Jordan, S. Kekre and K. Srinivasan (1997). 'New Product Development Structures and Time-to-Market'. *Management Science* 43(4): 452–464.

David, G. C., D. Chand, S. Newell and J. Resende-Santos (2008). 'Integrated collaboration across distributed sites: the perils of process and the promise of practice'. *Journal of Information Technology* 23(1): 44–54.

de Vries, H., H. de Vries and I. Oshri (2008). *Standards – Battles in Open Source Software: The Case of Firefox*. London, Palgrave.

DeSanctis, G. and R. B. Gallupe (1987). 'A Foundation for the Study of Group Decision Support Systems'. *Management Science* 33(5): 589–609.

Donnellon, A., B. Gray and M. G. Bougon (1986). 'Communication, Meaning, and Organized Action'. *Administrative Science Quarterly* 31(1): 43–55.

Dyer, J. H. (2001). 'How to Make Strategic Alliances Work'. *MIT Sloan Management Review* 42(4): 37–43.

Ebert, C. and P. De Neve (2001). 'Surviving Global Software Development'. *IEEE Software* 18(2): 62–69.

Eisenhardt, K. M. (1989). 'Building Theories from Case Study Research'. *Academy of Management Review* 14(4): 532–550.

Elfatatry, A. (2007). 'Dealing with Change: Components Versus Services'. *Communications of the ACM* 50(8): 35–39.

Espinosa, A. and E. Carmel (2003). 'Modeling Coordination Costs Due to Time Separation in Global Software Teams'. *Workshop on Global Software Development, part of the International Conference on Software Engineering (ICSE)*, Portland, Oregon, USA.

Espinosa, A., J. N. Cummings, J. M. Wilson and B. M. Pearce (2003). 'Team Boundary Issues Across Multiple Global Firms'. *Journal of Management Information Systems* 19(4): 157–190.

Espinosa, J. A., S. A. Slaughter, R. E. Kraut and J. D. Herbsleb (2007). 'Team Knowledge and Coordination in Geographically Distributed Software Development'. *Journal of Management Information Systems* 24 (1).

Evaristo, R. and P. C. van Fenema (1999). 'A Typology of Project Management: Emergence and Evolution of New Forms'. *International Journal of Project Management* 17(5): 275–281.

Faraj, S. and L. Sproull (2000). 'Coordinating Expertise in Software Development Teams'. *Management Science* 46(12): 1554–1568.

Firesmith, D., B. Henderson-Sellers (2001). *The Open Process Framework*. Addison Wesley.

Gabarro, J. J. (1990). 'The development of working relationships'. *Intellectual Teamwork: Social and Technological Foundations of Cooperative Work*. J. Galegher, R. E. Kraut and C. Egido. Hillsdale, New Jersey, Lawrence Erlbaum Associates: 70–110.

Gallivan, M. J. (2001). 'Striking a balance between trust and control in a virtual organization: a content analysis of open source software case studies'. *Information Systems Journal* 11(4): 227–304.

Ghosh, P. P. and J. C. Varghese (2004). 'Globally distributed product development using a new project management framework'. *International Journal of Project Management* 22(8): 669–678.

Ghosh, T., J. Yates and W. Orlikowski (2004). 'Using communication norms for coordination: Evidence from a distributed team'. *Proceedings of the International Conference on Information Systems*, Washington DC, USA.

Graham, I., B. Henderson-Sellers and H. Younessi (1997). *The Open Process Specification* (Open Series), Addison Wesley.

Granovetter, M. S. (1973). 'The Strength of Weak Ties'. *American Journal of Sociology* 78(6): 1360–1380.

Grant, R. M. (1996). 'Toward a knowledge-based theory of the firm'. *Strategic Management Journal* 17(Winter): 109–122.

Greenberg, P. S., R. H. Greenberg and Y. L. Antonucci (2007). 'Creating and sustaining trust in virtual teams'. *Business Horizons* 50(4): 325–333.

Gremler, D. D. and K. P. Gwinner (2000). 'Customer-Employee Rapport in Service Relationships'. *Journal of Service Research* 3(1): 82–104.

Grinter, R. E. (1995). 'Using a Configuration Management Tool to Coordinate Software Development'. *Conference on Organizational Computing Systems*, Milpitas, CA, USA.

Grinter, R. E. (1998). 'Recomposition: Putting It All Back Together Again'. *Conference on Computer-Supported Cooperative Work*, Seattle, Washington, USA.

Grinter, R. E. (1999). 'Systems Architecture: Product Design and Social Engineering'. *International Joint Conference on Work Activities Coordination and Collaboration*, San Francisco, CA, USA, ACM Press.

Grinter, R. E., J. D. Herbsleb and D. E. Perry (1999). 'The Geography of Coordination: Dealing with Distance in R&D Work'. *International ACM SIG-GROUP Conference on Supporting Group Work (Group 99)*, Phoenix, Arizona, USA, ACM Press.

Handel, M. and J. D. Herbsleb (2002). 'What is Chat Doing in the Workplace?' *Conference on Computer-Supported Cooperative Work*, New Orleans, LA, USA.

Hansen, M. T. (2002). 'Knowledge Networks: Explaining Effective Knowledge Sharing in Multiunit Companies'. *Organization Science* 13(3): 232–248.

Hart, R. K. and P. L. McLeod (2003). 'Rethinking Team Building in Geographically Dispersed Teams:: One Message at a Time'. *Organizational Dynamics* 31(4): 352–361

Herbsleb, J. D., D. L. Atkins, D. G. Boyer, M. Handel and T. A. Finholt (2002). 'Introducing Instant Messaging and Chat into the Workplace'. *ACM Conference on Computer-Human Interaction*, Minneapolis, MN, USA.

Herbsleb, J. D. and R. E. Grinter (1999). 'Architectures, Coordination, and Distance: Conway's Law and Beyond'. *IEEE Software*: 63–70.

Herbsleb, J. D. and A. Mockus (2003). 'An empirical study of speed and communication in globally distributed software development'. *Ieee Transactions on Software Engineering* **29**(6): 481–494.

Herbsleb, J. D., A. Mockus, T. A. Finholt and R. E. Grinter (2000). 'Distance, Dependencies, and Delay in Global Collaboration'. *Conference on Computer Supported Cooperative Work*, Philadelphia, Pennsylvania, USA.

Herbsleb, J. D. and D. Moitra (2001). 'Global Software Development'. *IEEE Software* **18**(2): 16–20.

Herrera, M. (2002). 'Globally Distributed Software Development: The need for integration of Object Oriented CASE tools with Groupware'. *Department of Decision and Information Sciences*. Rotterdam, Erasmus University: 120.

Herzum, P. and O. Sims (2000). *Business Component Factory: A Comprehensive Overview of Component-Based Development for the Enterprise*. New York, Wiley Computer Publishing.

Hill, N. S. (2005). *Leading Together, Working Together: The Role of Team Shared Leadership in Building Collaborative Capital in Virtual Teams*. Emerald Group Publishing Limited.

Hinds, P. J. and M. Mortensen (2005). 'Understanding conflict in geographically distributed teams: The moderating effects of shared identity, shared context, and spontaneous communication'. *Organization Science* **16**(3): 290–307.

Hirschheim, R. and H. K. Klein (1994). 'Realizing emancipatory principles in information systems development'. *MIS Quarterly* **18**(1): 83–109.

Hoegl, M. and H. G. Gemuenden (2001). 'Teamwork Quality and the Success of Innovative Projects: A Theoretical Concept and Empirical Evidence'. *Organization Science* **12**(4): 435–449.

Hofstede, G. (1993). 'Cultural constraints in management theories'. *Academy of Management Executive* **7**(1): 81–94.

Holmström, H., B. Fitzgerald, P. J. Agerfalk and E. O. Conchuir (2006). 'Agile practices reduce distance in global software development'. *Information Systems Management* **23**: 7–18.

Homann, U., M. Rill and A. Wimmer (2004). 'Flexible Value Structures in Banking'. *Communications of the ACM* **47**(5): 34–36.

Huang, J. C., S. Newell, R. D. Galliers and S.-L. Pan (2003). 'Dangerous Liaisons? Component-Based Development and Organizational Subcultures'. *IEEE Transactions on Engineering Management* **50**(1): 89–99.

Huis, M. A. A., J. H. E. Andriessen and M. Soekijad (2002). 'ICT Facilitation of Distributed Groups and Communities'. Building Blocks for Effective Telematics Application Development and Evaluation, Delft University of Technology: 39–46.

Iacovou, C. L. and R. Nakatsu (2008). 'A risk profile of offshore-outsourced development projects'. *Communications of the Acm* **51**(6): 89–94.

Jalote, P. and G. Jain (2006). 'Assigning tasks in a 24-h software development model'. *Journal of Systems and Software* **79**(7): 904–911.

Jarvenpaa, S. L., K. Knoll and D. E. Leidner (1998). 'Is anybody out there? Antecedents of trust in global virtual teams'. *Journal of MIS* **14**(4): 29–64.

Jarvenpaa, S. L. and D. E. Leidner (1998). 'Do You Read Me? The Development and Maintenance of Trust in Global Virtual Teams'. *Is Anybody Out There?: The Antecedents of Trust in Global Virtual Teams. Journal of Management Information Systems* 14, 29–64.

Joshi, K. D. and S. Sarker (2007). 'Knowledge transfer within information systems development teams: Examining the role of knowledge source attributes'. *Decision Support Systems* **43**(2): 322–335.

Karolak, D. W. (1999). Global Software Development: Managing Virtual Teams and Environments. Los Alamitos, IEEE Computer Society.

Kim, S. D. (2002). 'Lessons Learned from a Nationwide CBD PROMOTION PROJECT'. *Communications of the ACM* **45**(10): 83–87.

Klein, H. K. and M. D. Myers (1999). 'A set of principles for conducting and evaluating interpretive field studies in Information Systems'. *MIS Quarterly* **23**(1): 67–94.

Kobitzsch, W., D. Rombach and R. L. Feldmann (2001). 'Outsourcing in India'. *IEEE Software* **18**(2): 78–86.

Kobylinski, R., O. Creighton, A. H. Dutoit and B. Brugge (2002). 'Building Awareness in Global Software Engineering: Using Issues as Context'. *Workshop on Global Software Development, part of the International Conference on Software Engineering (ICSE)*, Orlando, Florida, USA.

Kotlarsky, J. (2007). 'Reengineering at LeCroy Corporation: The Move to Component-Based Systems'. *Journal of Information Technology* **22**(4): 465–478.

Kotlarsky, J. and I. Oshri (2005). 'Social Ties, Knowledge Sharing and Successful Collaboration in Globally Distributed System Development Projects'. *European Journal of Information Systems* **14**(1): 37–48.

Kotlarsky, J. and I. Oshri (2008). 'Country Attractiveness for Offshoring and Offshore-Outsourcing: Additional Considerations'. *Journal of Information Technology* **23**(4).

Kotlarsky, J., I. Oshri, K. Kumar and J. van Hillegersberg (2008). 'Towards Agility in Design in Global Component–Based Development'. *Communications of the ACM* **51**(9): 123–127.

Kotlarsky, J., I. Oshri, J. van Hillegersberg and K. Kumar (2007). 'Globally Distributed Component-Based Software Development: An Exploratory Study of Knowledge Management and Work Division'. *Journal of Information Technology* **22**(2): 161–173.

Kotlarsky, J., I. Oshri and L. P. Willcocks (2007). 'Social Ties in Globally Distributed Software Teams: Beyond Face-to-Face Meetings'. *Journal of Global Information Technology Management* **10**(4): 7–34.

Kotlarsky, J., P. C. van Fenema and L. P. Willcocks (2006). 'Case Research in Global Software Projects: Coordinating Through Knowledge'. *International Conference of Information Systems* Milwaukee, WI, USA, Association for Information Systems.

Kotlarsky, J., P. C. van Fenema and L. P. Willcocks (2008). 'Developing a Knowledge-Based Perspective on Coordination: The Case of Globally Distributed Software Development Projects'. *Information & Management* **45**(2): 96–108.

Kotlarsky, J., I. Oshri and P. C. van Fenema (2008). *Knowledge Processes in Globally Distributed Contexts*. London, Palgrave.

Kraut, R. E. and L. A. Streeler (1995). 'Coordination in Software Development'. *Communications of the ACM* **38**(3): 69–81.

Kumar, K. and L. P. Willcocks (1996). 'Offshore Outsourcing: A Country Too Far?'. *European Conference on Information Systems*, Lissabon, Portugal.

Kunda, D. and L. Brooks (2000). 'Assessing organisational obstacles to component-based development: a case study approach'. *Information and Software Technology* **42**: 715–725.

Lau, K. K. and Z. Wang (2007). 'Software component models'. *Ieee Transactions on Software Engineering* **33**(10): 709–724.

Lee-Kelley, L. and T. Sankey (2008). 'Global virtual teams for value creation and project success: A case study'. *International Journal of Project Management* **26**(1).

Lee, G., W. Delone and J. A. Espinosa (2006). 'Ambidextrous coping strategies in globally distributed software development projects'. *Communications of the ACM* **49**(10): 35–40.

Lee, O. D., P. Banerjee, K. H. Lim, K. Kumar, J. van Hillegersberg and K. K. Wei (2006). 'Aligning IT components to achieve agility in globally distributed system development'. *Communications of the ACM* **49**(10): 49–54.

Lee, S. C. and A. I. Shirani (2004). 'A component based methodology for Web application development'. *Journal of Systems and Software* **71**(1–2): 177–187.

Lyengar, P. (2004). 'Application Development Is More Global Than Ever'. Gartner: 2.

Mahmood, S., R. Lai, Y. S. Kim, J. H. Kim, S. C. Park, H. S. Oh (2005). 'A survey of component based system quality assurance and assessment'. *Information and Software Technology* **47**(10): 693–707.

Mahmood, S., R. Lai and Y. S. Kim (2007). 'Survey of component-based software development'. *Iet Software* **1**(2): 57–66.

Majchrzak, A., R. E. Rice, N. King, A. Malhotra and S. Ba (2000). 'Computer-mediated inter-organizational knowledge-sharing: Insights from a virtual team innovating using a collaborative tool'. *Information Resources Management Journal* **13**(1): 44–54.

Malhotra, A., A. Majchrzak, R. Carman and V. Lott (2001). 'Radical Innovation Without Collocation: A Case Study at Boeing-Rocketdyne'. *MIS Quarterly* **25**(2): 229–249.

Malhotra, A. and A. Majchrzak (2005). 'Virtual workspace technologies'. *MIT Sloan Management Review* **46**(2): 11–14.

Massey, A. P., M. M. Montoya-Weiss and T. M. O'Driscoll (2002). 'Knowledge Management in Pursuit of Performance: Insights from Nortel Networks'. *MIS Quarterly* **26**(3): 269–289.

Meyerson, D., K. E. Weick and R. M. Kramer (1996). 'Swift trust and temporary groups'. Trust in organizations: Frontiers of theory and research. R. M. Kramer and T. R. Tyler. Thousand Oaks, CA, Sage.

Mockus, A. and J. D. Herbsleb (2002). 'Expertise Browser: A Quantitative Approach to Identifying Expertise'. *International Conference on Software Engineering*, Orlando, FL, USA.

Mockus, A. and D. M. Weiss (2001). 'Globalization by Chunking: A Quantitative Approach'. *IEEE Software* **18**(2): 30–37.

Mohtashami, M., T. Marlowe, V. Kirova and F. P. Deek (2006). 'Risk management for collaborative software development'. *Information Systems Management* **23**(4): 20–30.

Morch, A. I., G. Stevens, M. Won, M. Klann, Y. Dittrich and V. Wulf (2004). 'Component-based technologies for end-user development'. *Communication of the ACM* **47**(9): 59–62.

Murugesan, S. (1999). 'Leverage Global Software Development and Distribution Using the Internet and Web'. *Cutter IT Journal* **12**(3): 57–63.

Nellore, R. and R. Balachandra (2001). 'Factors Influencing Success in Integrated Product Development (IPD) Projects'. *IEEE Transactions on Engineering Management* **48**(2): 164–174.

Nelson, K. M. and J. G. Cooprider (1996). 'The Contribution of Shared Knowledge to IS Group Performance'. *MIS Quarterly* **20**(4): 409–432.

Nonaka, I. and H. Takeuchi (1995). *The Knowledge-creating Company*. Oxford University Press.

Olin, J. G., N. P. Greis and J. D. Kasarda (1999). 'Knowledge Management Across Multi-tier Enterprise: The Promise of Intelligent Software in the Auto Industry'. *European Management Journal* **17**(4): 335–347.

Olson, J. S. and G. M. Olson (2004). 'Culture Surprises in Remote Software Development Teams'. *Queue* **1**(9): 52–59.

Orlikowski, W. J. (2002). 'Knowing in Practice: Enacting a Collective Capability in Distributed Organizing'. *Organization Science* **13**(3): 249–273.

Orr, J. (1990). 'Sharing Knowledge Celebrating Identity: Community Memory in a Service Culture'. *Collective Remembering*. D. Middleton and D. Edwards. London, Sage.

Oshri, I., J. Kotlarsky, P. C. van Fenema and L. P. Willcocks (2007). 'Expertise Management in A Distributed Context: The Case of Offshore IT Outsourcing'. *IFIP WG 8.2/9.5 Conference on Virtuality and Virtualization*, Portland, OR, USA.

Oshri, I., J. Kotlarsky and L. P. Willcocks (2005). 'Before, During and After Face-To-Face Meetings: The Lifecycle of Social Ties in Globally Distributed Teams'. *International Conference of Information Systems*, Las Vegas, NV, Association for Information Systems.

Oshri, I., J. Kotlarsky and L. P. Willcocks (2007a). 'Global Software Development: Exploring Socialization in Distributed Strategic Projects'. *Journal of Strategic Information Systems* **16**(1): 25–49.

Oshri, I., J. Kotlarsky and L. P. Willcocks (2007b). 'Managing Dispersed Expertise in IT Offshore Outsourcing: Lessons from Tata Consultancy Services'. *MIS Quarterly Executive* **6**(2): 53–65.

Oshri, I., J. Kotlarsky and L. P. Willcocks (2008). 'Missing Links: Building Critical Social Ties for Global Collaborative Teamwork'. *Communications of the ACM* **51**(4).

Oshri, I. and S. Newell (2005). 'Component Sharing in Complex Products and Systems: Challenges, Solutions and Practical Implications'. *IEEE Transactions on Engineering Management* **52**(4): 509–521.

Oshri, I., S. Newell and S. L. Pan (2007). 'Implementing component reuse strategy in complex products environments'. *Communications of the ACM* **50**(12): 63–67.

Oshri, I., S. L. Pan and S. Newell (2006). 'Managing Trade-offs and Tensions between Knowledge Management Initiatives and Expertise Development Practices'. *Management Learning* **37**(1): 63–82.

Oshri, I., P. C. van Fenema and J. Kotlarsky (2008). 'Knowledge Transfer in Globally Distributed Teams: The Role of Transactive Memory'. *Information Systems Journal* **18**(6): 593–616.

Paasivaara, M. (2003). 'Communication Needs, Practices and Supporting Structures in Global Inter-Organizational Software Development Projects'. *Workshop on Global Software Development, part of the International Conference on Software Engineering (ICSE)*, Portland, Oregon, USA.

Paul, D. L. (2006). 'Collaborative activities in virtual settings: A knowledge management perspective of telemedicine'. *Journal of Management Information Systems* 22(4): 143–176.

Peters, J. F. and W. Pedrycz (2000). *Software Engineering: An Engineering Approach.* New York, John Wiley & Sons, Inc.

Pfister, C. (1997). *Component Software: A Case Study Using BlackBox Components.* Zurich, Oberon Microsystems, Inc.

Polanyi, M. (1967). *The Tacit Dimension.* London, Routledge.

Rafii, F. (1995). 'How Important Is Physical Collocation to Product Development Success?' *Business Horizons*(January–February): 78–84.

Ravichandran, T. and M. A. Rothenberger (2003). 'Software Reuse Strategies and Component Markets'. *Communications of the ACM* 46(8): 109–114.

Repenning, A., A. Ioannidou, M. Payton, W. Ye and J. Roschelle (2001). 'Using Components for Rapid Distributed Software Development'. *IEEE Software* 18(2): 38–45.

Rodriguez, I., M. Nunez and F. Rubio (2004). 'A formal framework for analyzing reusability complexity in component-based systems'. *Information and Software Technology* 46(12): 791–804.

Sarker, S. and S. Sahay (2003). 'Understanding Virtual Team Development: an Interpretive Study'. *Journal of the Association for Information Systems* 4: 1–38.

Sarker, S. and S. Sahay (2004). 'Implications of space and time for distributed work: an interpretive study of US-Norwegian system development teams'. *European Journal of Information Systems* 13(1): 3–20.

Selby, R. W. (2005). 'Enabling reuse-based software development of large-scale systems'. *Workshop on Mining Software Repositories held in conjunction with the 27th International Conference on Software Engineering (ICSE)*: 495–510. IEEE Computer Society: St Louis, MO.

Scott, W. R. (1992). *Organizations: Rational, Natural, and Open Systems.* Englewood Cliffs, New Jersey, Prentice-Hall.

Shachaf, P. (2008). 'Cultural diversity and information and communication technology impacts on global virtual teams: An exploratory study'. *Information & Management* 45(2): 131–142.

Sinha, P. and A. Hanumantharya (2005). 'A novel approach for component-based fault-tolerant software development'. *Information and Software Technology* 47(6): 365–382.

Smith, P. G. and E. L. Blanck (2002). 'From Experience: Leading Dispersed Teams'. *The Journal of Product Innovation Management* 19(4): 294–304.

Starr, M. K. (1965). 'Modular Production; a new concept'. *Harvard Business Review* 43(November–December): 131–142.

Storck, J. (2000). 'Knowledge diffusion through "strategic communities"'. *Sloan Management Review* 41(2): 63–74.

Szyperski, C. (1998). Component Software Beyond Object-Oriented Programming. New York, Addison-Wesley.

Taweel, A. and P. Brereton (2006). 'Modelling software development across time zones'. *Information and Software Technology* 48(1): 1–11.

Taxen, L. (2006). 'An integration centric approach for the coordination of distributed software development projects'. *Information and Software Technology* 48(9): 767–780.

Terwiesch, C. and C. H. Loch (1996). 'The Role of Uncertainty Reduction in Concurrent Engineering: An Analytical Model and Empirical Testing'.

Törngren, M., D. J. Chen, I. Crnkovic and I. C. Society (2005). 'Component-based vs. model-based development: A comparison in the context of vehicular embedded systems'. *31st EUROMICRO Conference on Software Engineering and Advanced Applications*, Oporto, PORTUGAL, Ieee Computer Soc.

Traas, V. and J. van Hillegersberg (2000). 'The Software Component Market on the Internet: Current Status and Conditions for Growth'. *ACM SIGSOFT* 25(1): 114–117.

Trevor, J. (1994). 'RAD takes developers across the waterfall'. *Computing Canada* 20(2): 22.

Turnlund, M. (2004). 'Distributed Development Lessons Learned'. *Queue* 1(9): 26–31.

Ulrich, K. T. and S. D. Eppinger (2000). *Product Design and Development*. McGraw-Hill.

van den Heuvel, W. J., J. van Hillegersberg and M. Papazoglou (2002). 'A methodology to support Web-services Development using Legacy Systems'. *Engineering information systems in the Internet Context, IFIP 8.1 EISIC*, Kluwer Academic Publishers.

van Fenema, P. C. (2002). 'Coordination and Control of Globally Distributed Software Projects'. *Department of Decision and Information Sciences*. Doctoral Dissertation. Rotterdam, The Netherlands, Erasmus University, Rotterdam School of Management: 572.

van Fenema, P. C. and K. Kumar (2000). 'Coupling, Interdependence and Control in Global Projects'. *Projects as Business Constituents and Guiding Motives*. R. A. Lundin and F. Hartman. Boston, MA, Kluwer Academic Publishers.

van Hillegersberg, J. (2003). 'Component-Based Systems Development: The AEGON Bank Project'. Executive class, Florida International University, Miami, FL, USA.

Verbraeck, A., Y. Saanen, Z. Stojanovic, E. Valentin, K. van der Meer, A. Meijer and B. Shishkov (2002). 'What are Building Blocks?' Building Blocks for Effective Telematics Application Development and Evaluation, Delft University of Technology.

Vergara, N. M., J. M. T. Linero and A. V. Moreno (2007). 'Model-driven component adaptation in the context of Web Engineering'. *European Journal of Information Systems* 4: 448–459.

Vitharana, P. (2003). 'Risks and Challenges of Component-Based Software Development'. *Communications of the ACM* 46(8): 67–72.

Wallace, L. and M. Keil (2004). 'Software Project Risks and their Effect on Outcomes'. *Communications of the ACM* 47(4): 68–73.

Wang, H. and C. Wang (2001). 'Open Source Software Adoption: A Status Report'. *IEEE Software* 18(2): 90–95.

Webster (1992). *Webster's Dictionary*. Oxford University Press.

Wegner, D. M. (1987). 'Transactive Memory: A Contemporary Analysis of the Group Mind'. *Theories of Group Behavior*. G. Mullen and G. Goethals. New York, Springer Verlag: 185–205.

Weick, K. E. and K. H. Roberts (1993). 'Collective Mind in Organisations: Heedful Interrelating on Flight Desks'. *Administrative Science Quarterly* 38(3): 357–382.

Weick, K. E., K. M. Sutcliffe and D. Obstfeld (1999). 'Organizing for high reliability: Processes of collective mindfulness'. *Research in Organizational Behavior*. B. Staw and L. L. Cummings. Greenwich, CT, JAI Press. **21**: 81–123.

Willcocks, L., P. Petherbridge and N. Olson (2002). *Making IT Count. Strategy, Delivery, Infrastructure*. Oxford, Butterworth Heinemann.

Yenne, B. (2002). *Inside Boeing 777: Building The 777*. St. Paul, MBI Publishing Company.

Yin, R. K. (1994). *Case Study Research: Design and Methods*. Sage: Newbury Park, CA.

Zhou, J., K. Cooper, H. Ma and I. L. Yen (2007). 'On the customization of components: A rule-based approach'. *IEEE Transactions on Knowledge and Data Engineering* **19**(9): 1262–1275.

# Index

advanced development, investing in
analysis, 233–234
LeCroy case, 94
TCS case, 155
application sharing *see* collaborative
technology
awareness, of others, of company, 257
analysis, 208–209
LeCroy case, 79
SAP case, 107
TCS case, 137–138

Baan
background, 161–168
discussion, 196–200
organisation and management,
168–195
bug and task tracking
analysis, 212
LeCroy case, 80
TCS case, 141

case studies
case analysis, 208–236
limitations, 249
participation criteria, 66
practical contibutions, 246
similarities and differences,
**205–206**
theoretical contributions, 244
CB (component-based) architecture,
128, 131
ease of customisation, 37
in the LeCroy case, 95
in the SAP case, 102
in the TCS case, 155
non-software-related industries, use
in, 4
software components, 5
software development, with, 4
software industry, adoption by, 3
CB (component-based) system *see also*
components and CBD

(Component-Based
Development)
about, 39
characteristics of, 43
components, 40–43
Waterfall model, compare to
CBD (Component-Based
Development) *see also*
components, CB (component-
based) system, CB (component-
based) architecture, and reuse
and global teams, 4
end-user integration, 36
in the software industry, 36
methodology, 3
monolithic system, compare to,
36
organisation and management,
50–64
reuse, 46–50
software component technology,
38
success factors, 64, **65**
vendor integration, 36
change, continuous
in management, 177–179
in organisational structure, 180
with detailed planning, 141
collaborative technology, 113–115
application sharing, 87, 113, 148,
185, 220
Baan case, 184
case comparison, **220**
email, 114, 149, 185, 220
Intranet, 115, 149, 220
LeCroy case, 87–89, 96
online chat, 87, 184, 219
overview, 25–29
phone, 87, 113, 148, 184, 219
SAP case, 113–115
TCS case, 148–149
teleconferencing, 87, 113, 148, 184,
219

types of, 26
videoconferencing, 88, 114, 148, 186, 220
collective knowledge, 17, 34
  discussion, 228–229
  LeCroy case, 92
  SAP case, 119
  TCS case, 152–153
communication, 17, 18, 19, 20, 21, 24, 25, 29, 30, 34, 63, 76
  analysis, 160, 169, 224
  Baan case, 176, 181, 184, 190, 193, 198
  between key people, 180
  LeCroy case, 89, 96, 99
  problems in, 193, **196**
  SAP case, 101, 111, 117, 119, 122, 123
  TCS case, 134, 140, 157, 158
Component-Based architecture
  *see* CB (Component-Based) architecture
components
  CB system, 40–43
  communication via interfaces, 42
  deployment, 42
  granularity, 42
  Maui project (LeCroy), 73
components management *see also* advanced development, reuse, and vendor integration
  analysis, 231–236
  Baan case, 166, 195–198
  LeCroy case, 94
  SAP case, 121
  TCS case, 154–156
coordination, inter-site *see also* awareness, bug and task tracking, communication (systematic), division of work, and flexibility (work schedules, PM techniques)
  analysis, **207**, 208–215
  Baan case, 168–183
  LeCroy case, 79–81
  overview, 20–24, 50–52
  propositions, **237**
  SAP case, 107–111

cultural awareness, 24
cultural differences, 2, 6, 15, 17, 29, 31, 49, 61, 103, 118, 214, 257
  analysis, 225
  Baan case, 188, 191
  constraints of, 17
  LeCroy case, 97
  SAP case, 119, 124
  TCS case, 159

division of work
  analysis, 138–140
  Baan case, 170–175
  LeCroy case, 79
  SAP case, 108
  TCS case, 138–140

email *see* collaborative technology
end-user integration, 37

face-to-face meetings *see* social ties
flexibility, PM techniques, 213
  LeCroy case, 80
  SAP case, 109
  TCS case, 141
flexibility, working conditions
  analysis, 212
  LeCroy case, 80
  SAP case, 109
  TCS case, 140
follow-the-sun, 2, 51, 147

GD CBD (Globally Distributed Component-Based Development)
  ad hoc revolution, 5
  breakdown factors, 31
  increased interest, 5
  Information Systems (IS), 6
  management of, 15
  related research streams, 8
  success factors, **29**, 32, 34, **35**, 50, 60–65, 95–98, 121–124, 156–159
  success, obstacles to, 168–195
  theoretical basis for studying, 7
  various types of, 7

GDSD (Globally Distributed Software
  Development)
  breakdowns, 16–18, 19
  definition of a unit, 16
  increased interest in, 3
  inter-personal communications, 19
  inter-site coordination, practices
    for, 20
  limited research, 16
  management and organisation,
    18–30 *see also* Baan, LeCroy,
    SAP, and TCS
  social aspects among teams, 30–34
geographical distance, 2, 5, 8, 15, 19,
    23, 30, 49, 61, 63, 64, 74, 155,
    235
  Baan case, 167
  LeCroy case, 97
  SAP case, 104, 123
  TCS case, 132, 158
Global distribution *see* GDSD
  (Globally Distributed Software
  Development)
  problems associated with, 2
globalisation, software industry, of
  growth in past decade, 2
  unrealistic expectations, 5
Globally Distributed Component-
  Based Development *see* GD CBD

ICT (Information and
  Communication Technologies),
  24, 25, 78, 85, 98, 106, 112, 136,
  147, 207, 218, 241, 248
ICT infrastructure
  case comparison, **218**
  LeCroy case, 85–87
  SAP case, 112–113
  TCS case, 147
Information and Communication
  Technologies *see* ICT
inter-personal communications
  issues in GDSD, 19
inter-site coordination *see*
  coordination
Intranet *see* collaborative technology
intuition *see also* knowledge sharing
  analysis, 230
  managing by, 120, 126, **207**, 258

knowledge sharing *see also* collective
  knowledge, intuition, learning
  curves, and transactive memory
  analysis, 227–231
  Baan case, 175–177, 192, 190–195
  changing organisational structure,
    with, 190
  cultural gaps, 191–193
  LeCroy case, 92–94
  overview, 32–34, 61
  SAP case, 118–121
  TCS case, 152–154

learning curves
  analysis, 230
  new technology, 93, 154, 193,
    257
LeCroy
  background, 70–76
  discussion, 98–99
  management and organisation,
    76–98
  success factors, **77**, **78**

management
  continuous change, 177–179
  of component interdependencies,
    54, 82, 217, 248
managerial practices *see* components
  management, coordination,
  knowledge sharing, social ties,
  and tools and technologies
  case comparison, **207**
*Managing Component-Based
  Development in Global Teams*
  academic contribution, 10
  book outline, 10
  objective of book, 6
  practical contribution, 10
monolithic system, 3, 37, 43
  LeCroy case, 71

online chat *see* collaborative
  technology
Organisational Behaviour (OB)
  in Globally Distributed (GD)
  teams, 7
OSS (Open Source Software)
  GD CBD, a type of, 7, 9

phone *see* collaborative technology

relationships *see also* social ties and
    trust
  Baan case, 186–189
  LeCroy case, 90–91
  SAP case, 116–118
  TCS case, 149–151
requirements
  not clear, 177–179
reuse, 8, 38, 41, 42, 44, 58, 62, 254
  analysis, 231–233
  Baan case, 199
  benefits and challenges, 46–50
  LeCroy case, 94
  SAP case, 121, 126
  TCS case, 154–155

SAP
  background, 100–104
  discussion, 125–126
  organisation and management,
    105–124
  success factors, 121–124
social ties *see also* trust and
    relationships
  analysis, 221–226
  Baan case, 186–190
  LeCroy case, 89–91
  overview, 30–32, 60–61
  SAP case, 116–118
  TCS case, 149–151
software development, 3 *see also* CBD
    (Component-Based
    Development)
  advanced development, investing
    in, 94
  CBD, 3, 5
  component management, 36
  coordination mechanisms, 23
  global distribution, 15
  management in global
    environment, 15
  non CB, 6
  offshoring outsourcing of, 16
  OSS, 9
  outsourcing, 18
  software components, 5
  tools specific to, 28

software development methodology
  Joint Application Development, 19
  overview of, 18
  parallel (overlapping) approach, 19
  prototyping, 19
  Rapid Application Development, 19
  Waterfall (sequential) approach, 18,
    **19**, 44
software development tools
  Baan case, 184
  case comparison, **217**
  LeCroy case, used in, 81–85
  SAP case, 111–112
  TCS case, 143–147

TCS
  background, 127–134
  discussion, 159–160
  organisation and management,
    134–159
  success factors, **135**, **136**, 156–159
teleconferencing *see* collaborative
    technology
tension, social *see also* relationships
    and trust
  between cultures, 186–188
time-zone differences, 2, 6, 15, 30, 33,
    49, 63, 89, 96, 98, 124, 149, 204,
    212, 217, 222, 237
  constraint in GDSD, 16, 17
  LeCroy case, 97
  SAP case, 113, 123
  TCS case, 158
tools and technologies *see also*
    collaborative technology, ICT
    infrastructure, and software
    development tools
  analysis, 215–221
  Baan case, 183–188
  lack of compatibility, 182–183
  LeCroy case, 81–89
  overview, 24–29, 53–59
  propositions associated with, **221**
  SAP case, 111–115
  TCS case, 143–149
transactive memory, 34, 77, 222, 227
  Baan case, 190, 199
  definition, 33
  discussion, 227–228

transactive memory – *continued*
  LeCroy case, 92, 98
  SAP case, 118, 125
  TCS case, 152, 160
trust *see also* social ties and
    relationships
  Baan case, 189
  barriers, 29
  definition, 30
  LeCroy case, 89

rapport, compare to, 31
SAP case, 116
TCS case, 149

vendor integration, 37, 38, 131, 132,
    135, 150, 156, 160, 235, 236, 258
video technology *see* collaborative
    technology

Waterfall methodology, 18, 19, 44